THE ETHERIC CR

trip into the mysterious Third Tunnel located beneath the Romanian Sphinx in the Bucegi Mountains. On a specific mission to visit the underground chamber beneath Iraq, Radu and his team recover a powerful crystal that exists in another dimension but is housed in a container in this one. It becomes the basis for a new project to design a chair to facilitate out-of-the-body experiences in order for Radu to see beyond the veils of ordinary reality and to penetrate different dimensions. Based upon Radu's intuition as a result of the expedition to the Third Tunnel, the project is initially started privately by Radu and his mentor, Cezar Brad. When they run into financial blocks, they are unexpectedly embraced by Elinor, the enigmatic and wealthy alchemist who befriended Radu in *Transylvanian Moonrise* and facilitated his meeting with Repa Sundhi, the Tibetan lama who precipitated the entire series of discoveries of the Inner Earth revealed in the *Transylvania Series*. Through his role as Dr. Xien, a recognized adviser and representative of the Chinese government, the lama was loaned to the Romanian government in order to set up Department Zero, a secret branch of Romanian Intelligence dedicated to investigating and utilizing the paranormal. Playing a significant role in this new endeavor, Elinor helps Cezar and Radu take the project to another level.

The Inner Earth city of Apellos also offers their help with this project, and a whole new system and spirit of cooperation is set up between Department Zero and the Council of Apellos. Radu's mentor from Apellos, Méntia, comes to the surface world to meet Elinor in order to begin a collaboration that is designed to bring humanity back to a state of health and to raise the consciousness of Mankind.

✦

THE ETHERIC CRYSTAL
THE THIRD TUNNEL

Radu Cinamar
Edited by Peter Moon

SkyBooks
NEW YORK

The Etheric Crystal — The Third Tunnel
Copyright © 2020 by Radu Cinamar
First English language printing, October 2020
International copyright laws apply

Cover art by Creative Circle Inc.
Typography by Creative Circle Inc.
Published by: Sky Books
       Box 769
       Westbury, New York 11590
       email: *skybooks@yahoo.com*
       website: www.timetraveleducationcenter.com
              www.skybooksusa.com
              www.digitalmontauk.com

Library of Congress Cataloging-in-Publication Data

Cinamar, Radu / Moon, Peter
    The Etheric Crystal — The Third Tunnel
    220 pages, illustrated
    ISBN 978-1-937859-22-0
1. Body, Mind, Spirit: Occultism 2. Body, Mind, Spirit: General
Library of Congress Control Number: 2020943204

This book is dedicated to those who seek the answers.

OTHER TITLES FROM
SKY BOOKS

by Preston Nichols and Peter Moon
The Montauk Project: Experiments in Time
Montauk Revisited: Adventures in Synchronicity
Pyramids of Montauk: Explorations in Consciousness
Encounter in the Pleiades: An Inside Look at UFOs
The Music of Time

by Peter Moon
The Black Sun: Montauk's Nazi-Tibetan Connection
Synchronicity and the Seventh Seal
The Montauk Book of the Dead
The Montauk Book of the Living
Spandau Mystery
The White Bat — The Alchemy of Writing

by Joseph Matheny with Peter Moon
Ong's Hat: The Beginning

by Stewart Swerdlow
Montauk: The Alien Connection
The Healer's Handbook: A Journey Into Hyperspace

by Alexandra Bruce
The Philadelphia Experiment Murder:
Parallel Universes and the Physics of Insanity

by Wade Gordon
The Brookhaven Connection

by Radu Cinamar with Peter Moon
Transylvanian Sunrise
Transylvanian Moonrise
Mystery of Egypt — The First Tunnel
The Secret Parchment
Inside the Earth — The Second Tunnel
Forgotten Genesis

CONTENTS

INTRODUCTION

For those of you who have picked up this book without any prior knowledge of the circumstances surrounding Radu Cinamar and his previous work, I will lay out a background and summary.

During the Cold War, there was a natural alliance between the two communist nations of Romania and the People's Republic of China. Trying to keep up with the West in regards to the most advanced and esoteric methods of reconnaissance and espionage, the Romanians sought out the help of the Chinese as they did not really trust the Russians. As part of a cultural exchange program whereby Chinese students were able to participate in educational programs in Romania, the Chinese government sent the Romanians an expert in parapsychology who would set up a secret department that would deal with all abnormal occurrences. These were referred to as "K events", but in pop culture terms of today, these might now be termed as "X-File" events. Known as Department Zero, this special unit was only known to the head of state and the head of security. Besides housing and caring for paranormal subjects, Department Zero also trained them. The expert in parapsychology who set up this unique department is known to us as Dr. Xien, and he was introduced to us in the first book of this series, *Transylvanian Sunrise.** Although Dr. Xien is an intriguing character, we do not learn too much about him in that book. We do know that he was called in after the birth of another very interesting character who also turns out to be one of the progenitors of the *Transylvania Series*. His name is Cezar Brad, and he is born with an umbilical cord that is so thick, the doctors have to use an ordinary saw to sever it. As this is an anomaly, Cezar comes under the scrutiny and eventual tutelage of Department Zero and forms a close personal relationship with Dr. Xien from a very young age. Cezar is trained in a host of spiritual and psychic disciplines that would rival the best your imagination might offer.

As fate would clearly demonstrate, Dr. Xien was grooming Cezar to serve as a steward and guardian for what is arguably considered the greatest archeological discovery in the history of Mankind: a secret and previously inaccessible chamber beneath the Romanian Sphinx containing futuristic holographic technology that was put together some 50,000 years ago.

---

* The book you are reading now, *The Etheric Crystal*, is the seventh in a series of books by Radu Cinamar which are known as the *Transylvania Series* and include *Transylvanian Sunrise, Transylvanian Moonrise, Mystery of Egypt — The First Tunnel, The Secret Parchment — Five Tibetan Initiation Techniques*, and *Inside the Earth — The Second Tunnel, Forgotten Genesis* and Peter Moon's book *The White Bat*.

In what could be termed a virtual Noah's Ark that far exceeds the thinking and experiential capacity of those who lived in biblical times (or even in our own times for that matter), this chamber includes technology whereby one can place their hand on a table and see their own DNA rendered in three-dimensional holograms. Other devices on the table enable one to see the DNA of alien species from other planets with accompanying star renderings so that one can see where they actually originate from. By placing two hands on different parts of the table, one can also "mix" the DNA of two species so as to see how they might look if hybridized. As the tables themselves are six feet high, the creatures who built them were gigantic compared to humans of today.

This remarkable chamber also includes a "projection hall" whereby one can see a holographic rendition of the history of Earth that is particularly tailored to the individuality of whomever might be viewing it. This history, however, abruptly cuts off in about the Fifth Century A.D., perhaps because it requires some sort of software update. One of the more intriguing aspects of the Projection Hall is that it also contains three mysterious tunnels that lead into the bowels of the Earth and similar facilities in Iraq, Mongolia, Tibet and also beneath the Giza Plateau in Egypt.

Although Cezar, through the tutelage of Dr. Xien, was set up by fate to be the overseer of this remarkable archeological discovery, it was not his role to write the story of what was found and its implications. As these events were unfolding, Cezar handpicked Radu Cinamar to write these volumes. Serving as a mentor to Radu, Cezar gave him a rapid fire education in all of the political machinations going on behind this discovery while also introducing him to the world of psychic phenomena and esoteric studies. We learn about this in the first volume, *Transylvanian Sunrise*, but we are not told exactly why Cezar picked Radu. What I can tell you from what I have learned thus far is that Cezar is a remarkably adept individual, and he knew precisely what he was doing. His psychic sensibilities are quite formidable and proved to be accurate in this case. Radu got the job done, and with the release of this book, he now has seven volumes in English.

You might think that this discovery was a wonderful opportunity to enlighten Mankind and take advantage of all that this newly discovered technology has to offer for the benefit of humanity at large. Many, if not most, of the Romanians in the government who were privy to the discovery viewed it that way. Circumstances, however, dictated otherwise.

Cezar informed Radu that the actual discovery of this secret and previously unknown chamber took place when the Pentagon discovered it via the use of ground penetrating radar that operated through satellites. It is understandable that the Americans would use all technology at their disposal for reconnaissance purposes as well as to scrutinize all geographical anomalies and resources on the planet. Right or wrong, this is the purpose of the Department of Defense. What was most challenging about this intelligence, however, was that Masonic interests in the Pentagon funneled this information to a leader in Italian Freemasonry, a Signore Massini, who represents a hidden global elite that wanted access to and control of this chamber for themselves. Accordingly, Massini approached Cezar who was then the head of Department Zero and sought his cooperation. Cezar, who did not trust Massini, was forced to cooperate to a certain extent due to political circumstances. Thus, the evil interests of an Italian Freemason forged an unprecedented alliance between Romania and America with the former suddenly being admitted to NATO. The specifics of these political intrigues are detailed in the book *Transylvanian Sunrise* which is primarily the story of Cezar's life and his involvement with the uncovering of these amazing artifacts.

While the enigmatic and mysterious Dr. Xien set the stage for Cezar to uncover this secret chamber through rigorous training and education, he is a distant memory when the discovery is made and seemingly completely uninvolved in any tangible way with the political machinations and evil intrigues which allowed it to even take place. Dr. Xien, however, is an interested party and a definite progenitor of the information revealed in these books, and this comes into clear view in the second book of the series, *Transylvanian Moonrise — A Secret Initiation in the Mysterious Land of the Gods.*

Transylvanian Moonrise begins with an editor's note from the Romanian editor, Sorin Hurmuz, who includes numerous excerpts from the Romanian press that not only corroborate Cezar's story as told by Radu but give insights into why it is credible. Above and beyond these facts, it might interest you to know that a key area near the Romanian Sphinx is blacked out on Google Earth. Besides that, Americans were seen en masse during the time of the excavations that were taking place near the Romanian Sphinx in 2003. I have also spoken to several well-placed people in Romania who believe the general story to have merit. Exactly what has taken place and all of the details are still largely a mystery, but Radu's books offer us the only clues. In addition to that, they are remarkable stories and teaching devices which integrate the mundane aspects of politics with some of the most esoteric concepts of occultism as well as the cutting edge of technology.

Radu's narrative in *Transylvanian Moonrise* begins with a mysterious man named Elinor trying to contact the enigmatic author through his publisher, Sorin Hurmuz, who has generally been instructed to stonewall any people wishing to meet with Radu. In fact, Sorin has never met with Radu and only communicates with him by special courier or with a prearranged phone card. When it is eventually discovered that Elinor is speaking on behalf of a Tibetan lama, both Sorin and Radu change their tune and a meeting is eventually arranged. This meeting is filled with a panoply of metaphysical revelations which present an entirely new paradigm by which to view the events described in *Transylvanian Sunrise*. After an amazing indoctrination into the ancient art of alchemy and the prospects of immortality, Radu meets the lama who reveals himself to be none other than Dr. Xien and explains that he once served in the royal court at Lhasa under the name of Repa Sundhi at the time of the Chinese invasion of Tibet. Escaping that purge, he somehow ended up in the employ of the Chinese government and adopted a different identity as Dr. Xien.

Repa Sundhi has a very specific agenda for this meeting with Radu and it has to do with what is the focal point of the fourth book in the *Transylvania Series*: *The Secret Parchment — Five Tibetan Initiation Techniques* (more on that later). In *Transylvanian Moonrise*, Radu learns that the lama wants to take him to the Apuseni Mountains of Transylvania. Once there, a mysterious but well-described space-translation takes place that literally transports them (as well as Elinor, who remains in their company) to certain rarefied high peaks of Tibet which are inaccessible to humans by normal transportation means. Radu is escorted into a cave where he meets another progenitor of the *Transylvania Series*. Her name is Machandi and she is a blue goddess and tantric dakini who not only educates and initiates Radu but gives him an ancient manuscript which is to be translated from ancient Tibetan and published, first in the Romanian language. Having finally been translated into English, it is the centerpiece of *The Secret Parchment*.

While *Transylvanian Moonrise* refers to the characters in *Transylvanian Sunrise* and the lama is included in the dramatic events that take place, the two books are astonishingly different and offer complementary views of the overall scenario from completely different perspectives. The third book in the series, *Mystery of Egypt — The First Tunnel*, is no exception. Radu is recruited to join Department Zero on a journey with Cezar into the mysterious "First Tunnel" in the Projection Hall of the Bucegi complex. This leads to a hidden chamber beneath the Giza Plateau in Egypt. What they find there is no less astonishing than what has already been offered in the first two books. The purpose of the mission is to recover neatly organized slate-like tablets that are in fact a type of ancient "DVD" that project holographic "memories" of the history of the world. The tablets do not require a projector and are so numerous that they can only hope to return a portion of them to their home base, after which they will be sent to America for detailed study. Even though they cannot recover everything in one mission, what they do retrieve would take a team of viewers a considerable amount of time to view.

There is also an occult chamber containing a device consisting primarily of huge crystals that facilitates the projection of one's consciousness back into time. It is not a physical time travel device. It should be noted that it requires a certain amount of psychic and esoteric development to be able to withstand the rigors of projecting oneself into time, even if the physical body is not being utilized. We also learn that this device is bioresonant in that it is tuned to the physiological, mental and emotional conditions of the subject as well as their own past experiences. In other words, you would have different experiences than would I and so on.

Another intriguing aspect of the time device is that there is a certain amount of censorship present. When Cezar attempts to project his consciousness into time in order to see who created the device, he encounters blockages. While it is informative and useful in certain respects, it contains mysteries which it does not want penetrated, at least at this particular time. All of this gives rise to interesting speculation.

These censorship issues further fuel the controversy Cezar ignites by relaying his initial experience in the time device whereupon he returns to the time of Jesus in the First Century. Radu also recounts what he saw in his original experiences in the Projection Hall (beneath the Romanian Sphinx) when he witnessed events surrounding the crucifixion of Christ. This account contains UFOs wreaking havoc amidst a virtually insurmountable thunder storm while a fearing populace scrambles to save their own lives. It leaves us with a hornets nest of information, the result of which has been more than a few questioning the veracity of the authors. I should add, however, that most of the reading audience thus far has not blinked at the accounts given. They have enjoyed the book and are not judgmental about the authors. What is perhaps the most relevant aspect of this experience, however, is the fact that the device which facilitates it is bioresonant. Whether the events presented are indeed real in a conventional sense, they are certainly events that the collective consciousness has wrestled with for thousands of years.

What happens in Mystery of Egypt, however, is superceded by what occurs in the fourth volume, The Secret Parchment. Radu finds himself in the middle of the political and conspiratorial intrigue that is swirling around the effort to control the holographic chamber beneath the Romanian Sphinx. Accordingly, Radu is sent to the United States to attend a remote viewing program in the Pentagon, all in an effort to defuse the rising political tensions. As the conspiratorial intrigues escalate into a full scale political and esoteric war, there is an intervention by superior spiritual forces, one of which includes Radu being recalled to Romania in order to meet with Repa Sundhi to facilitate the translation of the ancient Tibetan manuscript or "secret parchment" which had been given to him by Machandi as described in *Transylvanian Moonrise*. While the parchment presents five invaluable techniques for spiritual advancement (these are not the same as the already known yoga exercises known as the "Five Tibetans"), its very presence in the world has ignited a series of quantum events extending from a bizarre structure emerging from the snow in Antarctica that serves an antenna function which is at the crossroads between signals to Jupiter's moon Europa as well as Mount McKinley and Transylvania. As incredible as the discovery of this extraterrestrial connection is, it only escalates the attempt to undermine the structure of Romania's Department Zero when the Americans learn that the signal to Transylvania reveals a passageway of solid gold tunnels extending miles into the underground and leading to ancient hieroglyphics embedded in gold indicating the locale as the nexus of the Inner Earth where "all the worlds unite". Not too far from this nexus, accessible through more passageways of pure gold, is an incredible room of golden thrones with panels of yet more hieroglyphics and a mysterious portal that appears to be a direct conduit to outer space; and, presumably, an outer space of another universe. These discoveries were made by a certain Professor Constantine who, upon reporting them and taking a team from the government to investigate, was whisked away and never heard from again. Although the investigators were killed, Professor Constantine was able to make a summary report to Cezar Brad — the file for such was deemed to be the highest state secret of the country of Romania. Even so, Department Zero was unable to find any access to these passageways and, despite considerable effort, no further discoveries were made. Although Machandi's secret parchment is translated and we are treated to its specific wisdom, *The Secret Parchment — Five Tibetan Initiation Techniques* leaves us with a very great mystery that is left dangling.

I also contribute to the book by revealing my own adventures in the area and learning of the ancient legends and how these fit into the scheme of Radu's adventures. It turns out that Professor Constantine was indeed a real character who disappeared, and I am even shown where he once lived. There is also a Valley of the Golden Thrones, and it is in this region that I make one of the most remarkable discoveries that I have ever stumbled upon.

Although it has not been mentioned in any of the previous books, I was led to a cave by a Romanian archeologist in 2014. Known as Cioclovina Cave, it is the site of one of the greatest archeological finds in Romania which indicate a civilization did indeed occupy caverns within the inner earth and in the vicinity mentioned by Radu. Cioclovina Cave represents a sort of grand central cave station with some seven other caves interlinking with it, representing at least seven kilometers of tunnels.

While the aforementioned findings concerning Cioclovina Cave are of great relevance with regard to Radu's claims, there is an even more startling confirmation from Dr. David Anderson, my scientist friend who originally brought me to Romania in 2008. In an interview conducted by myself in 2015, he revealed for the first time that Cioclovina Cave was the site of the largest discharge of space-time motive force ever recorded. Space-time motive force is a term Dr. Anderson coined to signify an energy that is released as a result of time dilation that occurs in the process of frame-dragging. If you are further interested in this aspect and would like a full explanation, you can watch the video series *Time Travel Theory Explained* at my website *www.timetraveleducationcenter.com*. This function is also explained in the appendix of the book *Transylvanian Moonrise*.

What all of this means in layman's terms is that Dr. Anderson's findings indicate that this area was the site of heavy duty time travel experiments or phenomena. He was completely surprised that I happened to come across this very area by happenstance during my adventures in Romania. Note that this area was never a targeted area of interest for me. I had an off day and was brought there by an archeologist I knew at his instigation. He had no idea of the time experiments or the like. The archeologist, by the way, told me that the stories I relayed to him about Radu's books, which he had not read at that point, correlated with many stories he had heard about the area.

While there are many so-called "side tunnels" or supplementary threads of great interest that involve Dr. Anderson and my other associates in Romania, I am getting off subject. Radu is very well aware of Dr. Anderson and is even interested to meet with him. It is quite possible that all of these different threads might coalesce into a single homogeneous thread some day.

Radu's fifth book, entitled *Inside the Earth — The Second Tunnel,* refers to what is referred to as the "Second Tunnel" in a series of three tunnels in the projection room located within the chamber beneath the Romanian Sphinx. The First Tunnel, named in the title of the third book in the series, *Mystery of Egypt — The First Tunnel,* leads to a chamber beneath the Giza Plateau. The Second Tunnel leads to underground cities and installations. The Third Tunnel leads to Iraq with an offshoot branch to the Carpathians (near Buzău, Romania) and then towards Tibet, and from there to Mongolia and the Gobi Plateau.

Inside the Earth — The Second Tunnel begins with a rather sober evaluation of geophysics and how it relates to the core of the Earth and the myriad misunderstandings that have proliferated about the enigmatic region which is often referred to as the "Inner Earth" and often incorrectly as the "Hollow Earth". Radu's old friend and mentor, Dr. Xien, gives him rather thorough explanations on these various aspects and gives remarkable new insights into the science and origin of black holes that will eventually reach into the halls of academe and revolutionize the way that science thinks about such topics. There is also an exhaustive explanation of the fatal error of the Cavendish Experiment, done in 1799, the "gold standard" for justifying that the Earth's core is a mass iron-nickel alloy surrounded by molten lava. You will learn that later experiments to justify this conclusion are based upon what amount to outrageous assumptions based upon an experiment which has not been subject to rigorous inspection and is, in fact, errant. You will also learn that what resides at the core of the Earth is indeed a black hole.

Beyond the science are Radu's remarkable adventures with Cezar where the two visit mysterious regions within the Earth and the multiple civilizations that occupy that region. There are lots of amazing meetings as well as descriptions of technology that facilitate transportation between the mysterious regions "Inside the Earth". Radu also provides us with a glimpse of the fabled city of Shambhala, a paradise at the core of the Inner Earth itself where balance and harmony are the basis of civilization. Whatever your final opinion of Radu's adventures might be, you will be exposed to a paradigm that is novel and will change your view of the world.

One of the most admirable aspects of Radu's book is that, while familiar aspects and characters are common to all of them, each one is unique and focuses on a different look. *Forgotten Genesis* is no exception and is the sixth book in the series which reveals the mysteries of how multiple extraterrestrial civilizations have influenced and steered the DNA of Mankind in order for it to evolve to a higher state. All of this knowledge is facilitated by Radu's new contacts in the Inner Earth civilization of Apellos who embrace him as an ambassador of information to share with the surface world. The core of this work, which includes seventy elaborate drawings meant to make the text easier to understand, concerns man's true origin and complex evolution over the ages. Some of the "hot spots" of human history, which have either remained unknown or have only been considered from mythological positions, are explained. They include Atlantis, Troy, Shambhala, and Hyperborea. Particular emphasis is placed upon the existence and manifestation of inter-dimensional chasms or portals at the "intersections" between the physical plane and the etheric plane. *Forgotten Genesis* also includes the back story and a description of the technology by which Radu was able to assimilate this information.

This latest edition of the *Transylvania Series*, and what you are about to read, *The Etheric Crystal — The Third Tunnel*, picks up where the previous book took off and features Radu Cinamar's first trip into the mysterious Third Tunnel on a specific mission to visit the underground chamber beneath Iraq where his team recovers a powerful crystal that exists in another dimension but is housed in a container in this one. It becomes the basis for a new project by Department Zero which concentrates on Radu's ability to penetrate different dimensions. Initially started privately by Radu and Cezar Brad, the project is unexpectedly embraced by Elinor, the enigmatic alchemist who befriended Radu in Transylvanian Moonrise. Playing a significant role in this new project, Elinor helps them take the project to another level. Like the other books in the series, this work is equally unique with new tangents to pursue.

Peter Moon
Long Island
July 28, 2020

CHAPTER ONE

THE ULTIMATE SECRET —
THE TUNNEL TO IRAQ

There is no doubt that the revelations about the origin of man on Earth and those of human history have marked me deeply. Pretty soon, I realized that the initiative of the man from Apellos who had arranged for me to access that information through the small "window" of time that I had available for something like this was very well calculated. The inter-dimensional helmet, a fortuitous gift which we had received from the people of Apellos, turned out to be a very technologically evolved device, not only for understanding the complex information we viewed, but also for the way this related to what would be our expedition through the Third Tunnel. It seemed like everything was arranged for a well-defined purpose, but it was a purpose which was unclear to me at the time. It did not take long, however, for light to be shed in this regard.

Satisfied with the richness and nature of the information I had accessed during the viewing of images of the past of Mankind, I was looking forward to what I felt to be the "icing on the cake": the expedition through the Third Tunnel. I had already accumulated considerable experience on previous journeys, and now I was feeling a general sense of fulfillment due to the fact that the last "act", the last mystery of the Bucegi complex – the Third Tunnel – would be revealed to me, albeit only partially, because we were only going to explore the branch to Iraq. I already knew that this was the most "accessible" branch in the rather complicated "architecture" of the Third Tunnel.

TREE STRUCTURE

Due to delicate issues on the diplomatic level, I am not allowed at this time to comment on the main line of the Third Tunnel, the one that goes to Tibet. Even though it has no access to this main branch, China has reserved the right to censor information regarding it, and we do not want any additional tensions in this regard. Recently, however, we have been getting different kinds of signals from the Chinese government, but due to the sensitivity of the subject, I prefer to address this in a future volume, provided I am given clearance to do so.

On the other hand, one of the secondary branches of the main line (of the Third Tunnel) – the one leading to Curvature Buzăului* – has a great strategic

---

* Curvature Buzăului can be interpreted as the "Buzău Curve" in English, and it refers to the curvature in the Carpathians (which run west to east, forming the southern border of Transylvania), curving upwards in a northern direction, forming the eastern border of Transylvania. The city of Buzău is near this "curve", an area which is known for its (*continued on next page*)

interest for Romania which also cannot be unveiled for now. This leaves the branch to Iraq as well as the further the extension (of the Third Tunnel) to the Gobi Plateau and Mongolia. As far as what I can share in this volume, the branch to Iraq is the only one that can be considered, at least to some extent, without there being unpleasant consequences. Generally speaking, I knew what I was going to see there, and even specifically what we wanted to find, but the emotion of the journey and the actual experience was nevertheless very vivid.

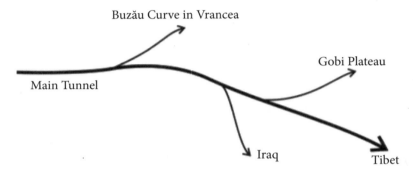

GENERAL SCHEMATIC OF THE THIRD TUNNEL WITH ITS BRANCHES

As I have said before, entering into the secret complex in the Bucegi Mountains automatically implies a vibrational leap of being, and that is why you never leave there being bored, tired or irritated.[*] On the contrary, after you enter the Great Gallery, the surrounding reality seems to be transforming, even if your mind tells you that nothing is different.

Access to the Projection Hall signifies an evidentiary leap, both in the vibrational frequency of the mind and the body. Inside this space, the specific field acts at a level so that the subtle influence on the psyche and mind is already a certain actuality which, in a certain way, can be described as a sort of "personality".

I knew the third tunnel was quite "technically accessible", but it was distinguished by its different branches. Over the years, Cezar made several expeditions into each of them, and I knew of their astonishing results from the reports I had read.

The main tunnel to Tibet offers the most direct access to extraordinary worlds. At the end of it, in one of the Tibetan massifs, there is a veritable

---

(*continued from previous page*) remnants of ancient civilizations that include mysterious "portals" and strange phenomena, all of which have been reported and observed completely independent of the works of Radu Cinamar.

[*] See Volume 5, *Inside the Earth - The Second Tunnel*, 2019

"launching pad", manifesting in both the subtle field of consciousness and in the outer physical world; but, as I said previously, further disclosures in this regard are imprudent due to certain political reactions, all of which need to be avoided.

On the other hand, the tunnel towards the curvature of the Carpathian Mountains – in an area corresponding to the surface of a rural landscape in the Siriu Mountains – is short and leads to an underground structure that plays a precise role at that point. For military and national security reasons, I am not allowed to go into detail, but I may return to this subject in one of the following volumes. All I can say for now is that at the end of this branch lies a complicated ensemble directly related to the main control panel in the Projection Hall in the Bucegi complex.

The fork to Iraq, however, is more accessible and simpler, and based upon what we discovered there, I had an idea that later developed in a very interesting way that led to remarkable results.

PREPARATIONS FOR THE JOURNEY

A day for rest and relaxation went very well. We had only a brief informal meeting with two American officers, neither of whom had never been in the Projection Hall before.[*] They, however, proved that they had done their home-work with regard to the documentation that they had access to with regard to the preparation of the mission. This also included intensive instruction on the characteristics of the Bucegi complex, the topography of the place and even the nature of space-time distortions in the three tunnels. By 2010-2011, together with Lieutenant Nicoară, we had developed a "manual" to prepare those who were to enter the Projection Hall to take part in the expeditions through the tunnels. The text was approved by Cezar and General Obadea, the latter still being alive at that time.

The experience gained in the first years after the great discovery in Bucegi demonstrated the need for a special protocol for those who were to enter the secret complex in the mountains and especially for the Projection Hall. We have established a set of precise rules as well as physical and psychological conditions that need to be met by "applicants" in addition to an ethical code of procedure. All of this proved necessary because, for the most part, those who entered there could not withstand the vibrational frequency of the specific energy field and artifacts in the Projection Hall. The special protocol that was worked on for several months was about two hundred pages long and treated these issues both theoretically and pragmatically. We have put together twelve specific tests and their evaluation grids. Therefore, it was a genuine

---

[*] These two officers were mentioned in the previous volume of the *Transylvania Series,* entitled *Forgotten Genesis.*

exam which the military had to pass. Save for myself, only nine civilians, all of them scientists, have thus far been allowed to enter the secret location.

The protocol also details how to make contact with advanced technologies, far superior to those currently in place on Earth, including technologies from "black projects" run outside of official governmental supervision. Those technologies are based on principles and approaches to the universe which are completely different from what is currently known, and that is why reverse engineering – which has yielded remarkable results in many other cases – could not be applied here except to a small extent. It is as if we must learn another physics, an extremely advanced one, which involves a deep knowledge of the mysteries of the Macrocosm*, unlike "orthodox" physics, a subject that only studies the universe in a partial and limited manner.

The American officers proved themselves to be very well prepared at all levels involving the Protocol, passing the exam brilliantly and thus gaining clearance for the expedition through the Third Tunnel. Certain restrictions, however, have been put in place over time, and here I am mainly referring to the Second Tunnel that leads to the interior of the Earth. These restrictions were imposed by some of the civilizations there, and we had to respect them, even though this created some tension in our relationship with the Americans. For example, Tomassis said from the very beginning that they did not want to work with the United States. This was a difficult condition to digest for the chiefs at the Pentagon, but the very wise Dryn remained very firm in this regard without giving further explanations. In the end, the Americans had to accept this, but the situation was not pleasant for us either.

Additionally, the leadership of Apellos requested that what we communicate outwards be just what they allow and nothing more. Censorship applies both to general information intended for the public – such as what I present in the books I write – and to those of a top secret nature which is intended for certain governments and security agencies. After my visit to Apellos, the city representatives requested to meet the functional "ambassador" of those on the surface. Cezar had already fulfilled this function for many years for those in Tomassis and for two other subterranean civilizations.

I wanted a brief discussion in order to make things better understood in the context of our bilateral relations with the Pentagon and those civilizations within the planet. Returning to our expedition now, through the Third Tunnel, the mission would take only a few hours according to the estimated schedule. In the evening, we would return to the Base.

The parameters of the expedition, which were fixed by Cezar, were clear and also provided for the thorough research of the occult chamber using the

---

* In previous volumes of the series, the author defined this term (Macrocosm) as the totality of the planes and dimensions of manifestation, from the physical to the causal universe. In other words, the Macrocosm includes both the physical dimension of Creation and its subtle dimensions.

special equipment brought by the two Americans, all of which was provided for in the bilateral agreement for the expedition through the Third Tunnel. This expedition would include procuring the tablets; studying the special "chair" therein and possibly finding the missing crystal which apparently represented the "pièce de résistance" in that site.[*] In order to identify the crystal, both Cezar and I had hope in the possibilities of the etheric helmet we had received from the people of Apellos, a technological piece of extraordinary finesse, the principles of operation of which were very advanced. Incidentally, the American side wanted to study that device in detail, but we had to refuse by reason of our agreement with the people of Apellos and their refusal to allow it.

American logistics, however, were not to be neglected either as the two officers had come up with a device to "scan dynamic exchanges of a quantum nature", a technological first we were told, with a high-resolution thermospectrometer with a peak range that can only be found in military equipment. None of these high-tech parts are for public use because they were part of the "miracle bag" of non-governmental projects.[**] This was not our business, however; and moreover, the American officers did not offer any further information to us on this matter.

We were apparently well equipped, but you never knew what surprises extraterrestrial technology might present itself to you in the secret complex in Bucegi. By that time, the research undertaken showed us that it was obvious that there was a point of incompatibility between earthly technology and that of the alien civilization that built that astounding complex, both with regard to principles and effects. As I said before, even reverse engineering could not help because the basics of the extraterrestrial technology could not be understood by modern science. We hope, however, to find certain elements that would hasten the realization of the fundamental leap that is required by science in order to gain access to a much deeper knowledge of the phenomena in the universe.

The next day, we got up early, but with all the preparations to be made, with the orders Cezar still had to give, plus the helicopter flight, we did not arrive at the Bucegi complex until noon. We remained for some time in the area of the Great Gallery to allow for the two Americans to be acclimated to the new energy level of reality with which they were now interacting.

Despite all of their preparation through the special protocol, their utter astonishment had intensified since entering the Grand Gallery and could not be contained. After we all arrived in the Projection Hall, it was necessary to take another half-hour break to allow them to adjust psychologically to what

---

[*] See Volume 6, *Forgotten Genesis*, 2019.

[**] The author is probably referring to so-called "Black Projects".

they saw on the outside and what they were perceiving inside of themselves. Meanwhile, Cezar adjusted the entrance to the Third Tunnel at the small control panel in front of it. As far as myself, as I do whenever I come to this amazing place, I retreated to the area of the golden yellow square near the Dome and sat there, trying to let all those subtle influences pass through me, feeding off of their strength and knowledge. I would say that I was practicing some kind of "communion" with that Hall which created a state of "floating" and even euphoria, both of which spread quickly throughout my being.

A SHORT TRIP

About half an hour later, everything was ready before the tunnel entrance. The two American officers were standing next to Cezar in front of the small console of the control panel. The enormous opening in the mountain was already activated, vibrating in a slightly phosphorescent greenish color, leaving it to be a little visible from within. I noticed that it was already becoming dark, a sign of the space distortion at the entrance, a common characteristic for each of the three tunnels. I expected the distortion to be a little deeper, but I noticed that it was relatively close to the entrance and quite strong because its specific pulsation was wider than in the first two tunnels.

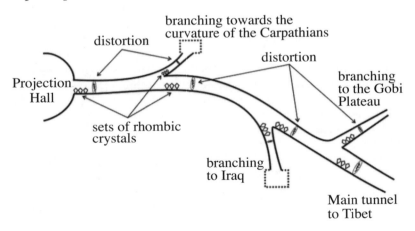

BRANCHES AND DISTORTIONS IN THE THIRD TUNNEL

Sensing my thoughts, Cezar said, "Each of the tunnels has its peculiarity. Here, the mode of transport is eased by some space airlocks...about the same as the tunnel to the inside of the planet."

He then activated certain commands on the console and a hologram appeared in front of us with the schematic presentation of the tunnel structure.

I noticed the strong nature of each distortion, marked by the accented indigo color surrounded by a dynamic bright-white halo. Each branch of the tunnel contained such a distortion a short distance from the entrance.

"Here we will be able to make a few 'jumps' and cover the entire distance," Cezar said.

I noticed that the American officers were quite excited, and I could relate to this very well from my own experiences upon entering the Projection Hall but especially when I went on expeditions through the tunnels. I joked a little with them, cheering them up. In their case, there was no question of apprehension or a feeling of fear, but it was rather about the emotion of mystery and experience that was intended for only an extremely small number of people on this planet. The huge mouth of the tunnel and the hypnotic pulsation of the distortion does indeed have a major impact on the human psyche and mind. It takes a good few minutes to align the body and mind to the huge subtle energy emanating from the Projection Hall as it is necessary for one's being to be a well balanced whole.

I briefly told the two officers what they should expect upon stepping inside the tunnel. It was, however, more of a recap because I knew all too well that nothing could replace the actual experience. Upon entering the tunnel, we immediately felt the specific sound insulation, and it suggested a break from the surrounding reality. I noticed that, as with the Second Tunnel that connects with the interior of the Earth, the colored crystals were situated in their places before the distortion, about fifteen meters from the entrance. Its surface rhythmically waved in the air, mildly altering the view to the other side.

I waited a few moments for Cezar who remained at the command console. After he entered the tunnel, he went through the distortion very relaxed and full of confidence, instantly disappearing from the sight of our eyes even though we could still see the continuation of the tunnel behind it. Already having experienced this kind of "crossing", I signaled the two majors to follow. After a brief hesitation, they quickly went through the distortion, disappearing suddenly. I then passed, feeling a slight tingling in the skin, the same feeling I had felt in the passage from the tunnel to the Earth's center. I immediately saw Cezar and the two officers waiting for me in front of a huge entrance to a branch of the tunnel.

The "displacement", in fact, was a "switching" between two areas of different space through a change in vibrational frequency. In that case, as the distances were relatively small, I assumed that the formation and maintenance of the distortion did not require a large energy source. Even so, this did and still does represent the greatest mystery to us: what is it that energetically supports all the amazing technology that is present in the Projection Hall, including the specific field there and the distortions that have endured in this way for tens of thousands of years?

The first branch, breaking off from the main tunnel to Tibet, took direction to the left and continued to the Carpathian curvature area. That tunnel was slightly smaller in size than the main tunnel. I estimated its height at seven and a half meters and the width about five meters. At the intersection, both on the main line and on the branch, we saw sets of colored rhombic crystals on either side of the tunnels followed by a distortion like the one at the entrance through which we had just had passed.

On the branch to the underground beneath Buzău, at the entrance on the right side, I saw one of the new electric cars and several sealed crates stored on the ground. I knew that shipment had arrived about a year ago from the Army and actually involved a lot more crates. From then until now, a single expedition had been organized with an exclusively Romanian team but for technical purposes only. I therefore assumed that the rest of the crates had been taken to their final destination, but I did not ask. From Cezar, I knew that it was logistical equipment and perhaps, in the near future, we were going to deal with its installation.

Cezar beckoned us to go through the next distortion, continuing on the main line towards Tibet, and we did so immediately. We then went off on a new fork that appeared virtually identical to the first branch, but this one was heading right towards Iraq, being smaller in size than the main tunnel towards Tibet. We were now at the crossroads of our expedition because our destination was on this path to Iraq.

"Another leap," said a smiling Cezar as we arrived.

I thought how convenient such trips are whereby you can arrive thousands of miles from the starting point within minutes, and I imagined how much Mankind could progress with such technology at its disposal. The acquisition of this technology alone, both conceptually and pragmatically, could change at least fifty percent of world trade, revenues, freedom and especially efficiency in almost all economic areas. The single pressing on an important button in the process of evolving science could trigger major changes in human life and destiny.

I also appreciated that expeditions through the Third Tunnel were the easiest to achieve, whether or not it was human displacement or transport devices, due to the extraordinary speed and efficiency with which they were achieved. The main line to Tibet retains a somewhat linear frequency without special disturbances, but the branches– that is, the ones to the Carpathian Curvature, Iraq and the Gobi Plateau in Mongolia – are consumed by large magnetic vortexes. I realized that the complex structure in Bucegi "explores" much of the planet in directions having different characteristics, suggesting the existence of areas where different but very old civilizations had developed, now covered by the "dust" of time that erodes everything.

DESTINATION: THE SECOND OCCULT CHAMBER

We all deviated from the main tunnel, entering the branch headed for Iraq. Behind the crystals, about ten meters from the entrance, lies the spatial distortion; and, as usual, we went through without any problems. Suddenly, we were on the last part of the tunnel of the secondary branch, maybe about twelve meters away from an opaque wall of indigo color. The light in the tunnel was no longer blue, but it had turned green, like the one at the entrance to the tunnel. There was a perfect resemblance to what we had seen in the tunnel to Egypt. The difference, however, consisted of what was at its end. In the tunnel to Egypt, its end was surrounded by a huge stone door, perfectly polished; whereas here, on the branch towards Iraq, the stone gate was replaced by an indigo color which slowly changes its shade. I had a hunch, but to be sure, I put on my helmet given by our friends in Apellos. I immediately saw the subtle field of the "gate" which was a dam of energy, and I was even seeing the interior of the space beyond it.

On the left wall of the tunnel, also encased in the same specific material, we saw the similarly distinct sign as that of the gate in the Great Gallery: a square inside which was engraved a triangle with the tip up. Cezar came before us, explaining.

"The protection system is redundant; but it in some sense, it is the other way around. That is to say, you cannot get access here unless you are recognized by the console in front of the tunnel in the Projection Hall. It seems that handling the control panel there leaves a biological or subtle impression that is recognized here. Only the one who commands that console can open the protection field here. But again, you cannot reach the console unless you get past the energetic dam at the gate of the Grand Gallery, and this is the real test for an intruder with unclean thoughts.

I wanted to check this out and I touched the triangle, but nothing happened. Cezar then did the same. Almost immediately, the opaque indigo background became translucent and then disappeared. In front of us, a fairly wide space appeared, a rectangular room more deep than wide and gently lit in a light blue shade that was very pleasant.

After we had all entered that room, Cezar told us that this was the occult chamber of Iraq, directing his attention towards the two American officers. It is a lot like the one in Egypt, but here we were particularly interested in the consciousness projection chair and the crystal that makes it work. In the other expeditions made here, there was more interest in studying the tablets.

I looked around and saw that the walls of the room had numerous niches of different depths where tablets were placed. This was different from Egypt's occult chamber because, here in Iraq, the shelves for platinum plates were replaced by types of niches in different locations. The room was smaller than that in Egypt, measuring a little more than half of it, about seven to seven and a half meters long and about six meters wide.

The niches were more deeply embedded into the walls of the room which were not made of stone but from the special material that permeated the tunnel inside: a special texture, seemingly a combination of something amorphous and something biological. The color of that material was indigo and was slightly phosphorescent on the surface. To the touch, it gave the impression that it was "veiled", but in reality, it was tough, both for the palms and for the soles.

Inside the room, the material appeared to be "molded" in different areas of the walls because we saw many niches of a rectangular or "L" shape filled with plates about the same size as those in Egypt. The niches were distributed on three of the walls of the room because the fourth remaining wall, through which we had entered, was in fact a subtle protective field. The distribution of niches seemed random to me, and the spaces between them were relatively large.

Each niche was filled with plates, but I noticed with astonishment that they, unlike those in Egypt, were all made up of perfectly transparent material, probably crystal. I approached one and took a tablet. I did not encounter any resistance, and that was another difference from the plates in Egypt. Here, they stood up, mysteriously adhering to a vertically stable position, as if they were attracted to a magnet. They had already been inventoried on a previous expedition, and Lieutenant Nicoară had the list of their distribution in the niches. There are slightly less than a thousand plates in Iraq's occult chamber which is far less than those in Egypt.

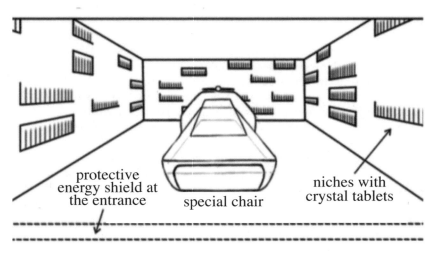

FRONT VIEW OF THE OCCULT CHAMBER

Cezar explained that the study of the crystal plates was deliberately postponed until a technology was designed to convert or extract information from the platinum plates in Egypt's occult chamber. It was considered that the crystal plates in Iraq are more difficult to decode than those of platinum.

A day earlier, when the two American officers asked him for further clarification, Cezar said that we did not want to mix the studies of these tablets. It was only a matter of time, however, before an advanced technology would be developed to retrieve this information and convert it into a format that would be easy to use for us. As we now have access to the platinum plates, it is time to turn our attention to the crystal plates as well.

THE MYSTERY OF THE CRYSTAL REVEALED

I did not understand the meaning of the niches in the walls nor the logic of their layout. But before I tried to figure this out, I was drawn to the main part of the occult chamber which was the special "chair". It was placed perpendicular to the protective energy wall, appearing as if it were "poured" into the floor, and it corresponded in size and shape to a humanoid being of at least two and a half meters high.

Compared to the dimensions of an ordinary human being, the seat seemed enormous to me as its walls were very thick with "inlays" that looked like cuneiform signs illuminated in a phosphorescent blue-metallic color. If we did not consider the crystal plates, the chair was basically the only object in the room, impressive in size and allure and complex in shape.

At first glance, it seemed to be cast in one piece as I did not see any joints. All its forms were cursive and rounded, giving it both a modern and somewhat aerodynamic but also a highly technological appearance. It looked like an ergonomic seat with the backrest at an angle of about thirty degrees, but it was very massive with many projections, curves and small recesses.

On the right side of the chair, I saw a lateral extension as an additional rectangular block with a width of about thirty centimeters which had an empty space in the middle with a rather complex structure on the inner walls. It was like an extension of the chair about fifteen centimeters in diameter which went about forty centimeters deep.

On both sides of that rectangular box, I noticed a few lighted blue signs. I immediately recognized the extension for using the crystal, just as I had seen in the images that were converted from the plates in Egypt. Even though the two American officers carefully searched the various areas of the occult chamber, using the equipment they brought for this purpose, they failed to capture any "anomaly" that might offer any indication about the crystal.

At the top of the chair, corresponding to the place where the head is placed, I saw two semicircular metal "strips" with a third that was perpendicular to

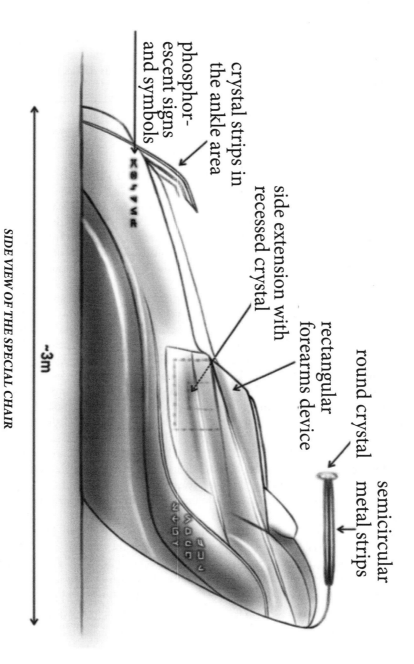

SIDE VIEW OF THE SPECIAL CHAIR

~3m

crystal strips in
the ankle area

phosphor-
escent signs
and symbols

side extension with
recessed crystal

rectangular
forearms device

round crystal

semicircular
metal strips

28

these, having at the lower end a large round crystal, probably near the forehead of the one sitting in the chair. In the middle of the seat, corresponding to the places of the forearms, were two devices of a somewhat rectangular shape but sharpened towards the tip. At my feet around the ankle area, I saw a wide "band" of crystal supported by a base which featured illuminated signs in phosphorescent blue.

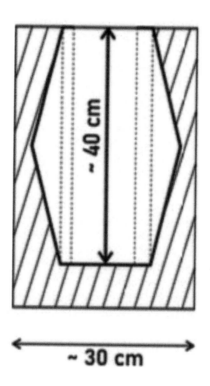

SIDE EXTENSION OF THE SEAT — THE PLACE FOR THE CRYSTAL

For the most part, we have little to do here," said Cezar. "We are to gather the plates and carefully look for the tetrahedral crystal."

We all looked at him in astonishment. Where would we look for the crystal?

With a hand gesture, Cezar showed me the helmet given by the people of Apellos. He was perfectly right because, after I used it to identify the nature of the opaque wall from the entrance to the occult chamber, I put it down, being concerned about the crystal plates and the special chair. I put the helmet on my head and realized I needed to focus as best I could, knowing that there is a close connection between my psychological state of mind and the object I was focusing on. With that helmet, the sight of the crystal plates turned into a real spectacle because each niche shined brightly due to the electromagnetic emissions they were emitting. It was a somewhat duplicate image with a sparkling light around the edge which indicated to me that the device was showing me the etheric level and its subtleties. Although I carefully took in a 180° panorama of the walls, I failed to notice anything special. Viewing the mysterious chair in the middle of the occult chamber, I knew with certainty that it only worked when it was coupled with the crystal we were looking for. On the other hand, the crystal was not there, and I considered this to be illogical as it had either been deliberately taken by the tunnel builders, which made no sense, or it was hidden. I was rather inclined to accept the second version.

I began to carefully examine the shapes of the chair while Cezar and one of the Americans took the crystal plates from the niches and placed them in the specially compartmented boxes which we had brought with us. While I was carefully investigating the special chair, the other American was paying close attention to my movements and how I proceeded. He had probably received instructions in this regard, but I did not see what they could do for him.

The chair seemed to be covered by a strong subtle field of energy that was phosphorescent indigo, close in color to that of the tunnel walls. When I reached the side extension that was intended for the crystal, I was in for a big surprise: it was empty, like a deep cylinder that appeared to me as being "full" with a cylindrical object which was also covered in a protective field but pink in color. I realized that I was seeing that "tube" in the etheric plane and that the same space would appear to be empty in the physical plane. At that time, we did not view anything on the recordings nor in the occult chamber because we only had the perspective of the physical plane. In fact, the crystal and tube in which it was "trapped" turned out to be in the subtle etheric plane and were therefore not commonly seen.

I was a little disappointed because I did not understand how the chair could work under these conditions. Approaching the side extension, I looked more closely at the cylinder inside the space that, without a helmet, I perceived as empty. Trapped in that space, it was somehow caught by protrusions I saw coming out of the walls of the empty place. It was perfectly transparent, and at the top and at the bottom, it had a thin ring on the circumference, silver in color. The ring was at the upper limit of the hollow cylindrical housing, and above it I noticed a transparent dome, slightly iridescent, as a field of protection.

Upon seeing the crystal inside the tube, I became filled with emotion. It was shaped like a tetrahedron with its tip down and was suspended in the middle area of the cylinder, probably in a field generated in that space. Although the helmet did not provide full depth perception, I could still see quite a bit of what was a beautiful blue crystal, quite large, perfectly polished on all sides, and reflecting from time to time the multicolored "spark" inside of it.

A comparison with an animated rendering of electrical connections between synapses in the human brain came to my mind. What I saw there was similar to that but in a more refined way. I felt the beauty and harmony that is intrinsic to a pure aesthetic object, something which you can hardly reproduce in words. Thanks to the headset, I even felt the sense that the etheric crystal was a consciousness. As I watched it, an almost hypnotic but deeply empathetic and beneficial connection was created between itself and me. The chair and the etheric crystal formed a subtle symbiosis, a mutual connection with myself that was not invasive. The level of vibration of the consciousness of the person interacting with this arrangement was directly influenced, and from here, I could anticipate a multitude of wonderful possibilities.

I took a deep breath and told the others what I had discovered. We were glad that we were beginning to understand the mystery of the crystal's "disappearance", but the enigma of how the of the chair functioned remained. Gathering around the crystal, we exchanged viewpoints about it when, at one point, Cezar suggested that I remove the cylinder from its place as I was the only one who could see it by reason of wearing the helmet tailor-made for myself. I extended my hand towards the "metallic" ring of the cylinder in order to try to pull it out of the housing. The others saw only empty space, but I was doing a "bioenergetic operation".

CHARACTERISTICS AND CHANGE OF STATUS

As I passed my hand through the small energetic "dome" above the cylinder, a short click was heard, and a slight vibration was felt throughout the chair that was accompanied by a slight hum. Some luminous signs appeared at the end of the chair, this time illuminated in red and pulsing. The chair seemed to come to life, waiting for operating commands. I did not know what that could mean, but Cezar was quite optimistic, foreseeing a fairly easy effort on figuring out the functions of that sophisticated device.

Through the headphone screen, I saw an instantaneous change of frequency spectra that were specific to the physical plane. The form's brightness disappeared as did the domed subtle field of energy, and the "inner" tube seemed to shrink somewhat due to the decrease in vibrational frequency. Basically speaking, it was a decoupling from the etheric mode of operation and an activation of the physical mode.

As Cezar smiled, his American colleagues uttered an exclamation of astonishment. Slowly pulling the transparent tube from it place, it came out effortlessly. As he came out of the room and I held the tube with the crystal, I felt a shiver run through my hand which went up to the top of my head. At the same time, I noticed a vibration in the chair with that specific hum. The discrete red lights at the top remained lit, pulsating slowly. While the chair obviously did not have any moving parts, I suspected that the hum and vibrational change were related to a specific frequency change, such as when switching from one operating mode to another. I repeatedly inserted and removed the cylinder with the etheric crystal from its designated place, and each time, I heard the same manifestations of sound, reduced in intensity but nevertheless clear. After that, we turned our attention to the cylinder.

I was holding the tube by the upper ring which had a metallic appearance that very much resembled titanium. I felt, however, that it was not titanium but an unknown material, the information coming into my cortex through the telepathic influence of the headset which I was looking through. I was trying to hold the object upright, imagining that this would avoid a possible disturbance of the position of the crystal on the inside. It was apparently supported by a mysterious force field as we did not see any source, attachment or other piece that would provide the energy needed for it.

To my surprise, the etheric crystal remained perfectly immobile as if it were embedded in that subtle energy field. In practical terms, it was levitating inside the cylinder, unobtrusively radiating a discrete light on its surface. The sight of that glow was as if it were from another world and its blue color generated in myself an inner state of bewilderment, something that seemed to penetrate into the deepest depths of my heart, reaching for unexpected strings of sensibility and even far away nostalgia that I did not quite understand.

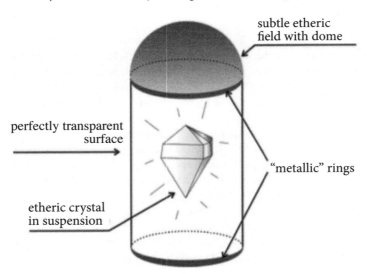

subtle etheric
field with dome

perfectly transparent
surface

"metallic" rings

etheric crystal
in suspension

THE ETHERIC CRYSTAL INSIDE THE CYLINDER

Then something amazing happened in my being because I felt a kind of mental "openness", like a telepathic transmission of some important information about that chair and the etheric crystal. It was like a block of knowledge which I could not decipher. Knowing it was important, I just accepted it, but I was not able to understand it yet.

I was awakened from my "dream" of the miraculous by the voice of one of the Americans.

"What are you looking at now? The cylinder is empty, but what do you see inside of it?"

I recoiled, feeling a chill throughout my being; and putting down the helmet, I also noticed that the physical cylinder I was holding was apparently "empty". It was extremely light, almost as if I did not feel its weight, and the circular wall was made of a material that, at first glance, resembled glass but created a feeling of great refinement, also being very thin. You could hardly tell that there was a protective layer between the outside and inside of the cylinder.

We all realized then that the lowering of the vibrational frequency included only the outer casing so that the tube took on a physical consistency, the technology for it probably only being relevant in case it needed to be replaced, removed from the housing or even for possible replacement of the etheric crystal inside through some special technique. The source of the transformations and experiences, however, the crystal inside the cylinder, remained etheric in nature. Perhaps this is even the same quality that enables the possibility of detachment and translation of the subtle bodies of beings in other planes of Creation. That extremely advanced and incomprehensible technology enables the etheric crystal to somehow be "trapped" in that tube and remain connected to the special chair to facilitate a phenomenon of separation between the physical and the subtle bodies of those who realize the experience. A kind of "affinity" was probably created between the crystal and the respective being and amplified by the technology of the special chair, but these were only my assumptions at that time based upon a momentary understanding.

Physically speaking, we were all looking at a simple hollow tube, but in reality, it represented a unique form of manifestation, having in its composition a physical part (its outer body) and a subtle etheric part (the crystal inside). Looking closely, even in the physical plane, one could see in the middle of the tube and only from certain angles, a very weak light, more like an extremely fine glow. This was obviously due to the strong subtle influence of the crystal which somehow penetrated from the etheric to the physical plane. This was, however, very discreet and could be observed only under certain conditions, at least as far as we could tell.

VERY ADVANCED TECHNOLOGIES

On the one hand, the discovery of the crystal delighted us because, after some necessary adjustments were made to make it fit the dimensions of an ordinary human being, it offered the possibility of experiments in the special chair. On the other hand, it was a cause for regret because our current earth-bound technology did not allow for the study of that extraordinary device, astonishing by its simplicity but still so efficient by the nature of the effects it produced.

In a brief discussion we had while studying the cylindrical object and the chair, Cezar expressed his concern about the nature of the experiments that would involve the etheric crystal and cylinder. I thought there was probably a need for some caution regarding the nature of the subtle fields to be engaged as there were few chances that other modern scientific methods that were either mechanical or chemical nature would have any effect on the cylinder. Cezar did not even react to the sophisticated equipment brought by the Americans. For example, the probe with the special scanning device indicated absolutely nothing, and the thermal spectrometer recorded only a slight variation of the parameters. It was quite discouraging for a start, but after all, the study and research of the artifacts in the secret complex in Bucegi was the job of scientists; and although their progress was minimal after all these years, it started to appear exactly in the sphere that interested us: the field of akashic recordings.

An immediate experience in the special chair was very tempting, but after some deliberations, Cezar decided that we would postpone this because several conditions had to be met first. The first was to adjust the position in the chair so that the body of the experiencer was coupled to all the necessary elements: head, hands and feet. Of these, only the head area could be accessed easily, but for the other two, the construction elements being much larger, a technical solution had to be sought. Before actual experiments could be conducted, a few preliminary expeditions were required to make the respective adjustments. Otherwise, the faculties of the chairs could not be explored.

I took the necessary photographic footage, checking the retrieval of all the tablets according to the inventory, and the cylinder with the etheric crystal was taken by Cezar. We stayed for almost two hours in that room, and although we were five, we felt no difference in the internal climate. The humidity and temperature were the same, and the oxygen level was perfectly normal. I exchanged a few words with Cezar about this and he told me that this aspect also caught his attention since the first expeditions to the two occult chambers in Egypt and Iraq. It was, however, a real mystery because you could not find any source that was maintaining the ambient atmosphere. The only conclusion that the scientists could draw that was indeed logical and relevant was that the atmosphere inside was somehow automatically regulated by the "intelligent" properties in the tunnel itself. Although this environment managed to meet all the biological requirements of a human being, it remained an unresolved mystery.

THE EFFECT OF SPATIAL DISTORTIONS

Pretty loaded with containers and containers, we left the occult chamber in the tunnel space and headed towards the spatial distortion. Following us, the subtle opaque field closed like a faithful guardian, occluding any image of the interior of the room. In a few minutes, we walked the road back, the same one we had arrival on, crossing successively the distortions along the tunnel. Due to the fact that the distortions were more numerous, the protocol recommended a recovery of several days in order to avoid certain unpleasant reactions at the level of the mitochondria, an effect that the researchers observed over time on those who took part in the expeditions through the three tunnels. After one or two passages through these spatial distortions, the influence on the fine structure of the human body was not noticeable, but after several successive "jumps", especially within a short time, the cells begin to react.

The effects are somewhat similar to those of nuclear irradiation, although they do not involve the same consequences. It has more to do with a destabilization of mitochondrial DNA as a result of the energy demand required during the pass-throughs. This can quickly cause states of weakness and even dizziness. There are exceptions, however, where such effects are not felt. Cezar, for example, is one such case. Even though he has gone on dozens of expeditions with frequent "jumps", he has always been found healthy at medical checks. Personally, I have noticed that he is even more vital after such expeditions, his skin seeming to be finer and more shiny. Researchers involved in this program, however, have hypothesized that, as time passes and with the repetition of experiences, DNA learns the specific imprint of the leap and adapts to it pretty quickly.

I arrived at the Projection Hall and then loaded everything into the electric conveyors outside the entrance to the Great Gallery. Quickly going through the administrative and other protocol stages, we handed the materials over to the scientific team for further inspection and climbed into the waiting helicopter.

In the evening, I spent a very relaxing time at the Base in the reading room, reviewing the main elements of the expedition from which we had just come. The journey through the Third Tunnel had been the fastest and easiest trip, very efficient in terms of time and access. Not once did I think about the amazing changes of scenery associated with moving very fast between realities belonging to different planes of existence. In only a few hours, one can travel thousands of miles back and forth, perform multiple spatial jumps and explore some of the most unique mysteries before returning to the Base where you can have an evening of pleasant discussion in the study or meeting room while drinking an aromatic tea. It is disconcerting for one's psychological equilibrium; but after a while, you get used to it and it becomes an integral part of your life experience.

In particular, I was very glad that the mystery of the crystal was solved because, through the use of the special chair in the near future, it could open a whole universe of unexpected possibilities of knowledge. Also, I reflected intensely at the moments when I had an unexpected subtle "communion" with the etheric reality in which I felt the "pulse" of the life of that crystal, something I perceived as almost a living entity. I did not suspect how fast and in what form I would return to that reality, it representing a major leap in my evolution and knowledge.

EDEN — A DERIVATIVE VERSION OF THE WONDROUS CHAIR

The two days we spent looking at the holographic images in the company of the man from Apellos embodied a mine of information essential to what the true history of humanity and its main points actually signify. It took me more than a month to synthesize this data based on hurried notes taken in front of the holographic screen. It was a huge volume of knowledge, elements and aspects which I felt responsible for presenting correctly, synthetically and intelligently.[*]

A few days after I started this work, I was at the Alpha Base and analyzing the file of the occult chamber of Iraq into which we had also introduced our latest reports. Looking closely at the photographs taken during the expedition, I suddenly felt an interest in a larger set of symbols embedded on the edges of the chair inside the chamber. Something drew me like a magnet to those symbols that I knew nothing about. I had a certain impression that I had seen them before, but I could not specify where exactly. A feeling that I had to make a decision was more and more on my mind, but I had no idea what that decision or action might be.

I turned my head to the window of the room, looking at the moon over the clear sky of the cold night which mysteriously reflected itself over the silent snow of the hills. For a few moments, enthralled by that enigmatic picture of the winter landscape, I felt that my mind seemed cleared of thoughts, but that only lasted a few moments because, almost immediately afterwards, the clear image of the chair in the occult chamber in Iraq came to my mind. An irresistible desire forced me to put on my helmet and go into playback mode.

THE ENIGMATIC SYMBOLS THAT CAUGHT MY EYE, ENCRUSTED ON THE WALLS OF THE SPECIAL CHAIR

---

[*] The author refers here to the contents of volume 6 of the *Transylvania Series, Forgotten Genesis*, 2019.

The images that I had clearly outlined in my mind with the chair immediately appeared, highlighting in detail the mysterious symbols that attracted me.

This was an important moment because I remembered that some of these symbols in the images on the holographic screen I had seen when we were looking at the data on the evolution of man and the modeling phases of his DNA. Whether they were universal symbols included in a galactic language or were part of a specific set of data, it was evident that they represented the traces of extraordinary alien knowledge.

I looked carefully at the set of data and information that appeared on the edges of the headset image and gradually began to "feel" those symbols, not just look at them. The sensation was well-known to me from the visions I had previously experienced because the inter-dimensional helmet facilitated my psycho-mental experience of what I saw, "projecting" me into the reality there. The symbols came "alive", loaded with a "conscious" energy which made me understand their essence intuitively.

At that moment, an intense emotion gripped me and my mind began to work with a feverishness. It was exactly the opposite of the state of peace I had experienced a few moments before, but I felt a sudden inspiration which prompted me to act immediately. I took off my helmet, sat down at the table and began to write down a few elements, even drawing some rudimentary sketches of the images that were quickly rolling in my mind.

At first, I just drew seemingly meaningless lines, trying to "connect" to the information I had in mind. I realized that everything had to do with building a chair like the one seen in the occult chamber of Iraq, but I still retained a considerable dose of skepticism in this regard. The technology involved there seemed light years away from what I knew I could do or understand.

For example, it was obvious that I did not have an etheric crystal nor the technology needed to work with it nor did I know the operating principles of the chair. However, I immediately found a foothold, a possibility by which I hoped to compensate for these big shortcomings, at least to some extent, in order to have the chance to build a similar device. I could not say exactly what was leading me to build such, but the effervescence I felt and the aspiration to do so amazed me.

In support of realizing that idea, I thought that important help could come from the recordings of the images in the occult chamber which I had access to thanks to the inter-dimensional headset. I had already used that important playback function and mastered how to get the recordings I wanted in order to interpret the images that were running fast in my mind. In fact, I mainly relied on the helmet and the details it offered which appeared on the edge of the lens because they involved symbols and even certain schematics and synthetic images. I hoped I could understand a lot of them, especially since I had some experience in interpreting such symbols and vibrations over a very wide range of frequencies, but I also relied on the telepathic influxes I could get through the headset as I have often been guided to look at the elements and information about the past of Mankind. In addition to this, I felt a certain inner impulse and a surprising confidence in going forward on that path and persevering in the practical realization of the idea. I could not explain it very well, but I knew somehow that everything had to do with the "block of knowledge" that I received in the occult chamber in Iraq when I had that state of "communion" with the etheric crystal that was referred to in the last chapter.

I put on my helmet again and lightly touched its rectangular surface on the left side of the head, next to the temple, to go into playback mode. I then focused on the chair, remembering what had happened in the occult chamber. An image was immediately clarified on the "glass" of the headset in holographic format. Basically, what I was seeing was a faithful rendering of the moments that had happened there a few days before, a perfect record of the period of time I had worn the helmet in that space. Indeed — at the top right-hand side of the image, I could see a series of symbols and shapes that followed one another quite quickly but which I could stop by mental control. As in the case of the holographic screen, the helmet indicates the most important elements through variations of light intensity while others were "described" by different frequencies which I perceived directly in the cortex.

In the beginning, putting the schematics and "equations" on paper was somewhat automatic. For me, it was quite easy to play them back from memory, but I did not understand much of the meanings of those equations. I could, however, see that the unusual symbols, signs, and notations that predominated combined with others that were quite similar to those known to me. Only later did I realize that they had the role of making me deconstruct and understand the substratum of the archaic symbols, some of which are even known to the current scientific world.

I soon realized that the first symbols and images were kind of physics lessons for me to learn some of the basic principles of new concepts and constructive ideas that were unfolding in front of my eyes on the lens of the inter-dimensional headset. Inspired by the telepathic transmissions that I was able to understand and that were provided to me through the highly developed headphone technology, I learned to somehow "translate" those symbols into a set of drawings and formulas that could be found, at least some of them, in contemporary physics.

Initially, I did not understand the relationships and symbols depicted in the immediate drawing, but I could still "access" them to the point where it was if I was "seeing" them somewhere in the back the head, in the occipital area. I then figured out how to decode them using a "key" that I was able to perceive.

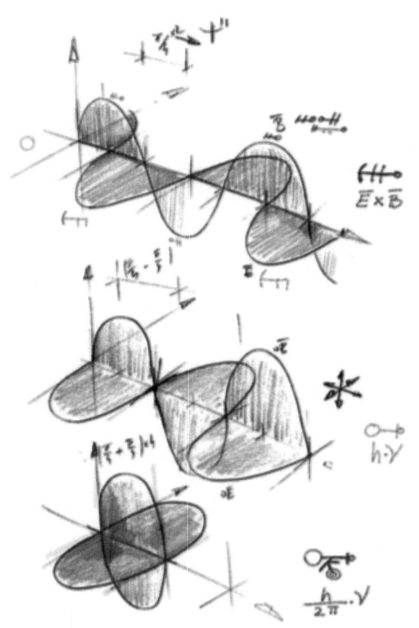

DIFFERENT TYPES OF ELECTROMAGNETIC
WAVES AND THEIR ASSOCIATED SYMBOLS

Each symbol I saw was accompanied by an explanation in terms of energy and an obvious correspondence in the Macrocosmic plane. It is possible that the very deep and intense impressions created by my long viewing of holographic images of the history of Mankind might have sensitized me to certain areas of the cortex but also to the mental sphere which made possible my extended understanding and interpretive intuition of the symbols I had seen. This probably opened a bridge to an alien civilization because I recognized many of the symbols that had already been "imprinted" in my mind from the holographic images which I had already experienced.

I gradually began to understand the connections that existed between certain symbols and the different images that were represented schematically as an electromagnetic wave in the form of "quantum" light. However, when deciphering the patterns I saw on the lens of the inter-dimensional headset, I realized that, besides the rendering of the magnetic and electric fields, there were some elements that I did not understand but which I tacitly accepted.

I noted that while I engaged in this process a clearer understanding of these elements gradually appeared in my mind. I made connections between different aspects, translated some symbols and even participated in rendering that information in its own proper order. Pretty quickly, I was able to make other correlations; and gradually, I managed to decipher a set of images that taught me to create a special device myself. It would be designed to generate electromagnetic signals similar to the ones I saw in the images, but there was still something in its composition that I could not understand yet.

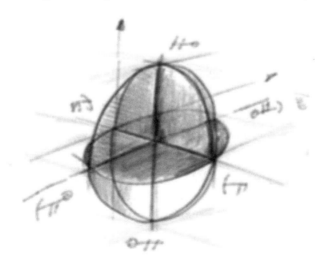

"QUANTUM" OF LIGHT

41

Without having any concrete proof, I somehow understood that, through those images, I was actually getting data on the construction of a chair similar to the one in Iraq. It was obvious that I could not achieve an identical construction, but nevertheless, I felt inspired to understand the main basics and the source of energy by which, at least to some extent, the effects of the special chair in the occult chamber of Iraq could be duplicated. Realizing that much of that experience was a knowledge that was given to me, I sensed the importance of such a device as well as to how it could contribute to the knowledge of the human being.

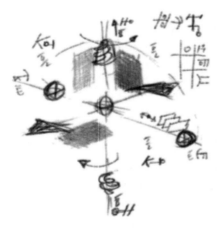

CONCEPTUAL DIAGRAM OF THE DEVICE CAPABLE OF
GENERATING A PARTICULAR ELECTROMAGNETIC FIELD

As Cezar had left for several days in Bucharest and because I did not want to forget any element, I had the time to put everything on paper and sketch the first images of the machine. I realized that the information did not come merely as an act of activated memory, but it was somehow integrated directly into my cortex when I viewed the different images or symbols and correlated them with a certain understanding. Access to them was very easy, but more than that, I was perceiving this data and information in a global way. I could, for example, individualize each element, but I also had the image of integrating it as a whole, of its functionality, and of the way it complemented other elements of the structure of the apparatus.

The first ideas of the general shape of the machine began to materialize about two days later. It was a kind of "rearranging" of the information in my mind, as if it had now become used to the multitasking data being transmitted to it. I could say that I understood, in a general way, both the design of the machine and its overall shape. I also realized that it was a modular construction which was transmitted to me for the simple reason of putting it into practice. Once I received this data, I also had an intuitive understanding of why the information was transmitted to me with the implication of what the device could do. In my opinion, these two aspects were correlated. On the one hand, there was the strong impression left by the special chair and the etheric crystal from our expedition through the Third Tunnel into the occult chamber of Iraq. On the other hand, the intensive viewing of holographic images were "days of fire" which showed me the true course of the origin and history of the human being on Earth. Therefore, the idea of constructing the device was related to those realities and would probably give me an easier way to access a certain type of information.

Later, it turned out that the function of the device was even more than that. Made precisely and in accordance with the specifications received, that device could induce in a human being an effect similar to that of the special chair in Iraq's occult chamber. I was increasingly convinced that it could actuate an efficient but especially conscious connection with the etheric and astral bodies, thus allowing the controlled exploration of some realities in the subtle but also the physical world. I also hoped that I would be able to access, at least to some extent, the space-time continuum and its mysteries.

In the following days, as I perceived the image of separate components of the structure, it created a specific field. The images then seemed to come together and give a consistency to the whole, clarifying the overall ensemble. I saw a circular frame with some attached elements that were laser-like jets or guns, serving as transmitters of some sort. Their construction and operation were based on crystals and a complex of alloys in which gold predominated. Only later would I realize that the frame consisted of a horizontal and a tilted component which together constituted the entire ensemble.

SKETCH OF THE CIRCULAR FRAME WITH DIAMETRICALLY OPPOSED "JETS" (TRANSMITTERS) WITH CRYSTALS

The "jets" had a complex interior structure, but on the outside, they appeared as concentric cylinders with a crystal of a certain shape and a certain size at the top.

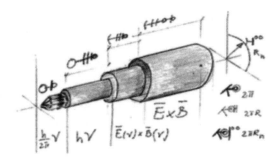

"LASER-GUN" TRANSMITTER WITH CRYSTAL TIP

The inside of these "laser guns" contained several types of crystals and other materials as well as three different types of coils, two of which were very complex.

The data I received also included that there should be an integrated seat in the central part of the construction. However, it had no "attractors" such as the chair in Iraq's occult chamber and was tilted at 15° in relation to the vertical plane.

As was the case of the special chair, this device had no obvious use of an etheric crystal for its operation, but it was my impression that its design and technology were adapted as much as possible to the suitabilities of the ordinary human being in order to achieve a notable effect. Even so, some requirements were challenging to fulfill, such as the gold and titanium plating of the exterior of the circular frames which we called "layers" or the special crystals that were a part of almost every component in the device.

Also, according to the information I received, some parts of the machine had to be made in red. These were needed to convert certain signals from the inter-dimensional helmet and from the crystal "laser-jets" because the specific action of the headset induced in the brain, and especially in the pineal gland, an expansion of the energy field on a certain frequency which was amplified by the crystals at the end of them. Additionally, a number of special spherical coils had to be made of an alloy of hafnium, ruthenium and neodymium which is, technologically speaking, very difficult to achieve. I knew all too well that those specifications are very difficult to meet, but I was hoping to find a solution in the future.

When the information I received became more crystallized in my mind, I could "see" the general outer form of the construction, but in reality, it proved to be much more complex. In order to have a reference, I gave it a name: "Eden". After first resorting to a sketch, I then elaborated on it more and more.

EXTERIOR STRUCTURE OF THE DEVICE

In its completed and final phase, the device also had a specially positioned chair so as to respect the specific angles of construction of the exterior shape.

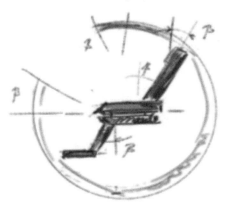

SPECIAL "ANGLE" VERSION OF THE DEVICE WITH A SPECIFIC ANGLE IN RELATION TO THE EXTERNAL COMPONENTS OF THE DEVICE

It took me a long time to understand why there was that permanent inclination to a vertical position. It could not be just for the relaxation of the body or for inducing a beneficial trance state. I carefully studied the symbols and representations that accompanied the recordings with the special chair in the occult chamber in Iraq where the incline was much higher, and I finally managed to decipher some of the complicated signs I was seeing. By comparison, I realized that the seat tilt of Eden was meant to facilitate certain important transformations in the body of the person who was reclining in it. The organism of the being was to absorb a series of waves that were emitted by the apparatus over a very wide range of frequencies, allowing the connections between the water molecules in its body to become very complex.

As I realized later, the water connections that were in the cells of the physical body, through a regular training or resonance with that device, came to align with a central signal, a kind of fractal "seed" which would in turn later develop into a series of other electrical and magnetic signals. In this way, I could become apt to receive certain information from the subtle planes and then be able to "see" them subtly but also to "feel" the subtle properties and acquire a broad knowledge of them. After that, I could access that information even with the senses of the physical body. I was trying to understand as well as possible the design of such a device and finally realized that it was actually a converter of information from the subtle planes into information that is specific to the physical plane which the ordinary human body is capable of receiving. After discussions we had in the next period with some of our specialists — without, however, giving them the overall view of the device — I came to the conclusion that Eden is a "machine" that creates a kind of temporary space tunnel, like a kind of "wormhole" that is spoken of in today's physics. Only then did I understand why receiving the images on the lens of the inter-dimensional headset also appeared on the image below, something I did not consider important at first.

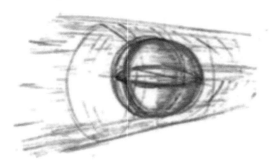

IMAGE WITH THE REPRESENTATION OF A SPACE-TIME TUNNEL WHICH CREATES A CONNECTION BETWEEN THE PHYSICAL AND THE SUBTLE PLANE

Based on the data I received telepathically, I made some adaptations and constructive solutions where things did not seem to go well due to blurred memory or a lack of clarity of information. Some of the elements I did not render in sketches, such as electronic devices from the outside of the "machine" like energy sources or sophisticated computing equipment needed to adjust the relative position of the human-device in real time.

Finally, I managed to create a more comprehensive sketch of the whole ensemble. After a fair amount of hard work, I was able to understand at least in part the intention of those who inspired me to start making this device. Basically, they telepathically guided me to build such a "personal use" device that was similar to the effects I had witnessed in the Occult Chamber in Iraq.

SKETCH OF A GENERAL VIEW OF
THE DEVICE WITH THE SEAT INSIDE

As soon as I reached this point with the general outline of the device and also acquired the understanding of its general operating principles, I called Cezar and told him that I had some important information. He was already on the way to the Base so we saw each other in just a few hours, and I was quite surprised. Cezar realized it was important so we retired to the protocol room to discuss this.

He listened carefully to me, very focused. I briefly told him how I had deciphered the "block" of information, showed him the first sketches and told him what I believe the device represents, correlating everything with the chair in the Occult Chamber that we had visited through the Third Tunnel. The main idea which I suggested was to build an apparatus at the department level with the support of our team of scientists based upon the information we received so that all of us could have access to it. This would offer the same type of results from using the chair in Iraq. It was already obvious that we could not move the chair from the Occult Chamber because it seemed to be an integral part of the chamber's construction. In addition, it was strongly magnetized. We were able, however, to find and even extract the etheric crystal and bring it back for study.

The problem with the device that I wanted to build, all of it based upon the information I had received, was of a different nature.

"If we present this to the authorities, be sure that we will not be believed, given the 'questionable' nature of the information," said Cezar. "No one will rely on information received 'telepathically', even if you have training in this regard. We do not have solid 'proof' to convince them for obtaining the funds, and as far as I know, they are not at all small. At this level of knowledge, very few are those with decision-making power and a tailor-made budget who would be confident enough in the results. Those who decide in this regard always face the practical side of the problem; and, in a sense, they are right. But their lack of training in such sensitive areas such as the border between science and 'unreality', as well as their poor understanding, would make them immediately suspicious and not believe in this information. Just by shaking the waters on this, we could attach a 'tail' to ourselves that we do not need."

I had to give him his due. After all, I could not even be sure of the results we would eventually get. There was no guarantee and no similar past experience, except for perhaps that of Maria Orsic and the medium transmission she received about the construction of a cosmic ship to Aldebaran.*

I, however, found it hard to believe that all the "infusion" of data I had experienced was pointless, and Cezar agreed with me. The idea then came to me that, if we could not formally use this information, we could yet prove to ourselves the truthfulness of the data by starting the construction of the apparatus in a particular order. Although he was initially surprised by my proposal, Cezar immediately smiled.

"And where could this be done without anyone knowing it?" he asked.

I thought a little and had the inspiration to suggest Elinor's villa. There, I had enough space in the basement near the alchemy lab; and besides, no one would have to know. The only impediment was the distance between Alpha Base and the capital, but over time, we were convinced that we could handle it. For our part, I had another asset: Lieutenant Nicoară, a specialist in physics and electronics who is also a man of perfect confidence and morality. Working with him would be a great help.

---

* The author refers to the leader of the Vril esoteric society, Maria Orsic (or Orsitsch), who, in 1919, presented to prominent members of two other secret societies (the Thule Society and the Lords of the Black Stone) written material following a medium transmission, edited by her, in a language later identified as a variant of an ancient language of the German Knights Templar. Maria Orsic stated that the telepathic transmission was monitored from an extraterrestrial civilization in the Aldebaran system located in the Taurus Constellation sixty-five light-years away from Earth. The manuscript presented the detailed technical data for the construction of a cosmic spacecraft capable of traveling to that planetary system. At the same time, Maria Orsic presented a second manuscript written in a state of media transmission which was in the Sumerian language and was translated with the help of specialists close to Thule Society and especially with the help of Sigrun, one of the the four women (Vrilerinnen) who made up the core of the Vril Society.

I weighed another two or three options with Cezar before we concentrated on this one, going into detail. Obviously, we could not miss too much time from the Base due to our many duties there. We, however, made a simple plan which could give results if Lieutenant Nicoară agreed to cooperate. We would then have every weekend available; and, from time to time, even more days that could be combined with other trips to Bucharest.

I then went through the analysis of the financial part because, according to my data, the amount of money required was huge. Accordingly, we provided for a slight adaptation of some of the materials and a few other small changes. Since the IT (Information Technology) field was essential in this project, I agreed with Cezar to call a friend of mine, a programming genius. In his case, we established a compartmentalization of labor, giving him only the software design themes, just as we have done with other specialists and designers in our service. I even had discussions with the scientists from the scientific team attached to the Bucegi secret complex, but generally speaking, I preferred to keep everything separate from the official side.

My intention here is not to present details about this amazingly positive device but just to give a general idea about its exceptional existence and its possibilities. In fact, the general sketches we have offered here were replaced with very precise and detailed drawings which made for amazing solutions that later made possible the construction of the device. It turned out, however, that its use required a long preparation until a "frequency agreement" could be reached between the user — who would be myself — and the device. For me, the use of this device represented a great qualitative leap regarding the correct understanding of some amazing realities, both of the physical world and of the subtle worlds or dimensions. I will detail some of these elements in the following volumes, and I hope that in this way many of the gaps that still exist in contemporary science that are related to the misunderstanding of the basic principles governing important phenomena in the Universe will be clarified or even eliminated from the burden of the current materialist conception.

CHAPTER THREE

New Projects in Development

Immediately after returning from the expedition, Cezar assigned the team of scholars the very important and urgent task of studying the etheric crystal. The plan for the construction of the device, which I generically named "Eden", implies a deeper understanding of how the space-time continuum works, i.e. the reality in which we exist. It was obvious that the technology of the etheric crystal and that of the special chair in Iraq's occult chamber could greatly help us in this regard, but we at least had to understand the general principles underlying those technologies.

A UNIQUE KIND OF BRAINSTORMING

The development of the chair's construction went somewhat in parallel with the scientific studies of the team of scientists. It seemed as if a new breath motivated and inspired them to work intensely, provoked by the amazing piece that was brought to them for research. They quickly realized that they would not be able to understand anything more about that extraterrestrial technology if they were to continue to use the "canonical" ideas and conceptions of contemporary science. Accordingly, they began to develop a new and very complicated mathematical reference frame which no longer adheres to the old principles.

Up until Einstein, Euclidean space was taken as the mathematical basis for describing the Universe.* After that, a major interest began to be given to the space of the phases "created" by the canonical equations of Hamilton in which several parallel dimensions are "seen" but are not, however, properly understood.**

---

* Euclidean space was defined by the Greek mathematician Euclid of Alexandria (300-400 B.C.) in his work *Elements* which served as a basic text in modern countries for understanding mathematics (especially geometry) until the 20th century. In contemporary mathematics, Euclidean space represents the fundamental space of classical geometry which can describe any spatial variety with an integer and a non-negative number of dimensions. This includes 3-D Euclidean space (with 3 dimensions) as well as the Euclidean plane (with 2 dimensions).
** Hamilton's first-order partial derivative equations are characterized by the fact that they provide a new (and equivalent) way of looking at Newton's classical mechanics. They do not, however, give a more convenient way of solving particular problems, but they do offer some prospects for a deeper understanding of classical mechanics and its links with quantum mechanics as well as other fields of science. Hamilton's canonical equations are very "attractive" given their simplicity and symmetry. They were analyzed from all points of view imaginable, from the fundamental mechanics to the geometry of vector spaces. We know a whole series of solutions of these equations for a lot of physical systems, but the exact general solution of the equations of motion for physical systems with more than two bodies which interact through a certain force field (for example, the gravitational field) is not yet known.

The spatial theory, however, that won the conviction of the researchers was Minkowski space*, especially after the elaboration of the *Special Theory of Relativity*** by Albert Einstein because, theoretically speaking, the number of dimensions of this mathematical space can be any integer greater than 1, meaning, at least virtually, there are an infinity of dimensions or planes of existence that can be formed in Minkowskian space, including both space and time. The problem is that those dimensions really correspond to another time and space, but they are also considered physical planes.

They do not show or explain what the subtle planes or dimensions of Creation, such as the etheric plan or the astral plane, actually mean in a way that is more accessible to ordinary human understanding and knowledge.

In a working meeting that Cezar, Lieutenant Nicoară, myself, and two other members of the Department had with a team of scientists after returning from our expedition through the Third Tunnel, Cezar suggested changing our paradigm of how we think about the space-time continuum by taking into account the factor of vibrational frequency. In the months that followed, this led to the initiation and development of a new thinking mechanism which needed special rendering tools. This is why the process of laying the foundations of a new mathematical method, which would describe this mechanism and thus lead to an understanding of this new approach, was initiated simultaneously. Because the problem was very complex, it also involved collaboration with two exceptional Russian mathematicians and physicists who had demonstrated some initiative in this regard.

The mathematical apparatus was so sophisticated and the solutions provided were so advanced that I was not able to understand it any better. In this meeting, however, I was allowed to present some aspects of the memorable

---

* Minkowski space, introduced by the German mathematician Hermann Minkowski, "mathematically" responds to the formulation and support of Einstein's Special Theory of Relativity. In the context of this theory, the three ordinary dimensions of space are "combined" with a fourth dimension which involves time to form a 4-dimensional representation of space-time. Formally, Minkowski space can also be considered as a pseudo-Euclidean space with 4 dimensions (Euclidean space has only spatial dimensions; the Minkowski space also has spatial dimensions, but in addition, it also has a dimension that involves time).

** The Special Theory of Relativity was published by Albert Einstein in 1905 in an article entitled About the Electrodynamics of Moving Bodies and generalizes the principle of classical relativity formulated by Galileo Galilei. This principle states that all uniform movements are relative and that there is no privileged reference system (or "source"), i.e. there is no absolute resting state. In that article, Einstein added a second postulate which states that all observers will get (following the appropriate measurements) the same value for the speed of light in a vacuum regardless of their uniform and rectilinear motion. The Special Theory of Relativity is practically a generalization of Newton's classical mechanics which modifies the notions of space and time in the sense that the measurement of distances and time intervals (depending on the observer's state of motion) is made with the help of light which has the same speed (in a vacuum) as any observer in an inertial reference system. Hence, the famous "equivalence" between matter and energy expressed by the famous formula: $E = mc2$.

discussion I had with Dr. Xien about the perception of space and time. I did not reproduce those elements in *Inside the Earth — The Second Tunnel* as they did not fit into the subject of that book. On the other hand, it seemed to me that it would have been too much for the ordinary concept of the world that we live in. In this new context, however, I find it appropriate to present the abstract notions that Dr. Xien shared with me, even if they might seem spooky to some people.

ANOTHER POINT OF REFERENCE: THE "WRINKLE" OF ILLUSION

I presented the respective information to the team of scientists during the brainstorming session; but in order to keep the spirit of the elements shared, I will replay the discussion I had with Dr. Xien in its original form. He pointed out from the very beginning the weakness of the current scientific concept.

"The problem I will tell you about now is posed in a way that science considers unlikely. In essence, there is no volume. If you look at an apple, you feel that it has an outer surface which is its shell, and you also say that it has something inside which is the pulp of the apple. In fact, none of this exists. Everything you see is actually just a box. It's like making a box out of a fabric and then painting it and arranging it to look like an apple. In reality, the respective 'apple' is the continuation of a surface. It is only a 'wave' or a 'crease' of the surface. I just have the feeling that there is something I call 'the inside', but it is actually nothing. And beyond that surface is also nothing, that is, the Void. Whatever object you look at, it seems to be how you see it and how you attribute its properties to it, but it really isn't. It is just 'a box of the universal surface', and beyond the 'wrinkle' of each object, you have access to Infinity."

At that time, I had not fully determined whether or not to take seriously the explanations offered by Dr. Xien. I was thinking, in fact, that he had not understood what interested me, and that is why I was making some jokes about "lack of volume". I spoke to him.

"I think you realize that, for scientists, what you tell me now is just a product of fantasy and that in the happiest case..."

Dr. Xien replied impassively.

"They can believe what they want, but do not forget that science reduces to the five senses, to formulas and to devices of measurement and control. No one has ever seen the wind, but it still exists. I do not speak to you in metaphors, but I seek to make you understand that the strictly materialistic contemporary vision is limited and insufficient to explain many of the enigmas of the surrounding reality."

I knew he was right, and that is why I did not extend the discussion in this regard, even though his explanation of "lack of volume" seemed a bit exaggerated. On the other hand, it was obvious that Dr. Xien wanted to stay within the sphere of the original subject regarding the reality inside the Earth. He suggested some additional subjects for discussion to point out certain issues. It was up to me whether or not I could listen to them and understand them. I suggested a new perspective on the issue of "volume".

"What if I break the object? If you cut the apple?"

"You then made a new surface," came the immediate answer. "When you fly from the apple, it is a new surface, but beyond your bite, it is not an apple but also the Infinite Surface. You need to understand this well. It is hard, it is abstract, but you have to understand it."

I was baffled. According to Dr. Xien, the idea of volume is false. There is no volume. There are only surfaces, the "wrinkled ones" of which we create our life experience. They are the "waves" of illusion that deceive people. With such a summary, I felt I was taken very quickly to an abstract field of discussion, but I did not understand it too well. Even so, I came up with a new argument.

"The fact that we are here cannot be denied. It's not an illusion."

"It is, but this happens only because our individual consciousness 'sees' it this way and believes that there is something it calls 'outside'. That makes the world exist. Otherwise, what is outside the 'skin', whatever it is, is nothing but the Infinite."

I was silent, indecisive. It was a real test of the conception of the world we live in. Seeing my uncertainty, Dr. Xien asked me a question.

"At this moment, tell me how far do you see the world around you?"[*]

"To the door. We're underground, what more could I see?"

"But you know from experience what is beyond it. You imagine the mountains, the trees, and then the cities with streets, blocks and cars that are difficult to get into in traffic."

"I can't imagine that. I know it is."

I was upset because I was not sure where he wanted to go. I realized that somewhere there was a weak point of how I was stating the problem, but in that discussion I still could not identify it. Impervious to me, Doctor Xien replied.

"Wrong. You do not know. You just assume you know, but you actually are living in an illusion. Things come to mind because you have their memory, but you might suddenly face another reality. Suppose this room is soundproofed. On the surface comes a terrible hurricane, tornado or devastating flood of which you know nothing. When you come to the surface, what world do you see? A world other than the one you had designed in your mind: a destroyed world, completely changed."

---

[*] According to what is reported in Volume 5, *Inside the Earth - Second Tunnel,* the discussions between the author and Dr. Xien took place in the fall of 2014.

"If so, then what can I say about the Inner Earth or anything else I don't know?"

"Basically, you can't say anything because there is nothing that correlates with what you already know. Remember that everything is just a 'box' on the surface of your consciousness."

Doctor Xien bent the table cloth to form a loop. He showed me its curvature.

"You know this box is a specific object, but behind the box, in the back, you see nothing. Theoretically, there is nothing from your perspective and angle of view. You just suppose it would be something. Observing the box as it curves means for you a specific curve of space and time. You send an energy which is your conception of what that thing should be, and that ray of energy 'hits' the surface of Reality and sends you an echo. If you stand in front of a huge wall and kick a ball, it hits that wall and then it curls in a specific way which is the echo I was telling you about. For you, that echo is your reality about that aspect, your conception of it. It is the echo that the box sends you, that is, that curve of space and time on the 'wall' of the Infinite. Wherever you are not actually seeing something but would expect to see something, that is the Supreme Reality, the Infinite."

"It is as if we are dolphins or bats," I said, reflexively associating Dr. Xien's explanations with what I knew, but now I understood his point of view better. They send waves which then return as an echo and their brain interprets reality, but they do not see it directly. I don't even see the box. What is there?"

"I told you: nothing you could feel, know or think. It is not the domain of the mind. Only you are."

His statement that "only you are" was unclear to me, but I left that direction of the discussion aside because, at that time, I was interested in the problem of understanding the interior of the planet. The subject of the "skin", however, or "covered layer" of the unseen reality that surrounds us particularly captivated me. Meditating on the problem, I soon realized that this is not in fact a "vision" or "hypothesis" but that the notions presented by Dr. Xien represent the very way we perceive the world around us. It is neither an assumption or an "idea", but it is indeed the reality whether we like it or not or whether or not we agree with it.

Some of the members of the scientific team took up the ideas that Dr. Xien offered and understood the theoretical aspects of the "volume" problem which I had laid out while the others started the research of the universal implications of the etheric crystal, using very sophisticated technologies to create instrumentation for measuring and interaction with this particular subtle plane. I was receiving weekly reports, and I must admit that there was significant progress during the next ten months that opened up the possibility of using the special chair. There were, however, many issues that needed to be worked out.

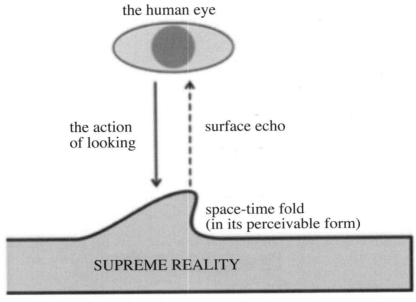

THE WAY WE PERCEIVE THE SURROUNDING WORLD

THE EDEN PROJECT: THE ASTROLOGICAL STAGE

Meanwhile, the secret construction of our own apparatus, rather its preliminary steps, had begun at Elinor's villa, and this was absolutely necessary for everything to go as smoothly as possible. Our approach, however, was different from that of the scientific team working within the Bucegi complex. Cezar's inclinations included some elements of an esoteric nature, none of which would have any meaning for scholars, at least not at that time. For example, the first step was calculating an astrologically appropriate time to begin construction of the device. Having seen the past of Mankind and the origins of man on the holographic screen of Apellos, as well as the way stars, planets, Moon and huge extraterrestrial ships have very precisely and methodically influenced the development of human DNA, such an initiative did not seem at all unnatural to me. The fact that contemporary science is so many light years away from this knowledge represents a deficit that it will probably catch up to in the future.

It is right, however, that the technology required to perform extremely complex calculations and analysis in the field of astrophysics — such as those made by the Sirians to choose the best moments and positions of the mother ships so that they aligned with other stars and with our planet — are almost completely absent at this time. As Cezar explained, however, it is necessary to take some actions to properly integrate the beginning of an important moment of a project of such magnitude. The case of the construction of the great resonators on Earth is an eloquent example in this regard because, as we have shown, their design was done in perfect harmony with certain stellar configurations whose specific energy was to act and support those huge constructions.*

This is why Cezar spoke to me about the correct integration of our action from an astrological point of view. Most people tend to trivialize this aspect, ironize it or simply ignore it, but such an attitude stems more from a deep ignorance of how the energies in the cosmos act than from bad intentions. At the same time, contemporary science is arrogant and baffled in terms of astrology, but this is due both to the incipient level of understanding of universal laws and to the technology that is currently available on Earth, none of which allows for the measurement of gigantic influences and changes with respect to subtle interstellar and interplanetary energy, let alone the specific applications of such.

We have spoken many times about the limitations of contemporary science and about its very narrow and materialistic vision which leads to a superficial and partial knowledge. This is a fact which cannot be denied. Under the guise of its "all-knowing" assertions of certainty that it makes, modern science is almost always placed outside of the phenomena it analyzes. That is why it cannot penetrate the essence, the real significance. Deep authentic knowledge cannot come only from observation and measurements. For this, more is needed. An overview of the Universe is needed on its multiple levels of existence, not just an arid and quite limited interpretation such as that of the physical plane. The true meaning of human existence and its universal integration must also be penetrated.

At present, the human being is viewed, analyzed and researched by scientists as a separate entity that is limited and isolated from what surrounds it. As I said before, however, man is a true microcosm, a true replica of what exists at the Macrocosmic level with all of its dimensions of manifestation, including the phenomena, beings and things that make it up.

---

* The author refers to the megalithic constructions (the pyramids) that were made in many areas of our planet (see volume 6, *Forgotten Genesis*, ch. 13, p. 273).

Belgian author and lecturer Robert Bauval, best known for his theory of the correlation between the construction of pyramids on the Giza plateau in Cairo and certain stars in the Orion constellation, had the courage to write in his book, *The Mystery of the Orion Constellation*, that Egyptian priests had at their disposal a sacred parchment which contained exact data for the beginning of the construction of some pyramids or for the reconditioning of some that already existed. These data did not coincidentally coincide, astrologically speaking, with special conjunctions between Sirius and the Sun at sunset or between the Moon and Sirius a few days before the Full Moon. That papyri contained data and recommendations for a period of about 10,000 years. The last important date that was mentioned was, by chance, the entry of Roman weapons into Egypt. (Romanian Editors's note)

At a certain degree of development and technological advancement, science is coupled with spirituality. At that level, things seem to be normal for a common man because, prior to that, he is not able to understand their real meaning. He does not understand the principles, causes, modalities by which information becomes accessible or is used and transmitted. What he considered until then to be science fiction or even impossible proves to be fully possible and real. Here it is necessary to change the paradigm of thought, without which we will remain prisoners of primitive and very limited conceptions.

This transformation of state in our conceptions must be adequate and harmonious, otherwise it will tend to become rigid. For this, a certain esoteric, spiritual and even initiatory culture is necessary or we risk falling into a well. For example, let us consider the case of astrology. In reality, it turns out to be a true esoteric science, but for many people, it appears as a fantasy and a bunch of childish beliefs, and that is just because modern science does not take into account factors other than using it as a charlatan would.

Astrology, however, is a profound science of subtle energy interactions between large celestial bodies (mainly stars and planets) and the microcosm of the human being which not only represents the physical body but also its subtle bodies: the ethereal, astral, mental and causal. In this way, the complex influences of the planets, stars and constellations are explained, but the science of human beings is more or less ignorant of this ancient subject. The psycho-mental condition of the human being, the tendencies, the state of health, even the evolution of the personality are influenced by these subtle influences which are the first and foremost characteristics of these great cosmic objects. We need to understand well, however, that we are not subjugated by these influences and their movements, and when they are not favorable to us, we can overcome them through superior discernment, knowledge and willpower.

There are those who are skeptical and might say that stars are too far away to have any power or influence on man or that the aspect of specific subtle energy emitted by stars and planets does not exist. We could say, for example, that we cannot talk about heat because it is an abstract notion which can be neither seen nor heard, but we nevertheless feel it; and further, that air does not exist because we do not see it, but we still breathe it. There are other examples along the same logical line, but in all of these examples, we do not see the agent that nevertheless exists and the influence of which can be felt. Then, why would this not be true in the case of planetary and stellar influences on the human being? The skeptics respond that no one has demonstrated this until now and the different behaviors of man and the changes that take place are based on other direct causes.

Obviously, not everything we do or feel is a direct result of planetary and stellar influences, but most of it is a consequence of them. In such a process, everything is interconnected because nothing is left to "accident" and is not, as scientists like to say, a work of chance. When the skill reaches a very high level of development, the barriers between the planes or dimensions of Creation are overcome and many things, unthinkable before, then become perfectly possible, just as I had the opportunity to see in the akashic records. All these cosmic influences then appear clearly figured out and interconnected; they are measured, interpreted and calculated very precisely, just as researchers would now follow the indications of an oscilloscope or other sophisticated devices.

On the other hand, there is the exaggeration of astrologers and preachers with all of their prophecies and advice, much of which is dubious or inaccurate.

In the case of the construction of our "machine", it was about making a fairly accurate calculation of the celestial configuration that was the most suitable to solidly support our initiative and the work of building the machine. For this, Cezar got in touch with two people he knew and considered very advanced in the science of astrology, asking them to calculate several variants in which the star and planetary configurations would be favorable to the beginning of our project.

This request might seem simple, but it involved very intense and complicated work on the part of the two people. It was also the first action of our project and the first collaboration with someone from outside. I also participated in several meetings and discussions on this topic until Cezar chose a planetary and star configuration that was to take place over almost four months, starting with the beginning of that duration. In a way, this was good because it allowed us to organize, design and plan in detail the stages carefully as well as to select the people we would collaborate with.

"ENERGY IMPROVEMENT" OF THE SPACE

The large hall in the basement of Elinor's villa, which was initially intended for the storage of instruments and substances for the alchemy laboratory as well as other logistics elements, was most appropriate for Eden's construction. The hall is square in shape, eight meters wide with a height of 2.8 meters. It would have been nice if it was a little taller, but we had to settle for what we had.

After I had completely emptied the room, however, it seemed very large and quite roomy for what we wanted to build there. First, some masonry work was required for an efficient ventilation system, but finally, after finishing, the place looked like new with perfectly white walls and a high quality laminate over the wooden floor. Initially, I thought the that the construction process would damage the wood, but Lieutenant Nicoară came up with the idea of stretching a thin rubber foil on the floor which could be easily removed in the end.

In the following days, a high-performance air conditioner was installed so that we had all the elements that provided an "adequate room climate". I felt a slight tightening of my heart, thinking that Elinor knew nothing about our plans or the small transformations we had made inside the basement of his house, but I was hoping he would understand and even enjoy our project. Cezar and I had already decided that Elinor should know about the construction of the "machine". After all, I was using his own villa for this; and moreover, he is a being who has reached a high level of spiritual evolution.

One of the important esoteric elements which Cezar carefully considered was the so-called "specific energy impregnation" of the room dedicated to the construction of the apparatus. I myself did not understand very well the necessity of such an initial action, but Cezar patiently explained to me that that stage of the process is, in a way, part of the economy of the universe.

"Any action we perform is within an external 'rhythm' with certain characteristics, and we have to choose our actions conscientiously. For example, if you want to go on vacation, do not start cutting wood, but do something about the upcoming vacation: buy what you need, book the room or do other things that suit your departure. Therefore, your intention must be in tune with the actions you are about to take. If these do not correspond to the nature of your intention, then you can expect all kinds of difficulties or obstacles and often even the failure of that action. It is the same as in the pistons inside the engine of a car. If they move chaotically, the engine crashes and gives no movement. If they move in a coordinated way, that is, they fit at a well-established pace with clear and correlated stages, it will work perfectly."

I thought for a few moments and then spoke.

"That would be for an internal combustion engine. But how is it for us? I mean, what kind of 'rhythm' do we follow in the construction of this device?"

"Here, it is much more subtle, even cosmic. Our intention is to build this very special 'car' (he is referring to the chair) and our actions so far must prepare for this. Let us say you intend to have a very hard winter. You do not wait for winter to come to see if you can survive, but you properly prepare for it. You make supplies, you ensure the heating of the house, you prepare your snow removal tools, etc. These are mundane actions, but by this example I wanted you to understand the idea of the process. In the case of our project, those mundane and obvious actions will be replaced by actions of a subtle nature, such as choosing a suitable astrological moment and subtle-energetic loading of the space where the device will be made. Such an integration cannot yet be understood by a so-called 'scientific' mind because it has no recognizable correspondence. It is not on the 'list' of modern scientific concepts and principles. It is a different way of thinking and approaching universal laws. Fundamentally, we are surrounded only by energy that vibrates on a myriad of frequencies. Matter is energy, our bodies are energy, atoms are energy and so on. Everything is vibration and that means rhythm. We do nothing but fit into the rhythm of our project."

"Good; and how do we find the rhythm we need?" I insisted, paying close attention to those explanations. "What's the beat of Eden?"

"It's like a kind of 'calling' by which you create affinity with the specificity of the future construction. You come up with something from the physical plane that corresponds to the initial idea, intention, plan or conception that you want to achieve, and by this you gradually 'tune' to what is the higher cosmic rhythm which corresponds to that frequency of vibration. Your car runs on gasoline. In order to use it, you will put neither water nor diesel in the tank. You will be looking for the best and most efficient petrol so that the efficiency of the car, at least in regards to the fuel, is the best. This means that you power the car and prepare it for the best performance. You can add other actions of the same kind: you will buy new tires, you will change the oil and do other things, all to make your travel with that car as efficient as possible. In the case of our project, we must find the element that best resonates with the specificity of the 'machine' to be built."

I understood the principle, but for the time being, I could not get used to the specificity of such an approach which, in our case, was especially subtle in nature. The normal mind tends to regard such as irrelevant.

"Is the integration that we do really that important?"

"Undoubtedly. The more important the action you start, the more you need to integrate yourself properly into the universal rhythm that corresponds to it because you will then be protected and helped by the huge energies carried by it. You are no longer an individual wheel lost among others with weak forces and a somewhat chaotic wandering. Instead, you are now part of the whole. You are helped, inspired and supported by its functioning, if you harmonize with it."

I asked Cezar how this integration of the beginning of an activity is pragmatically realized.

"There are several approaches and methods," he said to me. "In general, an ordinary person hardly understands these notions because he is limited by a set of conceptions and prejudices that he has nourished throughout his life. It is difficult to get out of this 'cage'.

"Good intentions and a desire to know more, however, can help. For example, a deep heart prayer or a well thought out prayer can mean a lot. It depends, however, on the nature and importance of the action you want to accomplish and integrate effectively because one might want to build a bicycle and another might want to make a rocket to fly in the cosmos. We need to understand very well that we are not 'isolated' in this universe, but that everything is interconnected. By such preparation, you can even convince yourself of this."

"But in the case of Eden, how will we proceed?"

"Here we will add some new initiatory elements which further facilitate entering into the universal rhythm of the idea and project we have proposed. There is already a strong impetus due to the perceptions you had about the constructive and conceptual elements of the 'car' (chair), and then there were our discussions and especially our firm determination to carry out the construction. But, we will also come up with new elements that will further the success."

MIDAS

The first "mission" was to find someone extremely well trained in the field of IT programming. Fortunately, we have no shortage of this in Romania. Cezar came with two prospects, and I with one. These were people who had been watching the SRI* for years. Two of them, which were Cezar's prospects, had collaborated, respectively, with the NSA** and Northrop Grumman in the field of U.S. military aviation. We had the records of these two people with excellent qualification ratings. I made up their profile which included a synthesis of the achievements each of them had.

The third prospect, which was from me, referred to a young man I had met several years ago in a circumstance that I am not allowed to present at this point. In the hidden circles of great programmers and IT people, he was known as Midas, probably by the name of the ancient Phrygian king. And indeed — it seemed that everything that he would "touch" in the computer field "turns into gold".*** His ability to "break in" through any firewall protection system, no matter how complicated, has earned him respect in the hacker community. Although he was intensely courted by U.S. agencies, including the Pentagon, he still refused to leave the country. His well known reply was: "Why should I leave here if I can still access any information?"

He was not interested in money or other material income, and this "saved" him because he did not slip into temptations that could become dangerous. He did, however, "break" all the protections of the great American agencies, one by one, but stopped exactly where he was supposed to. He would then send an e-mail to the general manager of that agency, describing the operation he had done and where the weaknesses of the system were so that the agency could resolve them.

In other words, he was a "white hacker", but he never specified how that system should be strengthened, leaving it to the care of the respective agencies. Even though his help was obvious and disinterested, there were still suspicions

---

* SRI refers to the Romanian Intelligence Service.
** NSA is the National Security Agency of the United States of America.
*** The author makes a metaphorical analogy with King Midas (the beginning of the second millennium B.C.), who ruled in the fortress of Pessinus in ancient Phrygia (approximately in central Turkey today). He was known for his ability to instantly turn everything he touched into gold, as a result of which, as legend has it, he died of hunger.

regarding him because, at one of the discussions between the representatives of the Services in which he took part, Midas said that he knows how not to be detected and leave no trace. Although that was considered to be practically impossible, his words still caused some stress among the generals and chiefs of the main institutions.

Because of this, he soon became frightened of international agencies and pressures were made to control his activity, even at the level of our Secret Services. This was included in a special program which I had access to, and that is why I proposed it as a very promising option to help us in our project.

In my opinion, Midas was a great genius in the field of computer science whose exceptional talent deserved to be fully utilized for the noble purpose we had set out to accomplish.

After presenting all this data to Cezar, he immediately approved of Midas's cooperation in the project, and he "officially" became our basic collaborator. From the beginning until the end of the project, he had contact with only Cezar, Lieutenant Nicoară and myself.

Lieutenant Nicoară spoke to him about the main work topics and what he wanted from him in order for the "machine" to work. Even though no additional data was presented to him about the project, Midas was very smart and quickly understood that it was something very special, he said the following to me after a week of "employment".

"What you ask me to do is not related to ordinary technology on Earth."

I smiled to myself, but I couldn't tell him what it was. I replied in a very general way.

"It is important that the job is done well."

Midas is a person highly touted by the main intelligences services* on the "market" and that is why he is included in a very special category in our country. Americans have often asked us to loan them this "asset" for certain tasks, but we considered that "better safe than sorry", elegantly declining the demand.

INFLUENCE OF THE SHIKHARA SYMBOL

In parallel with the training phase of our team of collaborators, Cezar continued the process of subtle integration with the Eden project. He defined that stage as being similar to a specific magnetic field which "loaded" the space in the room and prepared it for the operation, maintenance and success of the future "machine". After choosing the planetary configuration that was considered the most appropriate and exactly at the precise moment indicated, Cezar placed a rectangle of copper plated with gold in the middle of the large chamber. The dimensions of the rectangle were 20x32 cm and

---

* Espionage agencies and international secret services.

featured a laser engraving of a rather complicated symbol.

"By this, from a subtle point of view, we are preparing the realization of the project," said Cezar. "I told you that people in general are not used to such procedures because they do not understand either their meaning or substance. This knowledge belongs to the esoteric realm and has nothing to do with "magic" or other divinatory rituals. You can even say that it is pure science, but it is at an advanced level because it is based upon principles that are not yet known and even less credited by scientists as well as much of the population. Materialistic ideas are rigid and limited, and if you do not have degrees of freedom, you therefore you cannot see the whole. What we do here, however, is more special because it has a much wider spectrum of influence.

Using the information we had from our views on the holographic screen, we both worked on establishing the graphic form of the symbol. For the first phase, we decided on a compound symbol which could be translated as *su-(ka)-da* (*da* means "yes" in Romanian).

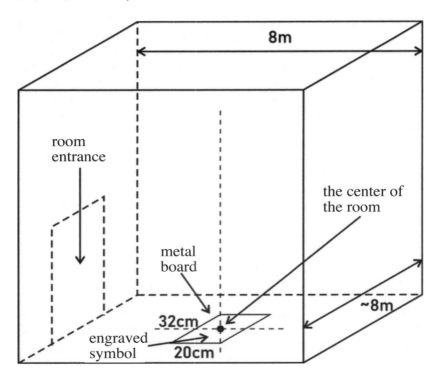

METAL PLATE WITH THE SYMBOL ENGRAVED ON IT, A RESONATOR FOR THE SPECIFIC ENERGY FIELD OF THE DEVICE TO BE BUILT

THE SYMBOL SU - (KA) - DA

SU shows the direction; *K (KA)* is always related to the vital energy — a fundamental symbol in Sirian writing — which in ancient Egyptian tradition was designated as *KHA*; and DA (meaning "yes" in the Romanian language) means "upward". In free translation, this means "energy that travels upwards", having the sense of sublimation, elevation, and increasing the frequency of vibration. In the Sumerian language, the meaning of this word was that of "ascension" in the purest spiritual sense.

Nevertheless, after several discussions and analyzing several variants of the symbols I had seen during the viewing on the holographic screen of the Apellos, we decided on another symbol, the so-called *SHIKHARA* or *SHI+KHA+RA* symbol.

THE SYMBOL SHI - (KA) - RA

In Chinese, *SHI* refers to the personal pronoun "he" or "she". *KHA*, as I said, represents the vital energy (in ancient Egyptian); and *RA* means "sacred (spiritual) light" in Sumerian, a term that was later taken by the Egyptians to refer to the Sun King (*RA*). Thus, shikhara means "vital energy that comes from the sacred (spiritual) light." The symbol can thus be correlated with the universal subtle energy (*prana* of the Hindu tradition) which "feeds" everything in an infinity of manifestations. By carefully analyzing this symbol, we were surprised to find out how ancestral Sirian symbols have been transmitted through time to this very day.

As a matter of fact, the word shikhara literally translates to "mountain peak", often mentioned in connection with the tops of temples in North India, resembling the seminal pools of the Himalayas.[*]

---

[*] In South India, the equivalent term for shikhara is the word "vimana" which, unlike the term used in the northern part of the country, refers to the entire temple building, and this includes the lower part referred to as the sanctum. Here, shikhara retains its original meaning, designating only the peak part of the vimana which is usually a dome, having over it a finial (a specific ornament located at the top of an important building).

It is very interesting to note that an analogy can be drawn between the specific structure of some Pleiadian "flying saucers" (see, for example, the cases documented by Billy Meier in the 1960s-1970s) and the structure of Hindu temples. Additionally, in ancient times, the term vimana also had the meaning of "flying vehicle" which, in the ancient Sanskrit texts of India, meant "temple" or "flying car".

The author even mentions in volume 6 of the *Transylvanian Series* (*Forgotten Genesis*, 2019): "On the other hand, temples in India, which are somewhat smaller in size but resemble the pyramids, though they are narrower at the base and more 'pursed' at the top, have a Pleiadian descent. As far as I could tell, the many details, inlays and roundings in their construction represent something specific to the Pleiadian civilization. I also recognized this feature in the Pleiadian ships that I saw in the holographic projections."

CHAPTER FOUR

EXTRAORDINARY CONSTANTS, SYMBOLS AND ARCHITECTURE ON EARTH

During the first viewing in front of the holographic screen that I had done with the assistance of the man from Apellos, I was able to see the basic elements of the creation of human DNA.[*]

I also became acquainted with several symbols of some extraterrestrial civilizations, especially those of the Sirian civilization, which expressed certain fundamental energetic realities at the cosmic level. Some of these were later found in different forms and versions in the cultures and civilizations of people on Earth. We talked extensively about those symbols, especially the *K* symbol, but during the viewing, I recognized several such forms and representations that are currently in use in science or even in everyday life.[**] It is amazing to see how many of the signs and symbols we consider to be trivial or simple "inventions" of ancient mathematicians or civilizations actually reflect the amazing energetic and even archetypal realities of the universe that were introduced into human civilization by some very advanced extraterrestrial civilizations and then adapted by Earth cultures throughout the ages.

SIRIAN SYMBOLIC WRITING

From what I could see on the holographic screen, most of the symbols that are reflected in our daily life have a Sirian origin. Their source goes back in time to the dawn of Mankind but much after Adam because, at that time, *E-N-L* beings were more meditative in character, being dedicated exclusively to spiritual evolution. After the first hybridizations and the increase in the number of *E-N-K* beings, we noticed that in order to counterbalance the decrease in the vibrational frequency of some DNA strands, there was a need for a certain type of knowledge transfer that included the content of the race memory from generation to generation.

Generally speaking, I realized that writing was not a determining factor in the period from the year 200,000 BC up until after the fall of Atlantis. In fact, it was not possible to speak of "writing" in the current meaning, but it was more about conveying symbols which, in their general structure, markedly

---

[*] See Volume 6, *Forgotten Genesis*, 2020, chapters 4, 5 and 6.
[**] See Volume 6, *Forgotten Genesis*, 2020, in which more cosmic symbols (*E, E-I, E-U, E-N* etc.) are presented.

resembled the cuneiform signs of the Akhadi and Hittite writings from ancient times. At that time, however, their arrangement and meanings were much more complex, being oriented in particular with the energies of the Universe which they reflected indirectly by the power of their occult significance. Gradually, with the passage of time, I saw that power diminished in intensity, precisely because humanity was beginning to forget the basic meanings of such symbols. The general forms of "writing" have remained, however, and can give one an idea of how the Sirians expressed themselves within their civilization.

I was, of course, curious to know more about this and allowed myself, with the approval of the man from Apellos, to enter a secondary branch of viewing for elaboration of the derivation of the symbols of the Sirian civilizations. Files with information were presented on the screen in a way that was very logical and quite easy to assimilate.

First of all, I realized that Sirian beings have a kind of symbols code which they can understand when necessary. This is used very rarely, however, because Syrians have strong telepathic abilities, and their existence is multi-dimensional in many cases. Most of the evolved ones choose to live in the etheric and even astral planes but coexist on the same ship with their peers in the physical plane, only at a higher level that is appropriate to their vibrational frequency and to the degree such is integrated with the structure of their large cosmic ships.

Sirian writing is not like ours but is rather made up of a set of rules by which Sirians can designate what has both concrete and subtle meanings. This mode of "writing" is very abstract but also very nuanced, being perfectly adapted to the capabilities and specificity of the Sirians who possess a great power of mental penetration and focus on very complex meanings of different types of manifestations, energies, phenomena, beings, and other things.

For example, specific signs of their "writing" — which are really symbols — can designate a graphic set of characters that represents a message. It can only be deciphered by the beings in their civilization or those who live in unison with their mental energy. If this condition is not met, understanding the forms and symbols included in the message is almost impossible because there is no affinity for the conception and knowledge at their original level of manifestation.

I thus realized that reading Sirian symbols occurs only on an upper echelon of thinking beings in contrast to ordinary ones. Given that this ability is already native to Sirian beings, it is logical to assume that their symbols will be understood anywhere in the galaxy on any of the planets colonized by the Sirian people. In fact, this was also the main purpose of their "writing": not necessarily to say something or to make poems but more to convey the essence of a fact or manifestation as an impression on the structure of space-time for those who were interested in that aspect.

Their symbols could also have the role of leaving a sign or a test to be performed, as we have often seen in different places on the walls of their ships or in other important areas. Due to the very nature of the activities carried out by the Sirian people, however, it is possible to talk about the existence of certain specific patterns which can be observed in different crews of the inhabited ships that have long missions. There are, therefore, certain characteristics that distinguish the Sirian communities, both on the planets they inhabit and on the ships they move in throughout the cosmos.

I will refer here to some of the main structures of specifically Sirian writings which are also found in different cultures or civilizations of humanity, being transmitted in a more or less pure form with regard to their original Sirian form.

THE BASIS OF SIRIAN SYMBOLS ARE THE LINE AND THE POINT

Generally speaking, the point represents the origin, the starting place of an activity or initiative. It shows us where to start reading a symbol or the basis from which to start to understand a certain graphic representation. This same symbol may have a completely different meaning, however, if the point is placed in different areas of the same graphic representation.

When multiple points are used in a symbol, it means that the drawing is very complex and requires a more nuanced understanding which encompasses multiple angles of view. As I could see, sometimes the essential area of a symbol with several points is enclosed in a circle; thus indicating that the area has strength and priority when interpreting the symbol.

On the other hand, the line in "Sirian writing" represents the connection between two or more points and generally refers to planets, stars or galaxies because this writing is, in a way, cosmic and even holographic. Indeed — in its abstract symbols we can find the entire unfolding of an action, from its macrocosmic level to the microcosmic level of the being.

The horizontal line represents a prolonged and repetitive action because it is a symbol of the yin nature of things.

The vertical line, which is of a yang nature, represents a "unique" action based upon an unexpected event or decided by higher beings. It may represent, for example, a connection between up and down, between heaven and earth, between two subtle planes, or between two types of energy.

The oblique lines represent, depending upon the degree of inclination to the vertical, different phases or stages between the two fundamental principles of Yin and Yang and the actions associated with their nature.

THE COMPLETE MEANING OF THE LETTER K

In the writings of Earth, regardless of the epoch or historical period in which they existed, some specific structures from Sirian writing can be recognized. Even in a brief analysis, it can be seen that those specific Sirian structures can be found in most of the letters in the alphabets of Earth's languages. One of the most eloquent examples in this regard is the letter *K*. This is, however, just a modified expression of a Sirian symbol which is close to representing the shape of the letter known to us as "*K*".

This symbol is very important in the life and activity of the Sirian civilization, especially with regard to the extent of its meanings and by the nuances it can have. At its base, however, this representation appears disarmingly simple, for it is made up of only straight lines and points.

The letter *K* starts from a vertical line that can be written in two ways. First, with the point or dot at the top of the line:

This symbol, in the Syrian world, represents the action of spiritually evolved beings upon those or to whom the will of God is manifested.

Second would be with the point at the bottom of the line:

This symbol represents the action of beings from the denser planes (such as the etheric plane or the physical plane) making a qualitative leap in their life in order to evolve spiritually. The point shows the place where the evolution begins (at the bottom) and that it tends towards the top, moving to the "top" of the line.

Next, the issue becomes complicated somewhat because another point intervenes in the middle of the vertical line which gives rise to two different interpretations of the specific rendering of the symbol.

In this case, there are two points at the top of the line:

This symbol represents the help offered by some spiritually subordinate beings to whom the will of God manifests. This action is mediated by beings in the middle planes of Creation: the higher astral plane, the mental plane or even the super-mental plan, the latter of which represents a transition between the mental plane and the causal plane such as your see in sages, spiritual masters or even celestial entities belonging to these dimensions of existence.

There is also a symbol with two points towards the bottom of the line:

In this case, this represents the action of beings from the coarser planes making a qualitative leap in their life to evolve spiritually, using the help of higher beings from the spiritual point of view who have the ability to communicate freely with other elevated beings from the upper subtle planes.

The addition of lines in the respective points represents the help given by different spiritual hierarchies, teachers, spiritual masters, etc. For example, a downward sloping line, starting from the middle of the vertical line with the point at its top, represents the fact that evolved beings transmit certain spiritual teachings in multiple ways in order to be understood by several different categories of human beings.

If the oblique line is oriented towards the top of the vertical line, this means that "intermediate" beings (such as human beings) receive support mainly from God when they fulfill an important mission, but are helped secondarily by different spiritual entities from the subtle planes of manifestation, as follows (see next page):

In the variant where the point on the vertical line is at the bottom of it, the addition of a downward oblique line shows that human beings can acquire spiritual knowledge both directly from evolved beings and through their own effort, as follows:

If the oblique line is pointed upward, then it indicates that human beings can acquire a certain knowledge by which they can reach divine wisdom and also understand the nature of its various manifestations in Creation:

Advancing with the presentation of the symbol *K* and its complex meanings, we come to the possibility of introducing two oblique lines which form a right angle between them. In the variant with the vertical line with the point at the top, the symbol represents the fact that the intermediate beings (humans) receive support mainly from God but also from different spiritually evolved celestial entities in order to succeed in their mission (the oblique line above). Thereafter, they transmit certain initiations in several ways in order to be understood by many different categories of human beings (the oblique line below):

If the two oblique lines are attached to the vertical two-point line at the bottom, then that means that human beings can reach different spiritual knowledge directly, either from highly evolved beings or entities (the upper oblique line) or through individual effort (the lower oblique line), thereby reaching divine wisdom. See below:

Finally, if there is a single point in the middle of the vertical line from which the two oblique lines start, then the symbol represents a spiritually initiated human being who can help others to evolve and orient themselves toward self-knowledge. This symbol is the one that signifies the connection between top and bottom:

It is very interesting that, starting with the symbol *K*, we find its form has meanings in different cultures and civilizations on Earth.

SYMBOL OF THE NUMBER PI (π)

One of the most important symbols derived from *K* is that of the number *Pi* (π), considered to be a mathematical constant. The graphic form of *Pi* starts from the Sirian symbolism that represents the eternal Wisdom of God, considered by this civilization to be the Great Spirit of Creation, the One and the Supreme.

The representation of Divine Wisdom is rendered in this symbol by the point of origin on the left, at the top. The "attainment" of Supreme Wisdom manifests itself at different times in history through highly spiritually evolved beings who serve "between people" (middle point, top) with precise missions of revitalizing and spiritually purifying civilization. To this end, certain highly evolved celestial entities or cosmic forces (continuous line from top right) are employed, the process being known as the "theme of avatars":

During their spiritual mission to Earth or to another planet in the physical universe, such a spiritual reformer appropriately interprets universal truths and laws that were known in some form in the past (the left oblique line) but still need to be adapted to the necessities of the time period in which he or she has manifested (point on the right, down).

In its evolution, a civilization registers both ups and downs, but its general tendency is ascending. To do this, "corrections" are needed from time to time to keep this trend going and not allow chaos to set in.

Such "corrections" or "balances" that are needed at certain time intervals in the existence of a civilization represent the various missions of avatars or beings with an exceptional level of spiritual elevation who incarnate in the physical plane.

I have been shown, however, that this symbol (Pi) has meaning only when the being who transmits the information so as to "update" the truth with respect to the current or "new" condition of space and time of that civilization is alive or their presence is clearly felt over time.

If the wise person or avatar is no longer alive; that is, he has left his physical body, his spiritual teaching can still be acquired by knowing some essential laws; and in this case, the middle point above is no longer useful. Variations of this symbol can be found in Pi's symbol, as follows:

Although it was simple to correlate the images of the symbol presented to me on the holographic screen with the presently known symbol of the number Pi, I was nevertheless directed to understand and shown by analogy that the initial points in the Sirian representation are presently replaced by the cursive rendition of a lowercase letter.[*]

---

[*] The Pi symbol of the irrational number 3.14 was proposed in 1706 by the mathematician William Jones and represents the sixteenth letter of the Greek alphabet.

This represents the understanding of the meaning that is connected between Heaven or the Divine plan (top line with the downward turning of the left side representing the Will of God in this situation and the Earth or the physical plane below it.) As the Divine Will manifests itself at different times in history through divine representatives, such actions are rendered by the lines that descend obliquely so as to make people understand the past (the left oblique line) and especially the future (the oblique line on the right, which is rounded).

During a break from the viewing, I talked with the man from Apellos about the precise aspects and nature of the number *Pi* in modern science and learned amazing things about what contemporary mathematicians and physicists refer to as a "constant." We were talking about the number *Pi* and the "irrationality" of it when the man from Apellos interrupted me.[*]

"The *Pi* number is, in fact, not a constant but an algorithm," he said in a very natural and loose way, after which followed a few seconds of total stillness.

"An algorithm?" I said in a jocular manner, without understanding anything. "What kind of algorithm?"

"A fractal algorithm, in the sense that certain values always change according to certain needs."

I did not understand anything.

"What do you mean by 'certain needs'?" I asked.

"The *Pi* number will have different values depending upon the domain or nature of the problem in which it is used. These differences are small, but they still exist."

For a moment, I thought it might be as in quantum physics where frequency and energy are very important quantities for determining certain processes. I was thinking that the higher the energy, the more significant those differences in *Pi* would be, and it might have different values depending on where they were used. This was like an inspirational flash in my mind, but I determined to analyze this correlation later. At that time, I was attracted to understanding the issues at a general level in order to form a solid basis for my understanding. I did not want to wander around the side paths without first mastering the main idea that the man from Apellos had brought up when he told me that *Pi* and other mathematical and physical "constants" were not actually constant.

"Okay; but how can such an algorithm be used in practice?" I insisted.

The man from Apellos began to "draw" in the air with his finger, making "pictures" as he explained to me.

---

[*] The number *Pi* represents the value of the ratio between the circumference and the diameter of any circle in Euclidean space. Nowadays, it is considered one of the most important constants in mathematics and physics because many formulas involve its use. The value of *Pi* is an irrational number (i.e. it cannot be expressed exactly as a fraction m/n where m and n are integers, and that is why expressing *Pi* in decimals has no end and is not repeated, being approximately equal to 3.14159...).

"In your mathematical language, the number *Pi* is a kind of function in the sense that it represents the transposition of a straight path into a curved movement. Since there is no such perfect curve or sphere in the Universe, mathematicians will come to the conclusion at some point that the number *Pi* is also changing "as needed". Rather, it can be called a "transpositional constant", having a different value depending upon what is required in that calculation, but is not a constant number by itself."

"However, if we divide the length of the circle by its diameter, the number *Pi* will always result," I timidly advanced, making a comment on what all the world knows.

"True, except that the length or circumference of the circle, as it is portrayed in your mathematics, is a conceptual mistake because it is a strictly mental conception with no connection to reality."

While the man from Apellos spoke and explained these aspects to me, I could already see with my mind the horrified faces of most contemporary scientists, shouting fiercely and with anger, "Blasphemy!"

I just smiled to myself, re-evaluating things with my imagination and returning to the discussion about the circle and sphere. With undisguised astonishment, I asked another question.

"Did you say that there is no perfect curve or sphere in the Universe? That would explain *Pi*'s 'variations' but still..."

"Give me an example of a body that is a perfect sphere," said the smiling man from Apellos.

A little confused, I realized that, at most, we can only talk about approximations of these perfect forms. A planet or a star, even if they seem to be perfectly spherical from a distance, this is not really the case. We are, in fact, dealing with an approximation of this perfect form. We prefer, however, to round off the values when we perform calculations with mathematical and physical "constants". That is why I have observed that other so-called "constants" may not be considered to be perfectly "stable" with regard to their numerical value.

With a nod of approval, the man from Apellos told me that this kind of "approximation" also applies to the speed of light. Although its value in a vacuum is considered to be constant, the speed of light undergoes certain fluctuations, even if the conditions in the environment in which the light is placed do not change. This opinion, in fact, seems to be already shared by a number of scholars worldwide.

"These numbers, which you call π and c, and which are considered to be mathematical constants, still suffer from small fluctuations, but these are not taken into account by your scientists," the man from Apellos continued.[*] It is the same with the perfect sphere, an absolute concept which actually does not exist in the universe. What creates the shape of a circle, bringing it close

---

[*] π = the number *Pi*, and c = the speed of light in a vacuum.

to perfection, are actually small circle arcs, one after the other so that, in the end, the resulting circle is an approximation made up of these small portions of the circle.

What the Apellos man referred to was actually a "quantified circle" or geometric shape consisting of a large number of fragments or "perfect" arcs that make up the circle. The end result is always an imperfection as a result of accumulating infinitesimal errors, but they are still errors. When I discussed these issues, I still did not suspect how quickly I would have to come to terms with their truth as regards the Eden project which I had started.

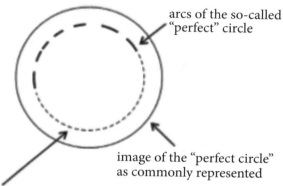

arcs of the so-called "perfect" circle

image of the "perfect circle" as commonly represented

image of the actual "quantified" and imperfect circle

A "QUANTIFIED" CIRCLE

My host continued.

"If you now understand that a circle is not actually a circle, since it is not perfect, then you must know that the center of the circle is not in the center either."

"Where is it then?" I asked, confused.

"On the circumference.; basically, everywhere."

I was dumb with amazement.

"Then," I said, "What sort of 'center' is that?"

"This is how people mentally represent the notion of a 'circle' and because of this, we can place a point in the middle of it as the 'center of the circle'. In reality, however, it is just a mental illusion because, wherever you look, you have the feeling of seeing this center."

I immediately made a possible correlation with Dr. Xien's explanations of "volume" and the "surface crease" which is merely an appearance of the inexpressible Infinite "beyond". Wherever you "increase" a volume, it is, in

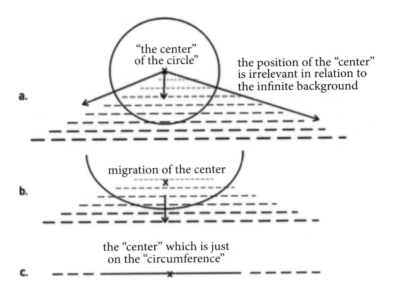

THE CENTER OF A CIRCLE IS ACTUALLY ON ITS CIRCUMFERENCE

fact, Infinity from which that volume appears. Likewise, wherever you place a circle or sphere, their center will be everywhere because there is no absolute spatial reference, and the "circumference" is actually a deployment, a surface. It is more a holographic image of the universe because, when the "center" is at the "periphery", the circle becomes a line.

Stunned by these simple but clear explanations while listening to the man from Apellos, I then returned to viewing the images on the holographic screen, only to find that the surprising influence of the Sirian *K* symbol does not stop only at the *Pi* symbol but that it can also be found in the ancient civilization of Egypt.

THE EYE OF RA

This is a well-known representation of the culture of Ancient Egypt with which, knowing some of the basic principles, we can now more easily analyze the notations and meanings of the Sirian "writing".

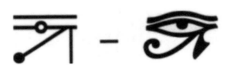

A first observation is that this symbol also derives from the universal symbol *K*, but this is less obvious than in the case of *Pi*, yet still clear enough to make a brief analysis of it, as it was shown to me on the holographic screen.

Obviously, the top line represents God's Eternity. In fact, everything in the original Sirian civilization is related to the Ultimate, Unique and Supreme Principle which is God. The Supreme Reality is the same for all because everything derives from it. With the Sirians in particular, I observed their aspiration to relate absolutely everything to this all-encompassing Reality because it is Infinite. In this deeply spiritual endeavor, the Sirian civilization is guided by its sages who have attained the highest level of spiritual perfection so that any action in which the Sirians are seeking to help, support or even to create is supervised by those very wise spirits.

Returning to the meaning of the symbol, the line below the "line of Eternity" represents the area of the higher plane (the causal plane) where the entity or being "holds" a certain knowledge which is close to the state of Eternity but still has a certain individuality in the scheme of Creation. Its presence is felt permanently in a present state, and this is represented by the circle that is in the middle of the line.

The presence of that entity or being manifested itself at a given moment in the past, an action symbolized by the slanting line to the left which has an end point. It will, however, have a message to be transmitted to the future when the time comes, and this aspect is symbolized by the vertical line to the right of the symbol.

Unfortunately, by a strange "twisting" of the meanings and by much manipulation, this ancestral symbol was overshadowed by the significance of the so-called "All-Seeing Eye", being self-attributed by the Organization and becoming a distinctive mark of it.

THE SYMBOL OF THE OWL

In ancient cultures and even in modern day esotericism, the owl is the symbol of wisdom. In fact, the fact that the Sirian symbol for such has the stylized appearance of an owl when viewed from the front has caused it to be associated with this bird.

In fact, the graphical representation is composed of several forms derived from different structures.

This symbol represents the eternal manifestation of God (horizontal straight line) which transmits knowledge at different moments from the past, present and future, symbolized by the three vertical lines. The three temporal dimensions are perceived in a balanced way by a being that can see the past and the future (the two circles) which unites them in a single manifestation in the present (the vertical line in the middle is longer).

There is also a simpler variant of the "owl" symbol which represents the eternal manifestation of God that directly transmits knowledge (the vertical line). This version corresponds to a reality that is accessible only to a small number of human beings, due to the fact that they must have high spiritual virtues and powers so as to observe the past and the future (the two circles) in a balanced way, uniting them in a single manifestation (the present one, represented by the vertical line in the middle).

Not coincidentally, these qualities are correlated with the correct and balanced vision over the relative time (past and future) involved, this being symbolized by the two circles that resemble two large round eyes. On the other hand, it also correlates with the appearance of the owl, an animal with a great visual acuity which also extends into the night. Here, the night is considered the "night of consciousness", that is, the ignorance and illusion which occlude the truth. The capacity of night vision symbolizes the power of penetrating consciousness beyond the deceptive waves of illusion (in which time plays an important role), thus succeeding in making the truth shine. This is the essence of the owl symbol.

JAPANESE DOOR SYMBOL

This is commonly found in the Japanese Shinto religion and actually even rendered in the construction of their Torii gates, but few are aware that the origin of this symbol derives from ancient Sirian symbols.

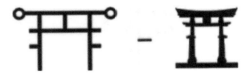

This symbol is more complex and requires a certain ability in order to be interpreted. It represents the eternity of God (the upper horizontal straight line) which manifests itself in the past and in the future, but at present, only those who have transcended the physical plane can reach it (the middle vertical line stops at the second horizontal line).

The two horizontal lines on the vertical lines are helpful methods of ascending or evolving spiritually, either by carefully analyzing the actions of the past (analyzing the past of one's life) or by transposing the human being into a higher state which one can reach through spiritual practice (the vision of the bright future). The being who attains the state of inner silence, however, will be able to attain wisdom through introspection (the gap below the middle line).

I wanted to take this digression on Sirian symbolism because I was deeply impressed by its extraordinary influence it has had, over time, on many civilizations of Mankind. Due to the depth of conception and the portrayal of universal realities, it can be a valuable aid in certain actions and initiatives through the high resonant energy that it activates. This was, in fact, one of the main reasons why we used Sirian symbols in the Eden project, even though they have remained a mystery to this day for other members of the work team.

CHAPTER FIVE

A SUPERIOR VISION OF MICROCOSMIC REALITY

During the interim between two stages of viewing the holographic screen, my discussion with the man from Apellos brought additional surprises besides the explanations regarding the impossibility of making a circle or a sphere or those about the "constant value" of the number *Pi* or the speed of light in a vacuum.

PHASE-SHIFT OF AN ELECTRON IN ORBIT

In the next break of relaxation, being preoccupied with these problems and seeking to understand their nature better, I made some observations to which I was waiting for an answer. Suddenly, and apparently without any connection to the topic of the discussion at that time, which referred to the position of the center of a circle on its circumference, the man from Apellos said, "The correlation you have made with quantum mechanics is correct."

I was surprised by the return to this topic and the way he mentioned it, even though I knew very well that the one I was talking to had telepathic powers. The man from Apellos was referring to the thoughts that had flashed through my head about a possible correlation between the "instability" of the value of *Pi*, depending upon the nature of the calculations in which it is used and the values for high energies and frequencies at the quantum level, all of which would favor this prospect. I was thinking that in such situations the differences around the "constant" would also become larger and more significant. Perhaps the inspiration to observe the variation of *Pi* at the microcosmic level originated from the man from Apellos. In any case, the topic seemed fascinating and I wanted to find out more.

"Some of your physicists in this field have observed that electrons that have a well-defined 'orbit' with a specific speed and energy — even if they do not appear around the nucleus in reality — show a certain phase difference after a period of rotation around the nucleus, that is to say, they emit a certain energy that should not then happen. Your scholars, however, do not understand this phenomenon and do not know what is happening at those specific times."

The phenomenon mentioned by the man from Apellos is a well-known one, although it was only then that I realized of its acceptance as such, even though I did not have a clear explanation from him. Normally, as the principles of quantum mechanics state, the electron should remain in orbit around the nucleus as long as it does not receive additional energy or give up energy to change that orbit. However, after a certain time in its rotation, a small phase difference appears "which should not exist".

"It is only when you put the problem this way that I think about it more seriously," I remarked with wonder.

I was, however, somewhat surprised that the man from Apellos insisted on focusing exactly on that phenomenon. Why precisely that phenomenon and not another? The process is simple, but it is true that, at least until now, it has not received a plausible explanation. I thought that perhaps it was not well documented enough, so I asked if there was actually any knowledge of the source of this phenomenon in modern quantum physics.

"So far, no, but what happens in this regard is fundamental to a deeper understanding of reality," the man from Apellos replied enigmatically.

THE IMPOSSIBILITY OF MAKING
A PERFECT CIRCLE OR SPHERE

Basically, I did not know what else to say. I expected some explanations to follow, but they did not come. After a few seconds, I preferred to ask directly.

"And what would be the reason behind this phenomenon?"

It seemed to me that I was trying to touch a dot on the ocean with my finger, but it was worth doing because I was very interested and absorbed the possibility of new information.

"I brought up this subject because it connects, in a way, with our discussion of the problem of the circle and the sphere," the man from Apellos began to explain to me. "Those small 'desynchronizations' in the motion of the electron in its orbit, which appear as a phase shift, occur due to changes in space and time. This precise 'alteration' of the space-time continuum generates the feeling of 'continuity' in the appearance of a circle or a sphere, giving the impression that they are perfect. In reality, a circle is 'born' and then grows like a child. At first, it is a point, then it grows more and more, and this growth continues indefinitely. Nowhere in the universe has there ever been a real and definitive 'circle' for the simple reason that it would then limit both space and time. It is, therefore, increasing as it continues, evolving in a continuous transformation and that is why we always assimilate the center with the periphery."

"Are you telling me here that there is no circle or sphere in the universe?! I can understand the concept of limitation which you have exposed, but what about the actual drawings or physical renderings? They look perfect."

"It's just an approximate perception. In reality, there is no perfect circle in nature. The circle is nothing but an idealization, a continuation of small arcs of a circle or, more correctly, a theoretical aspect derived from the notion of a spiral. The same is true for the sphere. The mental creation of a sphere starts first from an inner state, and then an imaginary vision of the sphere itself appears. It takes time to react and be creative."

I was now sure that I understood something very important. I realized that whenever we draw a circle or build a sphere, we must take into account the appearance of time, an aspect which is usually neglected. If we take this essential aspect into account, we will never make a circle, but what we will then draw, in reality, will be a spiral because we cannot return to the point from which we started, i.e. the initial time which we can identify as *t0*. We will never be able to reach *t0* at the same time, a point in space which corresponds to the exact location where the initial movement started, because a time interval has passed between the starting moment (*t0*) of the circle and the end moment (*t1*).

In this case, the fundamental mistake of contemporary science is to minimize the implications of approximating the space-time continuum to the scale of daily activities. Scientists simply ignore time as a coordinate of actual four-dimensional space, considering it to be negligible in terms of the scale within which we usually act.* In their calculations, they use only space and time in classical Newtonian mechanics where space and time are two separate notions and, moreover, where space is relative and time is absolute.**

Even physically or concretely speaking, if we draw a circle with the compass and a pencil on paper, we will get that "continuous" line made with the help of the compass, but it still requires a certain amount of time. For modern science, this time of creating the circle does not influence in any way the final shape of the resulting curve. At a closer look, however, drawing the circumference of the circle with the pencil fixed to the compass, its tip will blur a little because it is made of graphite. Thus, when the circle "closes", its radius will not be the same as at the start because there is now less graphite at the tip of the pencil. Even if it is a difference of only a few hundredths of a millimeter or even a few microns between the starting radius of the circle and its radius at the closing of the circumference line (because the pencil has lost some graphite) this difference still exists and distinguishes the hypothetical continuous circle from the one that is actually obtained by tracing.

Therefore, returning to the same point is impossible because, while we drew the line of the circle, a certain time has already passed, say *tn*. We will get close to the initial starting moment (*t0*), maybe even very close to it, but never at exactly the same point. This means we cannot overlap the last point of the line with the starting point because the end point of where the circle "closes" is in a different configuration of space and time than the one at the beginning. Indeed, at the close of the "circle", time has another value.

---

* If time is considered in addition to the three spatial coordinates within Minkowski space.
** That is, it flows in the same way in all inertial reference systems.

So, in reality, we have a spiral and not a circle. Whatever we do and whatever example we look for, the circle, as a mental notion, is impossible to obtain because you can never return exactly to the point from which you left with its tracing.

I would understand all this much better later, after the construction of Eden was completed. I then truly realized, in conjunction with the explanations of the man from Apellos on this subject, how important it is to pay attention to details in Nature because nothing is superfluous, meaningless nor done at random. In this connection, Einstein's words prove to be true and full of profound significance, even though they have generated much controversy.*

On the other hand, the man from Apellos explained to me that the line that is drawn as the circumference of the circle is actually made up of a multitude of small arcs of a circle. Therefore, that movement is, in fact, discontinuous. The feeling of continuity, however, appears at a macroscopic level precisely due to the approximations that are made. This leads to a mental "blockage" in the three-dimensional conception of physical space because, in the calculations related to daily human activities, the fourth dimension, which is time, is neglected. In theory, however, space and time are intrinsically linked and form an indissoluble continuum.

A problem arises when science considers that, in the ordinary circumstances of existence, this interconnection between space and time is "negligible". It is true that, from the point of view of ordinary human perception and the "continuity" of life, the mutual influence between time and space seems to be negligible, but it is precisely those "small negligible quantities" that actually make the difference between an approximate perception of things and a truly lucid perception, i.e. vigilance over the surrounding reality. Only some human beings, those who have an increased capacity to observe the mysterious connections in the universe, understand this interconnection and behave as such.

Of course, a "decision" to reform this concept in regard to today's mathematics and physics is difficult to make. The circle should be considered a spiral, and the sphere should be a concept of "puff pastry", a kind of "wrapping" of the surface itself. Likewise, the same principle should then be applied to other forms or "solids" that are considered to be "perfect". But, this "movement" of

---

* The author is probably referring to a famous quote from Einstein: "God does not play dice!" Einstein was making an observation in the dispute with the pioneers of quantum mechanics (Born, Schrodinger, Heisenberg, Pauli, etc.), highlighting some shortcomings in the theory of quantum mechanics. The quote appears in a letter that the genius scholar addressed to the physicist Max Born in 1926. The full passage in the letter is: "Quantum theory gives us much, but it hardly brings us closer to the secrets of God. In any case, I am convinced that He does not play dice with the Universe." Einstein wanted to say that nothing is approximate, left to chance or in uncertainty, including at the quantum level. His opinion was completely different from the conception of quantum mechanics which stipulates that all processes, interactions and phenomena that take place at the quantum level are the result of chance.

awakening from the heavy sleep of ignorance would be a disaster for modern science which should revise all their theories, calculations, theorems and science of mathematics and physics according to the new and correct vision. This would be about the same as the reaction you would expect to have from archeologists, paleontologists, historians and geologists before changing their paradigm of thinking based on dozens, maybe even hundreds of instances of evidence of the existence of very advanced civilizations that existed on Earth for thousands, tens of thousands and even hundreds of thousands of years before the "recognized history" of humanity, as we have exposed in the previous volume.[*]

"SPACE OF MOVEMENT" OF PARTICLES

The Apellos man then explained to me that what happens at the phase difference of the electron in its orbit is difficult for physicists to understand, especially because of their misconception about the meaning and existence of the electron.

"In reality, what they call the 'electron' does not move in orbit, but its motion around the atomic nucleus is just an approximation that scientists have given to that phenomenon in order to understand what is there inside the atom. Otherwise, they would not have had any conceptual reference unit."

I thought for a while, searching for my words.

"Are these phase differences, which in fact represent a discontinuity in the space-time continuum, separated from each other?"

"No. They are connected precisely by the respective discontinuity which allows a new 'path' for an electron to appear on a very close frequency but not the same as the previous one. The respective phase shifts pave the way for new approximate 'orbits' which shows that the electrons are actually 'moving' in spirals, not the circles or ellipses that your science claims at this time."

I intervened quickly.

"In any case, they're not closed, considering what you just told me about the circle."

In my opinion, this very phase shift, that is, the very discontinuity that occurs, confirms this.

The man from Apellos nodded at me, making a comment.

"Yes, you understand. In reality, there is no 'perfect circle'. It is illogical for your scientists, knowing this, to continue to approximate circular motion as a perfect circle because such a thing simply does not exist. They should modify their thinking to this new perspective, but this is not so simple."

"I wonder how this problem is posed at the quantum level," I said, reflecting more inwardly.

[*] Volume 6, *Forgotten Genesis*, 2020.

"The problem in the 'macro' world is an extension of the 'micro' world. Your scientists still follow the idea of a 'perfect circle' and a 'perfect sphere' because their conception of the basis of quantum mechanics is still too materialistic. It starts from the premise that there is matter and energy, even if a greater number of physicists suspect that the essence of everything that exists is only energy. If the calculations were made on the assumption of the existence of energy, and scientists finally understood that matter is only a local concentration of vibrations, then it would be acknowledged that the hypothesis of the perfect circle or the perfect sphere no longer makes sense."

Meditating later on these issues, I realized that the conceptual support of today's science still suffers from the superficiality or "laziness" of considering things at their exact and "correct" value. Approximations are always made which, in fact, "accumulate" and, in the end, offer a largely false result even if, at a glance, they seem to respect the laws of nature. One of the best examples is the space created by geometric figures, especially circles and spheres.

The problem with these "spaces" is that they, like many other notions and phenomena, are not yet well understood by mathematicians. The space that is "adopted" for calculations, be it Euclidean, Hilbertian, Minkowskian, etc, is an idealized space where events take place. But for them to take place, it is necessary to have another space beforehand. Therefore, we have a general space-time in which other space-times are created, as needed. For example, for things to "work", we use a system of axes and coordinates that are simply arbitrary and theoretical. If we really want to understand Nature, it is then necessary to take these coordinates out of the realm of theory and apply them "concretely". This means that there will be a designated space-time with a certain level of vibration in which there will be another space-time with a different level of vibration. There are permanent connections between these vibrational levels which are manifested by extremely small discontinuities. Scientists want to unite different structures or forms with each other without suspecting that each object actually represents a "particular" space-time, and the connections between objects represent the quantum union between several such "particular" structures of the space-time continuum.

Minkowski space is very convenient for such an approach because it considers time to be related to its fourth dimension, in addition to the three known spatial dimensions. In such a space, the objects themselves represent a "separate space continuum and an independent time". The union of objects represents the union of very close dimensions that would create this seemingly continuous dimension in which we consider that we live.

THE PROBLEM OF CONSCIOUSNESS IN THE QUANTUM WORLD

The difficulties of scientific conception do not stop here however. The man from Apellos pointed out a truth I had known for a long time from Cezar and Dr. Xien.

"Every atom is first and foremost an entity, a certain form of consciousness. I have noticed that there are scientists who have intuited this truth, but the vast majority of them ignore it. You can't consider an atom just by saying it is something very small and that's it. This is a vision that sets limits in itself. Even if you have somehow gone beyond the 'atomic barrier' in science and plunged into the world of elementary particles, it does not give you the proper understanding of the phenomena that takes place there or their mode of formation."

I was then reminded of several elements that initially define physics at the microcosmic level: the set defined by four quantum numbers to characterize the state of the electron in orbit around the nucleus,* the electronic layers and substrates in the structure of the atom, and the orbitals used to characterize the probability of an electron. The man from Appellos, however, pointed out that current quantum theory, even if it is quite complex, is not very useful as long as its foundations are not yet fully known.

"Rather," he said, "the situation is like that of a treasure hunter groping with a small lighted candle through a huge cavern in complete darkness. He hopes to make the great discovery, believing that it may be in a certain direction, but he is mistaken because he has not entered where he should in that cave."

"Well, that's how he could continue to look long and hard without getting any essential results," I said.

The man from Apellos nodded his approval of my comment and spoke.

"The point is, he only gets to a stalagmite or a puddle from time to time, but he never finds the treasure although often passing it. It's kind of a forever game of hide-and-seek."

I then asked him what the main causes were for this, and the man from Apellos told me that the first was their materialistic conception of science, and the second was a corollary of it: pride and scientific arrogance. I know all too well how things were in this regard, so I could only agree with him.

---

* Quantum numbers usually describe the energy of electrons in the atom but also indicate the various (quantified) values of their orbital and kinetic spin momentum. The four quantum numbers are: 1) The main quantum number n, indicating the number of the electronic layer; 2) The secondary quantum number or orbital kinetic moment l (as in the letter L), which determines the number of electronic substrates and the shape of the orbitals; 3) The magnetic quantum number m, quantifying the spatial orientation of the kinetic moment and indicating the number of available orbits in a sublevel; and 4) The quantum spin number(s) which quantifies the kinetic spin moment of the electron: the intuitive (though not entirely accurate) image of the electron spin that is due to the rotation of the electron about its own axis, and the kinetic moment of spin that "gives rise" to a magnetic moment proper to the electron.

"That is why," he added, "a radical change of vision is really necessary in the conception of your science." Not all the things you have reached are wrong, but you will not be able to make the decisive leap if you stay at this level. It's like waiting for an egg to boil in water at 70 degrees Celsius."

In principle, the initial model of the atom — based largely on the Sommerfeld model[*] — is not really wrong, although it is based almost exclusively on approximations.[**] For example, at the quantum level, we cannot talk about the trajectory of an electron or an elementary particle[***] but rather about the probability of the existence of an accumulation of waves in a certain area of that atom. Almost all phenomena related to the quantum world of the atom are described by models based upon uncertainties and approximations that scientists have made out of the desire that "things all must make sense in a certain manner that is otherwise well known by all those who have knowledge in the field".

ATOMIC MODELS

For example, there are still some today who still imagine electrons as particles that move very fast in the space around the nucleus of the atom, forming an "electronic cloud" but without any precise description about their exact trajectory or position inside the atom. This is the splendor of quantum phenomena because it is the best proof of the statement that "you get what you want to see and believe".

The planetary model of the atom is a good example of this. The world wanted to understand the structure of the atom, and this, in the beginning, was similar to the planetary system: as electrons rotate in elliptical orbits around the nucleus, so do the planets revolve around the Sun. It was quickly understood, however, that the electrons would fall into the nucleus and everything would collapse in a very short time. That is why the planetary model was completed with the idea of stationary orbits, a good idea which was already, slowly but surely, connecting with quantum mechanics. In this way, the planetary model became a pre-quantum model that appealed to the idea of quantifying the

---

[*] This model, which is a development of Bohr's model, assumes that electrons rotate around the atomic nucleus not only on circular trajectories but also on elliptical trajectories.

[**] The Bohr and Bohr-Sommerfeld models are pre-quantum models and were developed at the beginning of atomic physics. Non-relativistic quantum mechanics appeared about eleven years after the development of the Bohr-Sommerfeld model; and only after that, with the postulate of Erwin Schrödinger's equation published in 1926, was the non-relativistic quantum model of the atom developed which we could say is the contemporary model used today. The most rigorous current model, however, is the relativistic quantum model of the atom based on Dirac's equation.

[***] The author makes indirect reference to Heisenberg's uncertainty principle which states that the velocity and position of a micro particle (relative to the same direction of space) cannot be known simultaneously but only by one or the other of these quantities.

orbits of electrons. In this model, it is considered that the electrons move in orbits like concentric circles with each "orbit" actually representing an energy level.* This model demonstrates that the valences** of the atoms did not last long either, due to design inconsistencies.***

Quantum mechanics later showed that, in fact, electrons do not orbit the atomic nucleus and that they cannot be "found" in a certain place and at a specific time in the atom. Rather, they "cover" a range of probabilities of their presence inside the atom because they appear to exist simultaneously in different places at the same time. This situation is valid until the moment we perform a measurement on an electron, in which case we can find it in a certain area of the atom but not before the measurement takes place. That is why the model of the "electron cloud" around the atomic nucleus seems to present this situation satisfactorily because it at least gives a general idea of what is there, but that does not mean things have been fully understood.

In fact, the essence of quantum mechanics is not really understood even today. There are a number of phenomena that occur on a quantum scale that cannot be explained with the help of the mathematical apparatus of current quantum mechanics. One of them, famous in its own way, is related to the "experiment of the two slots" which highlights an extraordinary and still miraculous property of micro particles: namely, that they somehow "feel" that they are being observed.

THE PROBLEM OF QUANTUM UNCERTAINTY: IS IT HAPHAZARD OR PERFECT ORDER?

By its very nature, the probabilistic interpretation of quantum mechanics has a high degree of uncertainty,**** always being considered "strange" in relation to the "normal" conception and vision of classical physics and ordinary existence, but it is the defining feature of quantum mechanics. In reality, things would not seem so strange if we better understood how atoms appear and form in the physical plane. To cover this fundamental gap of conception, quantum mechanics imposes the idea of "haphazard", but there is a precise "descent" of the formation of each atom and a causality in its existence because, in reality, nothing in Creation, either at the macrocosmic or at the microcosmic level, happens "at random".

The dilemma between "chance" and "precise causality" has been the

---

* The Bohr Model which, in 1913, "dethroned" the Rutherford Mode.

** In short, the valence of an atom represents its ability to combine with other atoms to form chemical compounds or molecules.

*** For example, Bohr proposed his model almost twenty years before the discovery of the neutron in 1932 by James Chadwick although the existence of the neutron was theorized before by Ernest Rutherford in 1920.

**** The author indirectly refers again to Heisenberg's Uncertainty Principle.

apple of discord among physicists from the beginning. In quantum physics, for example, there is a lot of talk about location of particles and their quality while, in Einstein's relativistic physics, there is talk of energy as a concrete quantity which can be measured with various precise values. Therefore, we cannot always "swim" in the eternal "uncertainty" of waves and their general mode of manifestation because, while this provides more of an idea of how phenomena occur and how things are, it is not precisely accurate. Of course, from a certain perspective, both variants are valid because they offer different explanations in different conditions: sometimes things appear only in a general aspect or expressed in probabilistic terms, as in the case of waves; while other times they become concrete, as in the case of the involvement of observation in the experiment.

"The 'uncertainty' that one of the principles of microcosmic physics claims in your science arose from, in fact, was your inability to measure something," the man from Apellos said. "This has nothing to do with reality. It's like saying that, if you don't know what things are like in a certain place, then you assume that they could be 'something like that' with a certain probability, and you make this the 'end' of your knowledge in that direction. Further, if you do not know how to measure that, this doesn't mean you're right."

"Well, that's the controversy of the last hundred years which has tilted in the direction of the 'haphazard' interpretation,"* I said. "The followers of this idea,** however, did not say that they do not know how to measure quantum reality but that it can only be measured under certain conditions."

"They came to this conclusion by assuming that, if they cannot use photon-based measurement, which involves light, this means that there is no other method of measuring a quantum reality. In reality, the interpretation of quantum 'uncertainty' is wrong as you see it. This does not mean, however, that Nature is incapable of controlling or 'measuring' those quantum realities. If it were as it is interpreted in the Uncertainty Principle which your science has formulated, it would mean that there is no order in Nature and that everything is chaos."

"Then how should one understand this?" I asked, honestly surprised

"The idea is that 'uncertainty' should not be resolved but rather reinterpreted; and then, it is no longer uncertainty. You no longer start from the idea

* See the previous footnote about Einstein's statement that "God does not play dice!"
** Representatives of the "Copenhagen School Interpretation" were Niels Bohr and Werner Heisenberg as keynote speakers who defined a set of rules for understanding quantum mechanics. Einstein was reluctant from the beginning to adopt the "spirit of the Copenhagen School", denying it until his death. One of the opponents of the "Copenhagen School interpretation" was John G. Cramer who stated in his paper "The Transactional Interpretation of Quantum Mechanics" (1986) that, "Despite an extensive literature that refers to, discusses and criticizes the Copenhagen School's interpretation of quantum mechanics, nowhere does there seem to be any concise statement that fully defines this interpretation."

that 'you can't see the particle' because this is no longer important then, but by the correct understanding of the 'uncertainty', the seemingly linear motion of the particles is transformed into a kind of rotation of the particle, and you then immediately have angular momentum! You really want the particle to enter a state of 'rotation.'"

"How do I see it then?"

"You are no longer interested in seeing it, but you are interested in the fact that, through rotation, a certain specific radiation is produced which is, in fact, some electromagnetic waves which are specific to that rotational motion."

"Okay, but why don't I see it?" I insisted. "I understand. I have the specific rotation and waves of the particle, but I still don't see it. Why?"

"Because you can no longer see it with your current equipment. As I told you before, it also depends a lot on your technological measurement capabilities. Your scientists like to think they have everything in this regard, and if they can't measure or see anything with what they have as measuring instruments, they then think that reality doesn't exist."

I did not give up.

"And what's new in this? I haven't seen the particle before, and I don't see it now, even with these explanations. So, what's new from this point of view?"

"There are many other phenomena, including absorption. A vortex appears and then the particles will tend to move around a 'gravitational point'. The gravitational aspect is very important here."

"That's happening from the start of the rotation anyway."

"Yes, but the moment you reinterpret 'uncertainty', you can then arrange your devices to measure this new reality, and then you will see quantum phenomena that you did not know."

He was right because, in the quantum realm, reality changes according to what you want to pursue. I, however, had my doubts about the transformation of particle motion.

"It's still not clear to me how things are turning into a 'rotation,'" I said.

The man from Apellos was so patient that I would have liked to have had such a teacher in high school.

"It's a very important phenomenon. The rectilinear motion of a particle turns into a rotational motion, and then you can no longer see the particle."

"Why? A bullet coming out of the barrel of a pistol or an arrow released from a spring rotates and, at the same time, advances 'straight' at a certain speed."

"When you see a particle, what you see is dependent upon the wavelength of the photon you use, which appears to you as 'light'. If that particle moves so that you can observe its motion, you can tell where it is. But the moment you have the ability to observe and measure, say, within a range of 40 picometers,*

---

*A picometer (pm) measures 10 to the negative twelfth power meters. For example, a hydrogen atom has a diameter of 53 pm.

and the particle moves within a range of 10 picometers, you can no longer observe it.

"Okay, but there could be wavelength photons to observe the particle," I said.

"Indeed; but you do not have the necessary equipment to create such photons," the man from Apellos replied, telling me that it was still time to continue looking at aspects of the real history of Mankind. This topic was extremely attractive to me, so I set out to investigate it as deeply as possible because it seemed to me a cornerstone for a correct understanding of reality. In a series of exceptional experiences, which I later lived, I was able to delve much deeper into the true meanings of Heisenberg's uncertainty principle, but I will talk about all this in detail in one of the future volumes.

CHAPTER SIX

FIRST EXPERIMENTS IN
THE SPACE-TIME MACHINE

The year 2015, until the beginning of autumn, was very intense. The construction of the device, at least at the beginning, required a lot of preparations, discussions, meetings, tests and solutions. The distribution of tasks for other people was done on the principle of division of labor, in the sense that only the data strictly necessary for the part of the project that belonged to each respective member of the work team was provided. This is a normal and well-known practice, especially in military projects, as it prevents, at least in theory, the unwanted leakage of information.

I coordinated the project data together with Cezar and Lieutenant Nicoară. Cautiously, Cezar worked out confidentiality agreements with those who collaborated with us. In addition, the meetings took place in spaces closely monitored by us in order to avoid any unwanted "interference". In principle, the team was not numerous, but even so, we had to be very careful.

CHALLENGES AND OBSTACLES

Contrary to popular belief, large and complicated projects — whether governmental or not — are often less effective than those approached at a lower level. This is due in part to the rather complicated bureaucratic apparatus that appears at that level, including political or other interventions, as well as the large number of people taking part in the project. Usually, such a project represents a complex "entity" whose resistance is quite high. In the case of smaller projects, things can move much faster, but the resources and possibilities are also smaller.

From the beginning, the Eden project had two major problems which we had to overcome. On the one hand, it was necessary to design very complicated software which would ensure the specific functioning of Eden. Here, we relied on the extraordinary genius of Midas. On the other hand, the financial problem loomed on the horizon as a serious obstacle. Although we thought that funds would not be a problem at first, we soon realized that we were facing huge difficulties from this perspective. It turned out that the realization of the mere external skeleton of the "chair" itself, to which other basic arrangements were added, raised the expenses to a value that far exceeded both our current financial possibilities and the savings we had. And this was only the tip of the iceberg because there were also the payments to be made to our collaborators, and not only the contractual ones but especially those special materials which we have already mentioned. So, the initial estimated costs became much higher when we started to put the project into practice.

It was a difficult time, felt most intensely around the end of April. Neither I nor Cezar were willing to compromise as we had already adapted the project to a considerable extent so that it would still be accessible without losing too much of the possibilities that the device could provide. The production costs, however, were enormous. I confess that I felt the "pressure" of this fact, and even Cezar was concerned because the project had to go ahead.

Even though we were beginning to have to face these difficulties, the first experiments were already underway. The basic software of the device had already been designed by Midas, and the first tests of correlation with the two huge Tesla coils, which had been constructively adapted to our plans, were positive.

It was at about this time that I started the first training session, even if the device was in an early stage of development. The interaction with the frequencies modulated by Eden, which gradually became a "machine of controlled spacetime distortion," was obvious and powerful. Midas explained to me that this was mainly due to the modulated energy of the two special Tesla coils and that he still needed to make some programming adjustments. Basically, everything was a game of frequencies which had to be combined so that their action was as finely tuned as possible at the biological level. In the design theme, the frequencies modulated in a certain way by the basic software resonated at the same time with different glands of the body, especially with the pineal gland and also with different internal biological structures that included the structure of DNA itself. The software aimed at a permanent orientation of the frequencies according to the biological state of who was seated in the device. Feedback was expected at each external impulse. For this, special sensors were designed from scratch which were not on the market. This proved to be extremely sophisticated and required months of very intense effort on the part of Midas to find the solution to combine the frequencies. In a moment of sincerity, he confessed to me that, from his professional point of view, Eden's programming was the greatest and most difficult challenge he had faced until then.

"I'm still not happy with what I've done," he told me. "It works, but it's not perfect...I still need time … I insist."

A NECESSARY "UPGRADE" FOR CONTEMPORARY SCIENCE

I considered, however, that the results up until then were very good because I had seen how the technology that was born in our project tended to "break" the usual and old-fashioned patterns of current science. First, our work provided clear evidence of the existence of subtle planes of manifestation. I have touched on this topic many times in my books because I consider it to be of fundamental importance. Additionally, I do not see how contemporary science could take significant steps forward without understanding that the real structure of the universe is based upon the hierarchy of dimensions of existence with regard to the principle of vibrational frequencies of energy.

In the beginning, to make things clearer for Midas, I had to briefly explain some basic elements in this regard to be sure that what we were doing would reach beyond the limited concepts of today's scientists. We needed his free spirit and his very open thinking so that he could correctly understand the real way Eden was supposed to work. Fortunately, this proved to be quite easy with Midas as he already had some ideas about the subtleties and plurality of different worlds. It was only necessary therefore to summarize some aspects of it in this direction and to draw the correct line of approach to the theme of the project.

I have seldom had the opportunity to meet a person with such sharp intelligence. This young man managed to extract, in only a few phrases, the essence of complex elaborations which would have required perhaps lengthy discussions, and even more, to then correctly extrapolate upon the conclusions he reached. It was a pleasure to talk to him, but for that, it was also necessary to be yourself. Like any extremely mentally gifted and intuitive young man, Midas also had high expectations of his interlocutor, from whom he demanded good mental training. In his case, this attitude was justified because it was almost impossible to discuss a subject with him if it did not interest him nor if it did not really demand any contribution from his intellectual abilities.

Midas quickly caught on to the idea that the forms of manifestation of energy in the universe are endless, and that this implicitly leads to the existence of very complex worlds, plans and dimensions outside the physical plane in which we live.

"There are many so-called parallel planes, but they are potentials; that is to say, they are not 'active' until you become aware of them," I told him. "The plane or dimension of which you are aware is the one in which you exist."

"Do I only exist here, on the physical plane? You said that human existence is multidimensional, complex."

"That's right, but for now, you're only aware of the physical plane. For you, only it exists. The other dimensions you exist in, such as the etheric, astral, and so on, are just potential for you, at least for now. At most, you realize their existence in an indirect way through the effects that they produce and that you sometimes feel in your physical body, which is currently the only one that you seem to be fully aware of and convinced of its existence."

"But you said, however, that there are several such planes of existence. What else is there to believe?"

"That's a reality. I'm just confirming that. It's less important whether you believe that or not. What matters most is to become aware of the other dimensions of your existence."

"How?" he asked.

I smiled. Midas had a very concise, pragmatic and straightforward style of finding out. He was also very focused and staring, a feature that was especially visible whenever something interested him.

"By expansion. Think of a balloon. At first, it is almost deflated, and the volume it occupies is small. If you start blowing into it and inflating it, it grows in size and takes up more and more space. So does your consciousness. The more it expands, the more you become aware of the additional dimensions of the universe."

"You mean that I live simultaneously in several dimensions that are parallel," Midas said.

I was not sure if this was a question or a statement from him, but I answered back.

"Parallels are referred to by contemporary scientists. For them, the moment a plane exists, that is a physical plane. In their conception, it cannot be anything else."

"I read, however, about people who are aware of other dimensions or who have actually penetrated them, lived there and then returned. This means that

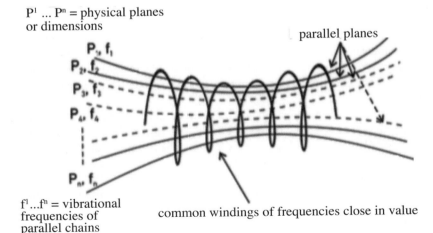

$P^1 \ldots P^n$ = physical planes or dimensions

parallel planes

$f^1 \ldots f^n$ = vibrational frequencies of parallel chains

common windings of frequencies close in value

**IN THE CONCEPTION OF CURRENT SCIENCE,
ALL "PARALLEL" PLANES ARE PHYSICAL**

they were and may still be fully aware of that plane or other parallel dimensions. What answer does science have for this?" he asked.

Midas was quite "incisive" but in a constructive way. He really wanted to know, to understand. I tried to explain to him with my own "weapons" of current science.

"It says that such planes of existence can exist, that they are 'parallel' with ours, but that they are all physical. Current science does not follow the idea that those 'parallel' planes or dimensions could be more refined than the physical plane. In other words, it does not accept that there may be planes of existence with a higher frequency of vibration than that of dense physical matter, in contrast to, for example, the etheric plane. For contemporary science, all that exists is the physical plane, whether it is conscious of it or not. The vibrational frequencies of these 'parallel' physical planes are close; that is, they are part of a 'common bundle' of a common envelope of frequencies, but in the end, for such scientists, it is also about physical matter."

Later, it was easy for Midas to understand that all current mathematics and physics are built on a "horizontal" model as opposed to a vertical one. Some scientists do not conceive, for example, that there could be a strictly energetic plane or dimension.

Even when they refer to someone's thoughts or emotions, they do not see this as a manifestation in another plane of existence but rather that those thoughts and emotions of people on the physical plane are only a chemical exchange between different sensors of the physical body.

"It's like a conceptual block," I explained to Midas. "In the conception of today's scientists, a subtle energetic plane has no way to exist. If you analyze this well, even the equations of mathematical physics are from the beginning designed to show and describe only the physical plane."

For contemporary scientists, there is indeed no hierarchy of planes of manifestation by reason of the vibrational frequency of energy. They do not even think of that. For them, anything is possible, but only on the physical plane. You can become what you want, open portals in another plane, and even make leaps in time, but all of this can only happen in reference to physical planes of manifestation.

Midas "adjusted" quite quickly to the basic conceptual structure of the universe and its main laws. I needed him to be convinced of this hierarchy of energy in order to properly program the source code and the necessary subroutines of the general software of the device. If his vision had been in line with the current paradigm of science, I do not think we could have succeeded in building Eden, at least not in terms of the space-time distortions that the "machine" could create. We needed a substitute for the function of the etheric crystal, and finally, Midas understood the mode of operation.

THE SUBTLETY OF AN ERROR

Around that time, an element intervened that would give a special impetus to the whole project. As far as I am concerned, this aspect also involved an emotional side which also alleviated the stress of the very intense period that had ensued since the beginning of the project.

In mid-June, just at the time of the stellar configuration that was calculated, the first assemblies of the device began. Construction proceeded fairly quickly, especially as many of the sub-assemblies had already been ordered or pre-assembled. After about two weeks, Eden was almost completely realized from an outer perspective. This was followed by work on the "interior" which included some electronic assemblies, certain finishes and especially the connection to the energy source.

From this last point of view, it was a difficult task to build the two large special Tesla coils. They can be considered the "heart" of the device and the source of the space-time distortions that Eden can accomplish according to clear and precise instructions released from the center console. I was strongly forbidden to present sketches or drawings of these coils, no matter how simple, or to offer other details of its construction or operating characteristics. The technical solution that was sent to me telepathically, which I was able to "extract" from the cortex without even understanding it too well at first, is truly amazing. Each component part of the coils were made in a different place to avoid any problems with security leaks and any unwanted connections or interference.

The smooth running of the construction and the experiments that followed, however, were not entirely without surprises. In July, I started the first training sessions, and the condition that enveloped my body as soon as I got in the chair and set the parameters that would determine the space-time distortion was absolutely amazing. I was so happy with what I had managed to do thus far that I spent hours on end, especially at night and in several stages, trying to adapt as well as possible to the subtle "energetic communication" with Eden. It being summer, the program was freer and I agreed with Cezar to make the most of that period so as to energetically stabilize my inner structure in order to adapt it to the specific energy of the device.

This was not a small task at all and it created a reverberation at very deep levels somewhere in my body. I usually felt the effects as waves or flows that created a feeling of immensity on a mental level. At first, it was really difficult because a feeling of dizziness appeared, as if the body could not sustain and control that energy. I, however, was not bothered so much by the intensity of the energy but rather by the ripple effects which the body did not seem to "understand" and to which my body was adjusting.

Somehow, the "chair" was trying to solve the task imposed by the programming of the desired space-time distortion through a kind of dissociation of energy levels in my being, or that was at least the feeling it created every time when the training session exceeded forty minutes. If I extended the meeting for an hour, the first signs of nausea and dizziness appeared. In fact, what bothered me was not so much the appearance of those symptoms but especially the feeling that something was not harmonious in what was manifesting. I was willing to accept a period of the body's adaptation to the new type of energy and the corresponding frequencies, but what I was regularly feeling and the same symptoms that were being accentuated could not be correct.

About a week later, I shared the results with Cezar. We had a long discussion, analyzing all aspects point by point. In the second part of that discussion, we were joined by Lieutenant Nicoară, and he caught the "weak link" in the situation quite quickly. He logically pursued the thread and deduced that it could be a programming error because that is where the "frequency distribution" originated. At first, I was a little surprised because I knew from the consultations with Midas that everything was very well understood and established, and I did not understand where the error could have crept in. I immediately arranged a meeting with him and Lieutenant Nicoară, and all three of us very carefully reviewed the lines of software code developed by Midas.

For me, that task was difficult to follow, and I had to ask for clarifications many times due to the complexity of the code. It was, however, a real pleasure to go through and understand, even if it was only a partial understanding, the exceptional way in which that programming genius had designed the operation of the device. It was, practically speaking, a combination of certain elements belonging to the physical plane and methods of tensor calculation which referred to the etheric plane. That source code and its "shells" were a true art of IT (Information Technology), replacing some of the subtle emissions of the etheric crystal.

Nicoară noted that although the values were to be calculated to the ninth decimal place for certain parameters resulting from a preliminary assessment, Midas had considered only the first five decimal places, these later being re-entered into the calculation flow.

As I recall, I think it was the first and perhaps the last time I saw Midas confused, surprised, and at the same time, upset. He explained to us that he simply did not consider that the results could be influenced by the seemingly very small values corresponding to the range between the sixth and the ninth decimal. His "rounding" of the values to the fifth decimal had seemed natural and sufficient. I, on the other hand, remembered the discussions I had with the man from Apellos in which he had shown me the similar mistakes that contemporary scientists were making, "neglecting" values that they considered insignificant but which, in reality, could cause some very fine effects of obvious importance for certain quantities corresponding to subtle planes.

Analyzing the problem, we realized that Eden was not only acting at the cellular level but even at much deeper levels, going as far as the quantum level. Here, any "quantity" is important because space and time are very subtle. If I had continued training with the initial set of values, the effects probably could have become very unpleasant and dangerous, even leading to a disorder of cellular functions.

After making changes and even improving some subroutines, which Midas completed in a very short time, we restarted the experiments inside the device. The changes turned out to be correct because the energy waves in my body now felt harmonious, and I could even prolong the sessions for more than two hours. I realized that it was all a matter of regular training. My physical cellular structure had to get used to the new energy frequencies and specific biochemical exchanges. In other words, I needed some time to adjust.

The construction of the device also permanently involved adjustments to the central software and the operation of the special coils, as well as to other component parts of the general assembly. It tended towards a perfect correlation of all these elements until a point of equilibrium of frequencies was actually reached, at which point Eden seemed to operate "on its own".

I had entered a correct flow of distribution of the waves and their harmonics, and I felt that I was advancing quite fast. I was, for example, doing bio-feedback between cellular transformations and my mental condition. This was nothing new in today's technology, but in Eden's case, things seemed much more complex and fast. After the start of the training had developed according to the settings I was making, the effects appeared almost instantly. I felt that it was an accelerated growth in the sense of refining one's being, even if the purpose was not yet very clear. In other words, I did not know very well what exactly those results could lead to.

UNEXPECTED VISIT

One month after the start of training, Midas announced to me that he was introducing a higher level of programming, a modulation of energy that would produce deeper changes at the cellular level. In the initial design meetings, we had set a reasonable value for the energy level gradient module, precisely to give the body and mind time to take in the energy information correctly. In this way, we gradually "chiseled" the body and the mind without knowing exactly what the real target of that technology was. I only suspected that it could be related to the easy penetration into the subtle dimensions of the universe to, in any case, facilitate "extensions" of consciousness in order to have access to higher information.

About that time, I was with Cezar in the living room one evening, just after a training session in which I had reached a kind of "threshold" of consciousness. I had noticed then that I could not say that I had slipped into sleep nor was I perfectly lucid. It was more like a semi-awake state in which the two states, dreamfulness and wakefulness, intertwine. I discussed with Cezar about the possible evolution of that condition, trying to find out if it could be done by extending the time given to each session or by changing other parameters, such as energy intensity or its spectral distribution. In the middle of the discussion, we both heard the door at the entrance to the villa open and then the sound of steps coming down the wide hall to the living room. It was like in a movie, waiting for an outcome. At that moment, both Cezar and I had the same telepathic perception, and I knew then that the one who had arrived was my old friend Elinor.

I quickly got up from my chair and took two steps toward the door. When it opened, I saw Elinor on the threshold. What a wonderful surprise! Astonished and at the same time very happy, I showed my outpouring of affection, hugging him and leading him into the room to meet Cezar. Meanwhile, I noticed the same "frozen" time of Elinor's appearance, somewhere around the age of 38; also, his calm smiling presence and radiant aura full of vitality and power of action.

Cezar had also risen from his chair, and I then introduced them. In a way, they already knew each other from what I had told them about each other, but they had never met face to face. I then had the opportunity to realize the deep respect that each of them had for each other. It may sound a bit emphatic, but I had the impression of two "titans" meeting to join forces to achieve something magnificently spiritual. They seemed to be "from the same world", both sharing the same aspirations and abilities to sustain the Good and help people. Through the game of fate, I had the opportunity to be around them, to listen to their teachings and to participate in some of the most amazing adventures, experiences which hardly find their place in the concerns of the common man.

The discussion started in a very natural way, being immediately oriented towards the Eden project.

"I know about your plan and what you started doing, but what brought me here were some of the blockages I felt in this far-reaching action."

Amazed and reflexively, I responded.

"But no one knows about our project in this location!"

Cezar and Elinor smiled discreetly, and then I understood at once. For those who have a high degree of spirituality, it is no longer necessary for knowledge to reach them by ordinary methods. At the level of higher planes, it can be transmitted directly.

Cezar replied to Elinor, highlighting in summary some implications at the political level as well as the somewhat ungrateful situation for which, for the time being, we could not proceed with this extraordinary project in an "official" manner. While we were talking and exchanging opinions, we all went down to the basement, to the big room where the device was being built. Elinor was impressed by the complexity and scope of the project, but especially by the speed with which we had advanced.

I then told him briefly about the etheric crystal and the telepathic connection between it and myself, the way I was inspired to start this project, but also about the fact that we were currently facing financial difficulties and how that could considerably delay the realization of it.

"Yes. It's a serious stalemate," Elinor admitted.

After a few moments of thinking, he continued.

"I have a proposal for you. If you agree, I will financially support this project from now on. I know it's important, and it needs to be developed carefully."

It was a wonderful surprise and one I did not expect in the least. It offered a new impetus and the possibility of refining the construction plans of the device as well as the opportunity for significant improvements. Of course, Cezar and myself both intuited that the sums available to Elinor came from the results of the science of alchemy, but I felt that it was not necessary to probe deeply into the subject. In fact, I later reflected with a bitter smile on the strange mentality of contemporary society: being deeply rooted in materialism, it ironically rejects some scientific fields, true knowledge of arts such as alchemy and astrology, but on the other hand, it is very suspicious and infers the concrete results that can be obtained by these ways. It is only a matter of an indoctrination of consciousness by which everything that is not understood or known by contemporary science is considered to be deceptive or that it cannot exist.

Next, we informed Elinor about the members of the work team, about other details of construction and ideas about our project. It was a very fruitful discussion which later extended to other related fields. As I said, I appreciated Elinor's proposal for financial support as a real stroke of providence which offered wonderful possibilities for the development of the project. Elinor's integrity and virtue were perfect, operating only in the spirit of selfless help. He did not ask us for anything, he did not demand anything, but we felt that it was our duty to inform him about the state of the works, especially since his ideas and intuition often prove themselves to be very valuable.

Given the new situation, Elinor told us that he would stay in the country for a while to help directly with the smooth running of Eden's construction and also to supervise my training. His presence brought a special impetus, and I am referring here not only to the exceptional financial help he offered us, but also to his very refined subtle influence. That contributed a lot to the first notable result I had working with Eden.

AN IMPORTANT STEP

About a week after Elinor's arrival, I sat one night in the seat of the chair, as usual, to begin my regular training session. A little later in the day than was typical, it was past one o'clock in the morning. I felt a little tired but not so much that I gave up training that night. I turned on the system, hearing the specific hum of Tesla coils which turned into a louder sound, but I was not tiring. Between the half-open eyelids, I saw the bluish-white light emanating from the coils as well as the unfolding of the digital information on the screen that I had fixed at a higher value than was usual with regard to their working frequencies and harmonics. I then fell asleep or at least I thought so. That was the first time something like this had happened. I had been preparing for almost two months, going through different phases and states, but I had never "fallen asleep".

Analyzing what happened later, I then realized that all the technical conditions were similar to those of other training sessions: the devices worked properly, even if they were adjusted to other parameters than on other days, the energy sources behaved normally, and the energy pulse variations were within the allowed limits. I, however, had fallen asleep. I thought that my state of slight physical fatigue could have determined this, but I remembered that this was not the first time I did the training sessions in such a condition, and those had been without any problems in this regard.

The most interesting aspect was that I did not lose consciousness of what I was doing then. Somewhere, in the background, my brain was giving me the information that I was "asleep", but in reality, I was quite self-aware. I realized, however, that something was somewhat "in the fog" but I could not say what. My consciousness seemed somewhat "difficult" and my perceptions were "slower". I sat in the chair of the device and heard the faint murmur of the appliances in the room, but I still noticed something strange: I could see my body, a little blurred, as I sat in the chair, and time seemed to freeze.

After I "woke up", I could not understand how I had "fallen asleep" since I was aware of those aspects, all of which seemed to have been identical both in the dream state and in the reality of the physical plane. "After all, did I sleep or not?" I wondered. I could not answer that question then. I reviewed the "movie" from memory up to the thought that I had fallen asleep, but I could not identify the transition period. I could not tell how exactly that happened: that which made me believe and say that I was awake but still asleep.

Thinking more clearly in the following days, I came to the conclusion that, at that time, there was no actual hiatus or "breaking" of consciousness, only a "slower" perception of it. In passing, I continued to be the same self, but in a different state of perception, and this probably led the brain to interpret that I was "asleep".

The next day, I told Cezar about that experience. Smiling, he told me that I had, in fact, experienced for the first time, modified by my own effort, the state of consciousness which involves etheric doubling. Even if this type of experience had been known to me for a long time (from the expeditions I took part in in the past), then it was the first time I had doubled "by my own forces", without the help of force fields or inter-dimensional devices. It is true that I also benefited from the advantages of technology, but the phenomenon actually occurred due to certain state transformations that took place in my being.

In the evening, I met Elinor at the villa and told him what I had experienced during the last training session. He congratulated me on this success and added that this type of "out-of-body" experience could be greatly helped by regular training and proper nutrition.

"This ability to consciously duplicate should become commonplace and fairly easy to do," he told me. "Consciousness is one, but it seems to be "divided" into several "consciousnesses" corresponding to each subtle body we have. Until now, you were mostly aware only of your physical body, but you have just consciously experienced the existence of your etheric body. The same will happen when you double in the astral plane or "wake up" while dreaming, being perfectly lucid and aware that you are during the dream."

"This ability to double down consciously came a little late," I said with some regret.

"This is primarily due to blockages of all kinds and impurities, both physical and subtle. It is not a necessary condition, but it is valid for most people."

He then recommended a series of three simple purification techniques to facilitate such experiences because a heavy physical body "clogged" with impurities cannot "follow" with sufficient accuracy the sometimes very rapid variations of the multitude of parameters at the cellular level of the human being. Impurities are accumulated over the years, either through a wrong diet or due to other unfortunate habits such as alcohol consumption, but especially smoking, which significantly decreases the frequency of vibration of the physical body. Under such conditions, the body cannot follow the fine variations of energy, and that is why it is very difficult, if not impossible, to make the transition from the physical plane to the subtle planes of existence. The greater the difference in the level of vibration between the physical body and the etheric or astral body, the more difficult it is to access experiences of conscious duplication in the etheric or astral plane.

The techniques that Elinor taught me are generally well known. One of them is the black fast, his recommendation being to fast for a day one or two times a week, during which time one only consumes water over a twenty-four hour period. The other two techniques are of Oriental origin and aim at a physical and partially subtle purification of the being.

Although I agreed with the process of purifying the being to get better and better results in my training, I was also aware that this could also be a matter of time. Physical and especially psycho-logical purification is achieved gradually because the inertia of such systems are based upon reflexes and habits settled over time, such as different body movements or attitudes, vices or misconceptions, and it is quite hard to change.

"What you're saying is true," Elinor said. "Most people live in a mechanical way and do not know simple principles of conduct for a healthy life. The vibration of bodily matter and that of the mind are, generally speaking, in close connection. You can't really say that a butcher has metaphysical feelings because that is like saying you want to glue a piece of steel with paper glue. There is always a correlation between form and content. In principle, one modifies the other. Changes in thinking and conception, at the level of the mind, determine adjustments at the physical level because what is higher and finer commands what is lower and coarser."

From an esoteric point of view, I knew quite well the law of becoming and transformation, about which Cezar and Dr. Xien had spoken to me several times. My concern, however, came from the fact that the process of purification of the being was no longer following a natural path in my case but was somehow tending to be "forced" by the very action of the apparatus I was employing. I already had the experience of training inside Eden and I could feel the energy influxes acting on my body very well. What I still did not know for sure, however, was to what extent those influxes and vibrational frequencies could act in my being and with what the effects were.

Elinor then told me that, in his opinion, Eden is meant to produce the expansion of individual consciousness and its access to higher subtle dimensions and realities. In other words, it was meant to make an accelerated contribution to my spiritual evolution if the energy "leaps" were not too great for my body structure to reject.

CHAPTER SEVEN

CONNECTION WITH APELLOS

As I had predicted, the energetic influence of the "machine" on my body was more intense and faster than the purification methods indicated by Elinor. The moderate solution would probably have been to dose an appropriate level of the energy intensity conveyed by Eden while continuing to practice the indicated purification techniques in parallel. In this way, I would have obtained a certain balance in the purification and preparation of my physical and subtle structure.

ELIXIR

I was, however, impatient. I knew and felt that I could have "taken" more, even if I was not yet perfectly prepared for it. The possibilities that Eden offered attracted me in particular, and the prospect of waiting for months to allow enough time for the structure of my being to adapt to the frequencies and intensity of energy did not satisfy me at all.

Speaking honestly with Elinor afterwards, I offered my point of view and asked him if the process of purification and preparation of the physical and subtle structure could not be helped by a special alchemical product. I knew all too well how I felt when, many years ago, he offered me a few drops of such an elixir.[*] Then, Elinor explained to me a great deal about the extraordinary importance of alchemical elixirs, substances which modern medicine does not even dream of. He told me that, in the case of these astonishingly effective substances, the transformation of the initial matter — which may be of a vegetable, animal, or mineral (metallic) nature — goes to the quantum level, owing to its extraordinary purity. The matter, which is the elixir itself, then somehow becomes intelligent. Moreover, this explains its action, which is holographic in the sense that it extends to all levels of being, not just the physical. Elinor pointed out to me, however, that such exceptional alchemical substances have different degrees of power and action on the human being, depending upon the stage they have reached in the process of the Alchemical Work.[**] The closer this stage is to the last phase or the Philosopher's Stone, the purer and more efficient the substance.

[*] February, 2005 (see volume 3, *The Mystery of Egypt - The First Tunnel*, published by Sky Books.)
[**] "Work" or "The Work" in the field of alchemy means the staged process of transformation of the Raw Material to the final stage, which is the Philosopher's Stone or Quintessence.

"However," Elinor told me, "there are very few pure alchemical elixirs. If the substance obtained is administered when it is still at an impure stage, there is a danger of poisoning the being or causing serious damage to its physical or mental structure."

"But the Middle Ages abounded in hundreds of types of elixirs and potions, some more powerful than others, that filled the pharmacies of that time," I rightly expressed my astonishment. "Does this mean that they were not good or that they were impure?"

"Let's not confuse the authentic alchemical elixirs with the so-called spagyric elixirs* or "second hand" ones, often obtained empirically or without a real knowledge of operations. The latter produced almost no results on the being and did not cure the sick person. Sometimes, the effects were even adverse and made one even sicker."

"Still, a lot of people were talking about and looking for these products," I said.

"Yes, but you had to take risks. Properly made spagarice is based upon operations specific to plant alchemy such as fermentation, distillation, separation, purification and reunification of elements in order to extract the essence of plants. Every seeker in the mysteries of alchemy strives to achieve this as he understands and knows how, with the technical means at hand. Enthusiasm alone is not enough because it must be doubled by great knowledge and impeccable patience. Many speakers obtained beautifully colored end products 'on occasion' which they then sold either in liquid form, like an elixir, or in solid form, like salt. Such operations, however, must be carried out with great care. Otherwise, you spoil the product and may not even realize it. The knowledge of the operations and the experience gained must be deep so that the elixir obtained is truly "alchemical". For this, it is necessary to take into account other principles and alchemical operations which do not make sense to talk about here. They do, however, require a divinatory knowledge from the alchemist and an initiation into the mysteries of these arts. Esotericism, Kabbalah and astrology are essential."

"Then, how do you explain the abundance of spagyric substances in that period? If many were inefficient or even dangerous, how could people still buy?"

"Know that there is not much difference from what you find on the market now. Many praise their products as 'miraculous' and even 'enlightening' when, in reality, they are based upon deep ignorance. As was the case long ago, you now find the same attitude towards such products: trade, deception, imposture, and gullibility. At that time, things like this worked due to the great

---

* The term spagirism was introduced by Paracelsus (1493-1541) and later by his disciples in the specialized works of the time, eventually coming to be associated, over time, with alchemy and even confused with it. It can be said in general terms, however, that spagirism represents plant alchemy.

ignorance of people, but the current situation is not too different because you can find countless types of drugs for "healing" in pharmacies which, in reality, do nothing. From a vital or energetic point of view, they are 'death'. They can apparently bring some improvements in certain diseases, especially if they are not too serious; or they can block the dangerous evolution of a disease for a while, but on the whole, it not only does not really cure that disease but also causes a whole series of side effects in the body which, in turn, can generate other problems. As they say, 'on one side you fill the gap, on the other side you dig a hole'. The same thing happens with many herbal remedies. You have to be a good connoisseur yourself to realize what it is really all about."

I smiled, seeing the direct and even radical way in which Elinor handled this. He was absolutely right because anyone with a certain culture in the field knows these things very well. Being synthetic, allopathic medicines destroys and impurifies the being more than healing it. For the body, it is more a work of Sisyphus because what is apparently repaired in one place, even if partially, spoils another area.

"As far as I understand, things haven't changed much in the last hundred years," I said.

"Those spagyric substances rarely produced any effect, in most cases being just plain colored oils. The pharmacists of the time either did not know the correct way to obtain a strong vegetable elixir through spagiriei or they were crooks.* This was probably one of the reasons that contributed, over time, to the rejection and ignorance of alchemy, even if spagiria is a distinct branch of it that related to the plant kingdom."

Following that discussion and the suggestion I made, Elinor agreed to speed up the process of purifying and vitalizing my being through a few daily doses of one of his alchemical elixirs which he offered me. I did not ask for "technical" details about the nature of that substance or how it was obtained because I was not prepared enough to understand those things. In addition, alchemy is probably the most "guarded" art that exists today because it is considered that the one who masters its supreme secret, that of obtaining the Philosopher's Stone, and is then even able to obtain this priceless product is, in a certain context, a "god" among men. Space and time influence it perhaps only to a very small extent. He then becomes a follower, a true sage, having access to a large part of the secrets of Creation because the Philosopher's Stone represents the quintessence of everything that exists in manifestation.

According to the instructions received from Elinor, I diluted each dose so that the absorption of the elixir was achieved as efficiently as possible by osmosis, without violating my physical structure.

---

* Spagiriei is a name used especially during the Middle Ages and refers to pharmacists, those who sold spagyric products.

Even so, for more than a week, I was "shaken" by the chills because I felt the vitality of an incredible freshness and power that penetrated every part of my being. The effect was colossal, without any comparison to any medicine or cure, even natural ones.

"Think that you have access to an ocean of energy that is very pure and refined," Elinor told me. "It's like introducing a miniature 'atomic plant' into your body. What you take now is enough for about three months, but most of the effects will extend over several months and even years, after which they will gradually diminish. However, an essence of them will continue to remain 'embedded' in your cellular level because there has been a significant energetic leap."

Indeed — I felt like I was living a new life. I then became fully convinced that everything is energy and that it penetrates every corner of Creation, nourishing and transforming it continuously. In the first training sessions that followed, I thought I would not be able to resist. I was losing sensation of my physical body, and I could no longer feel the contour of my body. The continual sensation was that of "lifting" accompanied by a state of such great inner exaltation that it was very difficult for me to concentrate. For a few days, I fully experienced the euphoria of the alchemical elixir, being closely observed by Elinor. Gradually, I began to control those states as "drunkenness of happiness", even keeping the ecstatic sensations in the background while the mind was focused inward to better modulate the specific frequencies of energy provided by Eden.

From the beginning, I realized that, compared to the training up to that point, there were big differences in my condition and efficiency during the concentration process. If I was "riding a bicycle" in the early stages, I could say that I was now "flying by plane". It is pretty hard to describe the expansion I was feeling then because it covered the space in a certain way to the outside, but at the same time, I felt myself focusing with great speed inwards, towards the atomic levels. The outward and inward movements were simultaneous, and this made me dizzy at first, but I then somehow managed to "suspend" myself: I was "watching" movements of energy from above without being influenced by them. My energy absorption capacity, as well as body purification, had greatly increased due to careful dosing of the alchemical elixir. It was a real miracle, I was fully aware of it and I was deeply grateful to Elinor, who gave me that opportunity in a very altruistic way.

"What you took during this period was only a modest elixir, if we are to make a rough hierarchy," Elinor told me one day, after I had thanked him for offering me the possibility of experiencing that alchemical substance. It is more accurate to say, however, that it is an essence.

QUESTION MARKS

We were with Cezar on the terrace in front of the living room, sitting comfortably in the large armchairs and enjoying a quiet and wonderful late afternoon. The green of the abundant vegetation in the garden and the colorful palette of flowers surrounded the lawn on the side of the villa that leads to the terrace where we were. Elinor continued with his idea.

"The substance is pure, very beneficial, but relatively limited in effects in relation to the elixirs of the higher phases and incomparable with the Supreme Elixir, it being based on the Philosopher's Stone itself."

I thought to myself that if I felt such extraordinary effects from this "medium to weak" elixir offered to me by Elinor, then what would happen if I took the Supreme Elixir? I was still a little confused, so I asked him a question.

"Am I taking a tincture or an elixir? And what kind of tincture?"

"It's not the same as the alcoholic tincture you're thinking of because, in alchemy, 'tincture' means something else. There is a distinction between substances that reach different degrees of evolution during alchemical operations. What I gave you is a substance that is plant based."

Cezar also spoke with interest.

"I understand that the power of action of alchemical elixirs is different, depending upon their stage of evolution."

"Not all alchemical healing compound are called elixirs," Elinor said. "Even if they have beneficial effects on the body, their power differs according to the degree of evolution they have reached via the sublimation of the alchemical process. Extracts have a lower effect on the body, and they are the most common products because they are relatively easy to obtain, but even here, a lot of attention is needed. Otherwise, the final product will be devoid of its active principles. The tinctures have a stronger action if they are carefully obtained, the essences are even more refined, and the elixirs are truly miraculous. They have no equal because they represent a "materialized energy", but it is extremely pure. At the top is the supreme elixir, the Philosopher's Stone."

"But are these elixirs different in power, depending upon the kingdom from which they are obtained?" I asked insistently. "You told me that what I took belonged to plant alchemy, so I suppose it is from a certain plant."

"Yes, from a kind of drosera.* And the elixirs are different. The strongest come from the metal kingdom. The vegetable elixir is also potent and can only be taken in high dilutions. You took some doses of an essence whose penetration power is average, but it still had to be diluted significantly."

Elinor then explained to me that by carefully dosing that essence that I had been taking for about three weeks, I had pretty much purified the astral flows that correspond to the planetary influences on the human body and

---

*A drosera is a carnivorous plant that lures, capture and digests insects.

even strengthened these influences in my being. The results began to appear during training when I had the first "mental transmissions" or rather the first subtle perceptions of akashic imagery. They appeared spontaneously during mental concentration although my intention was to improve my ability to consciously double.

ACCESS TO AKASHIC RECORDS AND AN UNSOLVED DILEMMA

One of those evenings, while I was quite deeply focused on the play of energy in my body and mind, I wanted to "expand" more, encompassing a fairly large area around me with my mind. I felt that my energetic state was the right one to get out of my body consciously, and this time I wanted to be able to move forward more with this type of experience. Cezar had advised me to gradually approach these "movements" with the etheric body, trying to remain as conscious as possible of every detail.

At one of the training sessions, however, an ambiguous situation arose for me. I felt that I was about to consciously "double", but instead, in the plane of my mental vision, scenes from the past of humanity suddenly appeared to me. I immediately wondered if those were images I had already seen in front of the holographic screen when assisted by the man from Apellos, or were they images I was then seeing for the first time? My uncertainty was that, although what I saw was familiar to me, some of the images were new, meaning I did not remember having watched them on the holographic screen.

From a certain perspective, this seemed natural to me. The Apellos device summarized what the viewer requested by focusing on the subject he proposed. There is, therefore, a kind of "feedback loop", a kind of feedback between my being and the apparatus, mediated by a very advanced technology. The question was, however, why did those images appear to me, and especially, why was I noticing some that I had not seen in the sequences presented on the holographic screen? It was like new information, but I did not know if it was something new or just a personal "upgrade" due to the alchemical elixir and the specific frequencies emitted by Eden.

The akashic images that appeared to me were clear, vivid and gave me the impression that I was in that very space and time. The reality was very close, as a way of expression, to what I had experienced when I encountered time travel with the "time machine" in the Occult Chamber of Egypt. I no longer actually saw the images, as in the case of the holographic screen, but somehow "witnessed" them from within me, feeling the atmosphere and the specific state of the places and beings of those times. I had a similar perception while watching the images on the holographic screen, but at a lower intensity. I presented the matter to Cezar, and after discussing it, I decided to ask the opinion of the man from Apellos as my experience involved the technology that they had made available. In fact, we had been thinking for some time that starting discussions with those in Apellos about Eden and our private project might help us to some extent, technologically speaking. It was now September, and I thought a new visit to their hangar would be nice because the weather was warm and the scenery beautiful.

THE APELLOS COUNCIL — A COLLABORATIVE DECISION

Already having a direct connection with them, Cezar had a long discussion in the screening room with the members of the Council of Apellos. After a successful collaboration between me and the man from Apellos, with the viewing of the images on the holographic screen and the intervention of the sage Dryn, the Council decided that the connection could become direct in order to facilitate a more efficient communication. Cezar told me that, based upon their mutual trust and their remarkable technological advancement, he had told them about the Eden project, what we were building, and the technological difficulties we were facing. The first issue was that we were working somewhat blindly, that is, not knowing exactly what such a device could do or clearly understanding what its purpose was. I had some ideas, but I was not absolutely sure. The plans I received telepathically were followed, but the efficiency and purpose of Eden's construction could only be proven by the human element; that is, by the experiences I could have there, inside the machine.

Cezar then raised the issue of akashic imagery during one of my workouts. On the one hand, the device helps to more precisely duplicate subtle consciousness in the etheric plane, as I had experienced myself; but on the other hand, it unexpectedly made possible the manifestation of the akashic in my field of my consciousness. It was undoubtedly a significant leap forward because the clear perception of akashic records is not exactly easy to achieve.

There was, however, a gap between what I had seen on the holographic screen and what I had perceived in that experience, and that created some confusion. What had then appeared to me in the visual field of my mind was, in fact, a succession of images which I already knew, from watching on the holographic screen, that were related to the Great Planetary Council of Teotihuacan and also to the conquest of Troy.[*] We could, however, speak of a difference, and this was exactly the main point of Cezar's discussion with the members of the Council of Apellos. He mentioned the extra images that came to me during training as being different from the ones I already knew. As a result, Cezar raised the issue of their verification, and this could best and easily be done on the holographic screen of those in Apellos.

---

[*] The Council of Teotihuacan was approximately 26,000 B.C. according to volume 6 of the *Transylvania Series, Forgotten Genesis*, 2020. The conquest of Troy is also mentioned in this book.

The Eden project had attracted the attention of Council members, and they asked for a short break to discuss the situation with their specialists. Returning a few hours later, Cezar told me that Méntia took part in the discussion, too.* She is the one I had the opportunity to talk to several months ago, being assisted by the man from Apellos while watching the images about the past of Mankind. She led the team of researchers in the field of medicine which, as I have said in a previous volume, is a science very different from today's medicine in our society: first, by their degree of understanding of the notion of health and then by the methods of research and healing used.

After a brief assessment of the situation, Méntia said that the problem seems to be more complex. She mentioned that what I "saw" during training was not necessarily true. They checked the recordings on the holographic screen; and indeed — the new images I told them about did not appear in those archives.

We were told that it was important to know what this meant. Méntia was especially interested in the fact that I had received those images which were not identical to what had appeared on the holographic screen. This meant that certain transformations that had taken place in the cerebral cortex primarily signified an evolution in the level of individual consciousness. Somehow, the "antenna" of my consciousness increased its reception area and mysteriously gained access to those new images.

I was slightly puzzled by the importance they attached to this, and I asked Cezar a question.

"Okay; and what's so special about that? I received some new pictures of those events. Well…and? Of course there is an evolution due to my training — that's what we're looking for, right? To be honest, I think too much emphasis is being placed upon an issue that seems natural to me."

"Méntia was interested in exactly this step you took, in what transformed in you," he replied calmly. "This is probably important from a research point of view. She even suggested we go to the place where you've been, the one on the holographic screen. She wants us to check out those images in real time."

REVIEWING THE HOLOGRAPHIC SCREEN

The meeting had already been scheduled for the next day, and we were already inside the hangar around noon. Due to the mutual trust and the higher level of collaboration that had been reached with those in Apellos, the usual security measures that had existed until then were no longer needed. There were, as usual, only a few people in the hangar. The man from Apellos was waiting for us. After a few moments, we introduced Cezar, and he motioned for us to follow him.

---

* Méntia is mentioned in volume 6 of the *Transylvania Series, Forgotten Genesis*, 2020.

We were led to the holographic screen room where we saw the recorded fragment about the Teotihuacan Planetary Council. With Cezar, I reviewed those images in summary. The new ones, which appeared to me during the training, appeared immediately after the general images about the construction and existence of the ancient city and before the images that presented snapshots of the actual development of the Council. Those images referred to a group of *E-N-K* beings who were taken with a Pleiadian ship from the spaceport area, some distance from Teotihuacan as we know it today. When they appeared to me in the field of consciousness, while I was in the seat of the device, I "knew" that those beings were taken to another star system in the galaxy, to a planet with a vibrational frequency slightly higher than that of the Earth, probably in order to diversify life there or to stimulate it.

With that starting point, the man from Apellos made the connection to the holographic screen himself to check if the images I mentioned really existed in the universal akashic records. Given his very good mental "dexterity" and the telepathic power he had, I could quickly see all three of the same images on the holographic screen, just as I had described them. This proved that they were not the product of my imagination, and moreover, that Eden could facilitate a certain kind of interaction with the individual consciousness of the human being in the chair so that one could have access to the "flow time".

After obtaining this result in the case of the Planetary Council of Teotihuacan, I verified in the same way the new images that I perceived in the case of the conquest of the city of Troy. These showed the presence of a delegation of three humanoid extraterrestrial beings, whose race I did not know, in an almost empty stone hall located inside the city. They were talking to the King. He was quite old and seemed very agitated. Empathetically, I already "knew" that I was witnessing the last moments of Troy. The man from Apellos then synthesized these images himself on the holographic screen, and so I now had sure proof that, through Eden, I could "see in time" but still did not have full conscious control over the process. For example, akashic imagery came to me spontaneously and without me thinking about it.

After reviewing these images, the man from Apellos contacted Méntia through the holographic screen to let her know the outcome of our meeting. Once again, in holographic form, I saw that special woman from the underground city of Apellos, and the impression she made on me was even stronger than the first time. She was undoubtedly a very beautiful and strong woman, both in terms of her personal vital radiation and her remarkable personality. It was precise, with a lot of "fire" and she manifested a special nature. Her dark brown eyes cast a great deal of strength and determination, contrasting with her very light, almost unreal white skin. Her black hair, featuring bangs and worn a little over her shoulders, had a special impact, similar to the women of Ancient Egypt, the darkness of her locks contrasting strongly with her almost white skin.

The discussion was short. After the situation was presented to her, she invited Cezar and myself to Apellos because she wanted to analyze this case, which she found interesting, with their advanced technological means.

"Preliminary tests show that Eden caused some transformations at the cellular level, and I think at the DNA level," she said. "This happened in a short time, and as far as I understand, this is remarkable."

She then turned in my direction and addressed me specifically

"I'd like to check the current structure of your DNA, and they will make other types of measurements. We are interested in this evolution because it is somehow unusual. It seems that there have been some remarkable 'leaps' and I would like to investigate the causes."

She had a style of speaking and moving that was very "clean" and at the same time strong. It was almost impossible not to be drawn to her and not to admire her deeply from the perspective of her feminine qualities, her very lively personality, and her superior mental abilities.

Both Cezar and I gladly accepted the invitation, and as far as I was concerned, I did feel a certain emotion, knowing that I would soon visit that magnificent inner city again.

SECOND VISIT TO APELLOS

Apellos immediately impresses with its brilliance, elegance, and harmony that can be seen in the shapes of the buildings, in the technology it has, and in the way it was created. It can be seen immediately that it is part of "another league" because the vibrational frequency of the energy specific to that place is also high. This is probably due to the extraterrestrial heritage because the inhabitants of the city represent an example of a higher category of E-N-K beings, deriving from a combination of E-N-K type DNA with extraterrestrial DNA. It can be felt immediately, almost from everything that is around you in that place: the people, the landscape, the construction, the means of transport, and the technology. Somehow, you always feel enveloped by a state of well-being, joy, and zest for life. People are very beautiful and benevolent but also firm when necessary.

They have a kind of uprightness and seriousness, something like what I saw in the Sirians, but they are also very pleasant at the same time, smiling and very intelligent. What I really liked is their harmonious pragmatism. Nobody wastes their time; everyone knows exactly what they have to do; and they are always exact with what they ask for; but above all, they are careful. It is that kind of subliminal attention they put into all of their actions, including their discussions, through which one can feel the living and attentive spirit in them which allows them to somehow remain "separate" from what they do in that moment. It is not a tense attention nor does it create the feeling of impatience or irritation, but on the contrary, it induces a feeling of calmness and security. They never seem to hurry and always give the impression that they are in control of the events around them.

Sharing all of these observations of mine from my experience in Apellos with Cezar, he told me that those were some of the distinguishing features of what the 4-D level of consciousness and living might mean. Apellos was like an underground "4-D enclave" that had prospered amazingly and was active in the surface cities, especially in our country, helping and sowing the seeds of exceptional future transformations in people's consciousness.

Under these conditions, it was a real pleasure to go back to their city where I was starting to feel very welcome and where I felt I was integrating perfectly. Méntia told us that we no longer needed to travel the route through Tomassis but that we could arrive in Apellos using their own means of communication through their special type of "elevator" which is actually a kind of semi-teleportation device.*

We were led by the man from Apellos and two more guards into the more secluded section of the hangar which was isolated from the rest of the room by high walls and where I had seen the circle-shaped translation device on

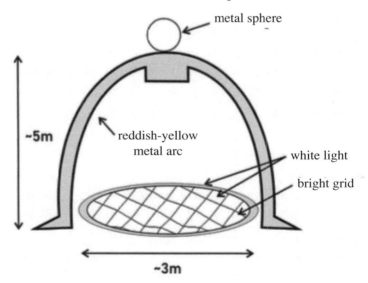

DEVICE FOR THE TRANSFER OF PERSONS AND GOODS FROM THE SURFACE OF THE EARTH TO THE CITY OF APELLOS

---

* See Volume 5 of the *Transylvania Series, Inside the Earth - Second Tunnel*, 2019.

my first visit. It was quite wide, and if we added the spectacular archway and the white lights that bordered the surface, it made a strong impression, but I did not notice any consoles nearby nor controls.

The translation was simpler than I imagined. Cezar, the man from Apellos, and I walked inside the dimly lit circle. The two guards stayed a short distance from him, outside, assisting the process. When I entered the circle, the lights on its surface, like lines and squares, became brighter, but then I noticed that the white light also had certain violet reflections which made it even more beautiful. The lighting on the edge of the circle, which was quite thick, pulsed at an even and fairly fast pace.

Basically, the translation process was activated instantly after stepping inside the circle. Indeed — I then felt a certain tingling sensation in my body, much like when I went through the distortion in the second tunnel starting from the Projection Room. Then followed a kind of "suction", a slight feeling of dizziness and the sensation of a trip by elevator with great speed, but everything was somewhat shrouded in "fog". Then, after a few seconds, the view cleared again and we found ourselves on a platform similar to the one on my previous visit to Apellos but a little smaller. We were also inside a circle of the same size and structure, but here the lights were blue.

We left the circle, and the man from Apellos invited us to follow him in a small shuttle, a kind of aerodynamic "capsule" which had four seats. I had never seen that type of shuttle in Apellos before. The capsule was at the edge of the platform in a built-in lift on a "line" with arches leading to the city center. Before stepping inside it, I stopped for a few moments to admire that beautiful city again with its extremely pleasant light and with a very fresh air carried by a light breeze. I gladly revisited the crystal-like buildings, their radiance seeming to touch the soul, and I let myself be "bathed" by the specific and continuous murmur that produced a state of deep relaxation in my being.

A 4-D WORLD

The journey by shuttle was short, the speed being considerable. The capsule stopped in front of a platform before a fairly tall building which the man from Apellos told us was the study and research headquarters of the city. I already knew that the headquarters was run by Méntia, with whom we were to meet. I entered a building in the city of Apellos for the first time. The impression was strong because the design, the shapes, the colors, the materials, and everything somehow gave a futuristic image. I especially noticed the roundness, the fact that there were almost no corners or angles, but everything was curved and then rendered pictorially by lines or other symbolic patterns that had a very relaxing effect on the psyche and mind.

In the very wide halls, I saw few people. As they moved unhurriedly in various directions, I noticed their dignified attire but especially the beauty and harmony which characterized them. They did not seem at all surprised by the presence of Cezar and myself there, although our clothing obviously contrasted with what the inhabitants of Apellos were wearing.

I had seen the interiors of some buildings in our world that are similar to the building we were in then, but the impression was still different. Maybe the difference came from the specific radiation of the materials, maybe from the way the shapes and constructive solutions of the space were arranged, but in any case, we seemed to be breathing a different kind of air in Apellos. Cezar even made a brief comment, certifying that the vibrational frequency of matter and the environment was higher than that of the physical plane at the surface. Once again, he told me that Apellos meets the basic conditions of existence in what we call the 4-D dimension of existence, superior to the 3-D dimension of the physical plane. Although the civilization of Apellos is still based on existence on the physical plane, the general frequency of vibration was still higher, towards the limit of passing into the etheric plane.

The physical condition of the inhabitants, their way of life, the form of social organization, and the construction and technology is all at a much higher level than what can usually be found on the surface of the terrestrial world. In my opinion, they are an example to follow, and their actions have proven that they support us and want us to evolve in order to overcome the vicissitudes of this critical period of humanity in which we now find ourselves.

We were led to the right side of the great hall at the entrance to that building where we saw what might look like an elevator in our world, only it seemed to have no walls but only an illuminated base that was round in shape. I could see, however, a certain semi-transparency which delimited the space inside the elevator from the outside, but I could not identify the material from which the surface was made. At a medium height on the wall was a circular and an almost transparent screen-like panel that remained dark as long as no one was in the elevator. When we entered the elevator, the screen lit up discreetly and several signs appeared on it but also a schematic structure of the building, represented holographically and with red and blue LED-like lights inside. The man from Apellos pointed with his finger at a certain route on that holographic representation, and I immediately felt the ascent, smooth at first, then faster and faster but without any feeling of discomfort. I could see everything beneath me, as if I were flying through the air. At first, it was quite scary, but there was something there that made you have full confidence. It was something I cannot describe well, but it acted in a very beneficial way on the subconscious.

RESEARCH LABORATORY

After less than fifteen seconds, the elevator slowed down and then stopped, and we stepped into a huge hall in which white and blue predominated. The space was lit everywhere by an even and very pleasant light, but I could not see any light bulbs or other lighting devices. I immediately realized that it was an ultra-sophisticated research laboratory. I saw assemblies and devices that were completely unknown to me, a technology much more advanced than the ones we know on Earth. At a glance, I could say that the huge laboratory was more focused on medical studies, but I also noticed some features that made me think that it could be about studies in physics and biology.

The first person I saw coming towards us was Méntia. I already knew that she was leading the scientific field of medicine in Apellos, but as I would find out later, she was entrusted by the Council with coordinating all scientific activity at the level of their civilization. In the back of the lab, I noticed several people, each working in front of a very large screen in front of a small monitor, just as we might work in an office. For them, the "monitor" was completely transparent with a translucent-like "glass" that was very large, about three meters long and two meters high. The projections on the surface of the screens were holographic, shallow, and the scientists worked standing in front of them, directing all sorts of changes to those projections with their hands and operating commands, especially through their voices. I noticed that, despite the very large space there and the fact that there were dozens of people working inside, the atmosphere was very quiet and relaxed, being dominated by a kind of general hum at a very pleasant frequency.

Méntia greeted us with a smile and asked us to follow her to the side of that room where we saw several devices suitable for medical study. I honestly had to admit to myself that this woman was gorgeous. But one detail struck me. When I saw her in the images on the holographic screen, she seemed taller, but in reality, I found that her height did not exceed, in my estimation, about five and a half feet. She was wearing a suit, molded to the body, as a kind of white jumpsuit with blue inserts and a distinct golden mark on the shoulder. Her almond-shaped dark eyes were filled with intense inner "fire" and accentuated her inner strength and strong personality. Méntia was very intelligent, and from the way she spoke and behaved, she demonstrated a sharp, well-structured and calculated mind.

We stopped in front of an ergonomic chair which featured many accessories and special equipment on its wide edges. I realized that it was used for study, especially since one of the large transparent holographic screens was only a short distance from it. Between the screen and that ergonomic chair were a few other devices of different shapes, but I did not notice any connecting cables. The civilization of Apellos had probably long ago passed this stage of technological evolution.

It was the first time I had met Méntia face to face, and when I got to the ergonomic chair, I caught her looking at me intently. She went straight into the subject, asking us what Eden does and what its purpose is.

"By and large, I understand how it works," she said. "There are directed and harmonic pulses of energy on various specific frequencies. It is clear that certain transformations occur in the biological structure, primarily at the cellular level, which can even go as far as DNA. We'll check this now, if you agree, but I still do not understand what the real purpose of the device is."

"We suspect that it is a 'gate' of access to certain space-time nodes and through them, to subtle dimensions," said Cezar.

Méntia thought for a moment, then spoke in a low voice, more to herself. "Makes sense. The one in the chair becomes the 'gate' himself."

She then headed for the holographic screen which lit up as it was approached, showing some graphics. Looking at it in profile, it was only then that I noticed that a small circle-shaped device was attached to the slightly raised frame of the cover which had begun to glow intermittently but discreetly, constantly changing color. Méntia changed certain parameters with her right hand directly on the holographic image while her left hand, held slightly to the side of her body, was placed on one of the rather complicated devices which seemed to be a kind of information converter. Her fingers moved in conjunction with the images on the screen, but I could not tell what she was going to accomplish. I could see many symbols, images, fragments of images, animations and graphics in a fast-paced way. It all took less than half a minute, but in that short amount of time, she seemed completely absorbed in what she was doing. Suddenly, her concentration had become total, as if we were no longer with her.

SCIENTIFIC ANALYSIS AND SOME ANSWERS — THE MISSING LINK

She then took a step back and addressed me directly, telling me that if I agreed, we could do some non-invasive scientific research together because their technology allowed for a very special analysis of biological structures, down to the quantum level. I sat down in that ergonomic chair, and immediately on her right side rose an arm that had a perfectly polished metal plate at the end. The arm "scanned" me in the head area, then withdrew. I could then see Cezar coming to the big screen, carefully paying attention to the changes that appeared in me.

Méntia then told him not to scare me because, in a short time, I would no longer perceive the outside but would be immersed in a strong white light.

She explained to me that a vitalizing and very penetrating energy field would completely surround me. She had barely finished speaking when, indeed, I saw something white with pearly iridescence rise from my right side like a wall, after which I suddenly felt myself enclosed in a thick white cloud. I could then feel the weak and strong areas inside my body. I perceived the organs that worked harmoniously, where there were certain problems, the degree of purity of the blood, and also the cellular "wear and tear". In a way, it was like a telepathic transmission, but in reality, I felt as if I was "reading" all of those results inside me, in a very free and natural way.

Then, after about a minute, the "white cloud" gradually dissipated, and I saw the ambient space of the laboratory again. Méntia motioned for me to come in front of the screen with Cezar to show us a cellular structure and an energy flow moving through it. To the right of that structure, on the holographic image, I could see the DNA macromolecule, but in its biological form, in what I could say is "real time". The images then began to follow one another quickly, showing a "penetration" into the structure of DNA to the level of atoms and covalent bonds.

Méntia explained, referring to me.

"Your body is going through a period of obvious acceleration of some internal biochemical processes, even showing us a kind of 'rearrangement' taking place. The devices record an increase in the number of photons in cellular exchanges. There are even some changes in DNA, especially in the bonds that potassium and zinc atoms separately make in DNA."

Pausing for a moment, she then turned to me and asked me to tell her how I had come to perceive the akashic images in Eden so that she would have a clearer idea of what had happened then. I looked at Cezar, and with his approval, I told him how it all began, from the subtle transmission in the occult chamber in Iraq, about the etheric crystal, to the telepathic perception through which I "saw" the plans for construction of the apparatus; and then the way it was built, its basic principles and the way I had trained. Méntia listened to me carefully, nodding to me from time to time as I repeated what she already knew, and finally spoke to me.

"Now I have a pretty clear picture of the situation. If I correlate the descriptions with the results I obtained from scanning your body, something unusual appears. There is a missing link. In all these 'adventures' you had with Eden, it was impossible to reach this stage of transformation of perceptions only by reason of the characteristics of the apparatus. The graphs show me, from interpolation, that the evolution in the training was not constant. There must be something else in this whole process that you have not told me about or that you either do not know about."

FINAL CONCLUSION

There was a pause of several seconds, and before it became embarrassing, Cezar replied.

"There is indeed an element which has not been mentioned. Not because we wanted to hide something, but out of respect and consideration for the person involved. His status is special and he doesn't want to be known, but in the context of things, maybe it's even better if we all know each other."

Cezar then asked me to talk about Elinor and the elixir he had given me to help me evolve during my training with the "space and time machine". We quickly summarized our connection with Elinor in a few words, briefly speaking about his extraordinary knowledge in the art of alchemy and pointed out that the elements of the "elixir" administered to me, which was a strong spagyric essence, had remarkably purifying effects on me. We also mentioned Elinor's involvement in our project but also the reasons that, up until then, we had not offered the path of its development.

At the end, I noticed that Méntia was really impressed and also very interested in what I told her. Her undisguised interest led her to tell us that, by the nature of her deep medical concerns — also correlated with other related fields such as biology and quantum physics — she had also partially studied the field of alchemy. I even noticed an effervescence in the way she spoke now and a certain inspiration in the way she was analyzing things with the well-known enthusiasm of the researcher who "seizes" a new idea and is about to unravel it.

"I didn't think of that with alchemy, but now things seem obvious to me," she said. "It is clear that that elixir contributed the most to the 'leap' you made because the device alone could not have caused so many biochemical combinations in your body and transformations at the cellular level that are as stable and 'clean' so as to facilitate your visions. This would probably have taken a much longer time."

Then she fell silent suddenly, preoccupied with an idea that seemed to grab her full attention. She was in front of one of the machines, quite complicated in structure, and was working on it in a way which I could associate with computer programming. After a few seconds, she spoke to us while continuing to work.

"If you had only used the possibilities of Eden, it would have taken about four years for those transformations to take place in your being. So, using the alchemical elixir, you needed about a month."

She then came before us and told us that she wanted to arrange a meeting between her and Elinor, if he would agree. For this, she would come to the surface, offering to help us with the project because she had a mandate in this regard from the Council of Apellos. She added that she wants to have an important conversation with Elinor in view of the help that Apellos aims to provide to the Romanian population.

"In some parts of the world, they do the same," she told us. "There are many other underground cities that have decided to help the surface population which corresponds to their underground projection area. It is a coordinated action."

We were glad that the connection with Apellos was getting stronger and stronger, and we gladly received Méntia's request to visit us. I, however, asked for a short break for the final answer because we needed a confirmation from Elinor.

CHAPTER EIGHT

ELINOR AND MÉNTIA: A MEMORABLE DISCUSSION

We returned from Apellos by the same method as our arrival, using the semi-teleportation "elevator". I arrived in Bucharest very late at night. Remaining at Alpha Base to solve some problems, Cezar would come to the capital the next day.

At the villa, Elinor was in his basement lab. I was not too surprised, even though it was about three o'clock in the morning. He never seemed to sleep or rest, or at least I never saw him do that, even though we have spent several days together on occasion.

ENDORSEMENT

I had arranged with Cezar to inform Elinor of the existence of the city of Apellos in the Earth's crust and of our connections with that civilization because we had to tell him about Méntia and her request to meet him. I was a little tired, but I still thought I should take the opportunity and summarize these issues. Elinor listened to me carefully, but I could tell he was not surprised by what I was sharing with him. From his tacit nods, I realized that he knew very well about the mysteries inside the Earth. I was a little unsettled at this, and at one point, I paused to make a remark.

"You seem quite familiar with the internal structure of the planet. You're not surprised when I tell you about the existence of cities there. Now, I can understand this from the fact that the internet contains many references on this subject, but even when I mentioned about Shambhala, your attitude remain unchanged."

"That's because I've been there many times," Elinor replied, smiling. "At some point, this becomes a necessity, especially in terms of important missions that must be performed on the surface."

I was speechless with astonishment. My surprise must have amused Elinor, for he went on to explain.

"You already know very well that when the body and the mind reach a high degree of purification, the frequency of personal vibration increases a lot, and you then have access to realities that the ordinary person not only does not understand but does not even the know the existence of, or worse, he strongly denies them."

I was a little silent because I felt my soul flooded with great joy and the desire to reach that so-called "mythical" realm which I already had the opportunity to see up close.*

I suspected how Elinor had access to Shambhala, but I nevertheless posed a "question" which was actually a certainty.

"I think that your study and accomplishments in alchemy gave you that chance."

Elinor did not answer verbally, but he nodded. I then tended to ask him more about Shambhala, its inhabitants, about what he actually saw there and especially what he did there, but I immediately felt, as a telepathic answer from him, that it was not the time for such a discussion.

I went back to what I was telling him about Apellos and Méntia, her position there and the trip to that city which Cezar and I had just returned from. I told him how we came to tell Méntia about the spagyric essence I took in progressive doses; and, of course, about who gave it to me. Finally, I shared the request of the special woman from Apellos to meet with him, noting that the civilization there wants to help the population of our country and that, most likely, Méntia saw an opportunity for this in the meeting that she wanted.

Elinor immediately accepted the proposal because, in Méntia's case, there was obviously no issue of confidentiality. By reason of its very status and level of evolution, the Apellos civilization is part of a higher category, a "world" common to that of Elinor, an individual who sees and perceives the nature of reality in an elevated manner.

By the way, this was the only time the issue arose for Elinor to meet someone through us. I already knew that the position in society of such human beings as Dr. Xien, Shin Li or Elinor must remain very hidden so that their missions can proceed as freely as possible. Such issues would be overwhelming to today's humanity who, for the most part, are not capable of understanding the nature of such actions or the causes that govern them. Due to the opacity of their conscience, people would stand in the way of such important spiritual missions which are, in fact, aimed exclusively towards the good of society. That is why, for some of these higher beings who are involved in complicated projects at different levels of humanity, the essential condition is one of perfect concealment. They live in society and seem to be integrated into it, but nevertheless never stand out, taking great precautions and being careful to "cross" whole epochs, hundreds or even thousands of years, almost without notice.

---

* See volume 5, *Inside the Earth - The Second Tunnel*, 2019.

NEW AND AMAZING DATA ABOUT MÉNTIA

The personality of this woman from Apellos seemed fascinating to me from the first eye contact.

We had agreed with Méntia, who seemed to be very efficient in everything she set out to do, to meet us in Bucharest during that day. If Elinor accepted the invitation to meet with her, it could take place right in his villa. As the response was positive, I met Méntia in town and then headed home, quite excited by her presence next to me. The impact of her subtle energy had been strong when I first saw her in the image on the holographic screen; and then, in Apellos, I admired her very intense presence and special mental nature. Now that she was physically to my right in the car, I could feel that her subtle radiation was even stronger, probably due to her state of mental concentration. She was quieter than at the meeting in Apellos, which had taken place the day before, more internalized, but at the same time, I felt from her attitude that she had somehow become more tolerant, probably because the connections between our civilizations were already beginning to take shape. It was obvious to me that she then was focusing on meeting Elinor, an event she considered important.

I was also excited about the special situation I was in, realizing that I was, for the first time in our physical world, in the presence of a being who was part of another civilization with strong extraterrestrial influences. Méntia probably perceived my thoughts and emotions because she said the following to me.

"Yes, the extraterrestrial influence is strong in our DNA, and in terms of epochs, relatively recent. First of all, it is a hybridization with one of the civilizations that you call "Pleiadian". The structure of our DNA, however, is much more complex and there are other branches of hybridization within it. There is one with the DNA of Sirius beings and one with the DNA of beings in the planetary system of the star Spica, as it appears in your astronomical charts.[*] For some reason, I did not want this to be known to you up to now, but the collaboration is beginning to be fruitful and some things can be shared."

Her Romanian was very correct and at the same time "sweet", a description I use because I cannot find another word to better express the weak but exquisite accent she had. I told her this and she thanked me, smiling discreetly. She then added that, in the language of Apellos, her name is not pronounced "Méntia", as it had been recommended to me at our first "teleconference".[**]

"'Méntia' is easier for you to pronounce, but in reality, my name is Mentiktla, which means 'ray of joy' in our language.

---

[*] Spica is the brightest star in the constellation Virgo, being a binary star (it is actually a two-star star system that orbits the center of mass of the system). Spica is 260 light-years away from our Solar System.

[**] See Volume 6, *Forgotten Genesis*, 2020.

The way she pronounced her name in her own language sounded very pleasing, evoking something of a Mayan style, although I did not know if there was any connection between Apellos and those ancient people. I then asked her if she often came to the surface, and if so, could she tell me what the purpose of such visits might be?

"Yes. I come to your world regularly and sometimes I stay for longer periods of time. There are documentation and support missions in various forms which they can assign, especially in the medical and biological fields. Our structures are quite well developed here in your world, and the actions we take are not out of the ordinary."

"And do you support this activity only in Romania?" I asked, curious to find out the extent of such in the world.

"No. Of course we work in other states. The collaborations are very extensive and complex."

"But how do you interact there?"

"What do you mean?" she asked.

"Speaking...how do you talk with them?," I said.

Looking a little surprised, she said, "I know twenty-three foreign languages and dialects very well and encounter no communication problems in the areas where we operate. We often combine spoken language with telepathic transmissions."

I swallowed hard as her performance was far above the standard of an ordinary linguist. In a way, however, this was explainable given her extraordinary intelligence and the special mental abilities of the Apellos civilization. In a conversation I had with the man from Apellos, right after the first "teleconference" with Méntia, he told me that, from the point of view of the way we consider and "measure" the intelligence of human beings, Méntia has an IQ of 174, well above the condition of genius. She also told me that she is ambidextrous and that she has a biological age of 41 even though, as I was able to ascertain, she looks like a woman of no more than thirty years old.

I looked admiringly at her profile and the look of her slender athletic body. When I first saw it, almost a year ago as an image on the holographic screen, it was a moment of surprise. Then followed the "synthetic" or "holographic" discussion between us where I could not focus too well on a person's characteristics.* In Apellos, on the other hand, the purpose of the meeting was precise and its duration quite short. Only now did I feel a certain relaxation in communication and had time to make more careful observations as my interaction with Méntia was much freer from the pressure of time.

It was getting dark, but the light of dusk made her very light white skin contrast even more with her black shoulder-length hair which was straight and shiny. Something in the profile of her image made me think of sculptures from

---

** See Volume 6, *Forgotten Genesis*, 2020.

ancient Greece or pictorial representations of ancient Egypt. One element that I noticed with some surprise was that, although she was very beautiful and elegant, Méntia was not wearing make-up and did not wear any accessories. I did not notice any earrings, bracelets, rings, medallions or other pendants. On the other hand, she exuded a refined noble elegance as a distinctive feature of her own body. Even in the encounters I had with her later, I never saw her wearing skirts or dresses with necklines, but always wearing clothes almost molded to the body, elegant and carefully combined. Several times, however, I saw that on the short collar of the blouse or sometimes at the bottom of the sleeves, a kind of band with a pattern that somehow imitated Romanian embroideries, and I concluded that they like it.

FIVE UNDERGROUND CITIES AND THEIR SUSPECTED HELP

The discussion continued regarding her actions on the surface of the Earth and especially in the area of Romania. She told me that she preferred more secluded areas with few people, such as small towns, communes and sometimes even villages, even though, being a specialist in medicine and biology, she could have found more opportunities for action and manifestation in big cities. She always preferred to work in mountainous areas and was never attracted to seaside towns.

"I think it's a specific feature of our civilization. We always prefer the heights of the mountains and their climate. Urban clusters are just your option — you don't necessarily need that. But your society has taken this path, and over time, you have created certain imbalances. I come to such places only when absolutely necessary. But, we are not the only ones acting in this way."

Not quite understanding what she meant, I asked, "Are you referring to other populations inside the planet?"

"Yes. There are five underground cities similar to Apellos which are relatively close to the surface, each with its own specific civilization. Over time, a network of communication was formed between those with whom we act in your world and those who come from the five cities. It's more efficient that way."

I remembered the revelations about this made to me by one of the attendants I had on my first visit to the Apellos hangar. Like Méntia, he told me that there are five main cities below the land area corresponding to Romania and even mentioned their general locations.[*] I mentioned this in the conversation with Méntia and told her about my visit to Tomassis.

"Tomassis is very deep and does not fall into the category of the five cities closest to the surface, such as Apellos. The one in the Dobrogea area corresponds approximately vertically to the city of Tulcea, and the one in the

[*] See Volume 6, *Forgotten Genesis*, 2020.

northeast of the country is under the Ceahlău mountains. The population of your country is well supported."

I smiled admiringly. It was comfortable to know that we were not alone and that we had support, albeit in a hidden way. But, I thought later, if there is still such a fairly intense movement of those in the "interior" and if they are so technologically advanced and want to support Romania, how is it then that they do not act more promptly to bring about much faster and more efficient change across the country? I also shared this confusion with Méntia. It was the first time I saw her charming smile.

"We're acting more than you can imagine. Sometimes, that has gone as far as sacrifice. It is true, however, that before, in the past centuries, it was easier to intervene because the structure of your society and the technological means at its disposal were precarious. Our interventions were more effective, without raising suspicions. Now, however, much more caution is needed. There have been, however, cases in your history in which certain people connected with us have manifested themselves directly and even sacrificed themselves for the good of your nation."

Surprised to hear that, I asked her to give me an example.

"She's even considered a national hero. In society, she was named Ecaterina Teodoroiu.* Even though she was and still is considered by almost everyone to be an 'ordinary human', in the sense that both her parents were human beings who belonged to the Earth's civilization, one of her parents was, in reality, from the 'surface' and the other from the 'interior', but not from Apellos. There, her name was Amnita. There is even a local story about her special birth. Due to the specific combination of DNA, she had the genes of subterranean beings, and this is what determined her impulse to act as she did. Such beings show a very strong spirit, but this does not mean that all those who have stood out as heroes or great leaders in the history of your country came from our underground cities."

I admit I would never have thought of what Méntia was telling me. It was amazing, but at the same time, I felt a wave of gratitude directed towards these beings from the "inside" who have been helping us to overcome the difficult moments of our history for centuries. On second thought, it was only then that I realized that today's territory of Romania was the target of numerous conquests, but when they reached the surface projection area of the cities inside the Earth, they became less efficient or were even stopped completely. In Transylvania, for example, no one entered or passed through the frightening forests or the gorge of the Apuseni Mountains for centuries and not even for thousands of years before that. Or, even after hundreds of years of Austro-Hungarian occupation, they retreated with almost no trace. Nothing was taken by the Hungarians or

---

* Born in 1894, Ecaterina Toderoiu died in 1917 in the battle of Marasesti as the head of an infantry platoon of the Romanian Army in the First World War.

Austrians, and there was no mixing of language, customs or traditions. It is the same in the north, in Bucovina. In the mountains, we have always found our defense and chances of success. And, the mountains also represent, generally speaking, the path through which those "inside" come to the surface. That is where the main portals linking to the "interior" exist. That is why it was no coincidence that Méntia preferred only mountainous areas and accomplished most of her missions in such a setting.

GENIUS, DNA, AND TECHNOLOGY

After allowing myself these inner reflections for a few seconds, we returned to our discussion of the mountainous areas that Méntia preferred.

"That means you have connections in such mountainous areas," I said, wanting to understand how all those who come "to the surface" interact with the locals.

"We work with a number of associations," Méntia said. "I am especially interested in helping children who are incarnations of special beings and who need support to manifest. You would expect them to come from big cities, but it's the other way around. Most come from less populated nearby areas. Our statistics also show a higher density of them towards mountain areas."

"But, how do you identify them?" I asked in astonishment. "There is no such thing as a 'reincarnation table.'"

"You don't even need that," she said. "We give an accounting of DNA through study. You have not yet discovered this technology, but inside the macromolecule, there are some specific groups or formations which indicate precise latent possibilities of manifestation, at a much higher level, of that person in this world. When we identify such a family of 'quantum signatures', we know that that child may have a special destiny."

Excited by such very advanced technological possibilities, I spoke.

"You can then use the holographic screen for additional information about that person in the future."

"The survey of the future takes shape only from a certain age, and in such cases, it is even more uncertain because that special person has several degrees of freedom and the time lines are numerous and difficult to follow, even for us. But, it is still true that this method sometimes gives us ideas for action so as not to interfere too much with other determinants of the child's life."

"I understand that it is more a general support of the person, following the principle that he develops as he wants."

"Even more than that, depending upon certain subsequent choices, we can say with great precision in which direction the special characteristics of those beings will manifest. Then, discreetly, we support these children or even young people in an 'unseen' way and seek to help them without those around them suspecting this. As they grow, we appear in their lives as either teachers or tutors, or we act through our companies."

"But, are they aware that they are supported in this way?"

"In general, they have happy opportunities in life, and we seek to strengthen this belief. We have refined our modes of action a lot and we can go almost 'undetected'. In very rare cases, however, some of them who are endowed with a special intuition begin to ask themselves certain questions. But, because we only have the desire to help, we can also withdraw immediately when things reach a certain limit."

I was not only impressed by the advanced degree of their technology but also by their human side with the altruistic help they offered.

"Have you done the same in other countries?" I asked.

"I haven't traveled much, but I'm always up-to-date with your latest discoveries in medical science, biology, and physics. Some of them, however, are never advertised, as I think you already know."

Amazed, I asked her questions.

"But how do you access them? Have you also infiltrated the Services?"

"No, we don't care about politics or your decision-making system. The backstage fights between the espionage and counterintelligence agencies are all far from our sphere of interest. We like what is clean, pure and superior, but our technology is more advanced than anything that now officially exists on Earth, and this allows us to enter, even where it is believed to be hidden or inaccessible."

"I mean on the dark web," I said, thinking I understood.

"Not just there. I told you, our technology is not limited to information-driven flows powered by electricity, as it is in your world today."

Méntia took out of her travel bag a kind of tablet, a little bigger than the ones on our market, but very simple. It was basically like a glass surface, rounded at the edges and about five millimeters thick. Certain points of different colored lights immediately appeared on its surface, especially at the corners. I could not look closely because I was driving, but I still realized that the presentation system was very close to what I had seen on the holographic screen. That "tablet", however, seemed to expose images only in a two-dimensional format.

Méntia probably perceived my thought telepathically because she immediately responded to what I was thinking.

"The two-dimensional option is only used here on the surface, so as not to shock. Otherwise, of course, I work on this tablet, as you call it, in a holographic system. Its search functions are much more sophisticated, but most importantly, it allows access to information that exists that is even beyond the electromagnetic connection. It does not matter whether or not the storage device is connected to the 'network.'"

ALIEN CONTACT: STATUS QUO IN SOCIETY

I was perplexed. Such "carrier" technology was still inconceivable to us at the surface, at least from what I knew until then.

"That's more like an alien acquisition," I said, somewhat jokingly.

Méntia, however, answered me in a very natural and serious way.

"Of course. We have many ongoing projects with some advanced alien civilizations. But, after all, this is natural in our case. I do not understand why you are so tormented by this meaningless denial of their existence."

"Well, there is the social impact that such revelations would have, but it is especially the occult interests that factor into this issue," I replied.

"Yes, we know all this, but the first reason is falsified, and the second is mainly related to the will of the population."

"Falsified? In what sense?" I asked for clarification.

"The negative impact on society, especially that of a religious nature, would not cause the chaos that your authorities expect. It is an intentionally calculated exaggeration of this effect in order to scare and cause the idea of disclosure to be rejected. There may be some outbreaks of dissatisfaction, but they will not proliferate much. The situation has changed in the last fifteen years."

"And we know that as we have studies done in secret. But, there is the opposition of some forces about which I see that you are also informed."

"Obviously. How else? We know well the underpinnings of the 'occult' interests and what these power-hungry beings actually want."

"Another idea was the direct contact of Mankind by at least one of the advanced civilizations. The question arose of their landing directly with their ships. I saw the documentation of such plans with measures, possibilities and their effects on society," I said, hoping to surprise her with this information.

"We know about that, too," she said, smiling. "At one point, the plan was indeed topical, but a closer analysis showed that the level of consciousness and will of Mankind did not meet the necessary conditions to make such a contact. This plan has been revealed by other groups of extraterrestrial beings with obscure interests to some secret groups of people on the surface of the planet."

Méntia had become thoughtful, and her voice had faded. She stared ahead through the windshield and seemed preoccupied with something.

"I think you already know these things," she added.

I had to admit that I did not know what she was alluding to.

After a time of silence, she continued to speak, but this time in an equal tone, almost monotonous and with great concentration.

"The representatives of these occult groups, having a great power of influence, have manipulated things in such a way that people are indoctrinated with the idea of xenophobia towards extraterrestrial beings. And then, if the alien

135

ships had landed on Earth, an indescribable chaos would have been created which could have nullified the beneficial intervention that was desired for human civilization."

Now, I understood much better all the media "bustle" that had appeared 10-12 years ago but to which I had not given any special attention.

"Come to think of it, Hollywood has seriously taken on the role of fabricating this perception in people's subconscious," I said. "Most of the so-called Sci-Fi series created over the last thirty years have been aimed at convincing the population that they should fight with a gun in hand against an imminent alien attack."

Méntia bowed her head, agreeing.

"Under these conditions, if the force and the initial plan had been followed, it would have been too direct, untimely, and almost harsh for the general mentality," she continued. "Our projections and estimates showed that there would have been a high degree of chaos which would have hindered the transition to a higher world instead of easing it."

"Perhaps it would have been good to follow that plan, even in such conditions," I said, "perhaps slightly modified, but one is at least entering another area of reality."

"It is never forced. We do not intervene if there is not a certain state of affairs. Your society has come here through a combination of ignorance and indolence which have been carefully cultivated through manipulation. This has proven to be an effective method. Manipulation is the main weapon of your occult world elite, and it was used on a huge scale. This has generated a number of chain effects which have even manifested themselves in people's physical health, all with direct implications for their DNA. By the way, that's the main point I want to discuss with Elinor."

THE HEALTH OF THE HUMAN BEING: A SPECIAL EMPHASIS

I commented a little on this topic, also discussing nutrition. Méntia told me that all of the people of Apellos are vegetarians and that, among many other things, the product we call "sugar" is a big problem for the surface population, especially since it is widely consumed. From the discussion, I understood that she likes fruits, especially strawberries and peaches, and bee honey is one of her favorite foods.

"In the research I do both in Apellos and here on the surface, I'm very interested in the biochemical structure of plants and fruits," she told me. "Their richness and variety is amazing, but people still don't seem to very well understand their importance with regard to health."

I resolutely approved of what she said, also mentioning the harmful legislation for cultivation and generally speaking of a whole chain of factors that seems to make the large-scale consumption of such natural products more difficult, instead of stimulating them. Méntia nodded slightly, affirming what I said with a slightly sad look.

"In Apellos, the flora is small, but we nevertheless consume many more plant products than you do and which you have at hand in an impressive variety. But, it is true that our technology for combining the active principles of plants and extracting them correctly is much higher than what you have now, but even so, the degree of what is natural and vegetable must be greatly increased in human nutrition."

"Maybe it's an educational issue," I said. "In any case, it is clear that the population should insist on this line. But, if I make a comparison, we are much better off than the West. Europe wants to seem to teach us what we need for our health, but it ignores a long tradition that we have in this territory, inherited from our Dacian ancestors. They had advanced knowledge of the virtues of plants which were then passed on to the Greeks, and from them to the Romans, and then to the rest of the continent. Somehow, this is 'inscribed' in our DNA, and even if there is still a great ignorance among the population about these things, at least compared to other countries in the West, pharmacies do not work very well in Romania because the population uses many natural herbal remedies. It's a big surprise for pharmaceutical companies."

Méntia confirmed this and stated that Western "education" presents things only from an empty physical and chemical perspective. In reality, the health of the human being always starts from the spiritual level, then involves through the emotional level, and finally materializes at the physical level which is our very body.

"The body reacts very well to plant principles, but it inhibits itself when eating meat products," she said. "Your medicine knows very well the effects and reactions that occur in the body in both cases. There are also complex studies in this area, and the theory is quite well developed. What is missing, however, is a deeper understanding of the constituents of plants, and here I am referring in particular to the subtle essences that exist in plants but which are not even suspected by your science. That's why you cannot get effective elixirs in a natural way."

"Over ninety percent of the products in pharmacies are synthetic drugs," I added. "I don't need to tell you what that means, what interests and industries are involved, and what harmful trends ensue. Things are well known to many people, but there are many more who simply do not care. That's why I suggested that, basically, it is primarily a matter of education. The formation of a healthy mentality in this sense should start from the school rooms."

Méntia told me that, although she did not know this expression, she still understood its meaning. She even gave me her own example as a child, having a very good education regarding the health of the being, especially since she comes from a family from Apellos that has a long tradition in the science of medicine.

THE MEETING

In the meantime, we arrived at the villa where Elinor was waiting for us. Cezar had also arrived some time earlier, and I found them both talking relaxedly in the large living room. I noticed that Elinor was very pleasantly impressed by Méntia's presence, and after a few introductory greetings, Cezar and I sat comfortably on the wide sofa with Elinor and Méntia in the two elegant armchairs in the room. I could not help but smile, remembering how many years ago, in the same chair where Méntia was now, sat Repa Sundhi, from whom I had learned extremely precious lessons. That magical night was also marked by the mysterious and terrible presence of the yidam and the subsequent journey that followed, representing a very important stage in my spiritual knowledge and evolution.*

On the table between the armchairs sat a bowl with several varieties of fruit, among which I noticed were a few peaches. I thought then that Elinor was quite inspired, given that Méntia liked that kind of fruit. Immediately, she turned her head halfway to me, speaking with a charming smile.

"Yes, I think I'll try them a little later."

We were all amused by that simple demonstration of her telepathic abilities, after I explained with a laugh what was the reason was for Méntia's comment. The atmosphere was relaxed and somehow I can best describe as "bright" in the absence of a better term to explain the very good feeling I had about those very special beings present in the same room. In a way, it seemed almost incredible to me where the adventure of life had brought me, and I was deeply grateful for it, primarily to Cezar. He completely changed my existence and made me see far beyond its usual limits while awakening in me unsuspected abilities. And now, I was taking part in a meeting which, from my point of view, I considered to be a meeting between the sages, given the elevated and very refined mental and spiritual condition of the three exceptional beings before me.

---

* See Volume 2, *Transylvanian Moonrise* for mention of Repa Sundhi, the Tibetan lama who was also the same person as Dr. Xien, the scientist who guided Department Zero into existence as described in Volume I, *Transylvanian Sunrise*. The yidam is also identified as a creature with super natural abilities that is generated by a lama using a sand mandala and can occupy spaces and dimensions which the normal body of a lama could never do.

THE PREMISES OF INDIVIDUAL
ASCENSION AND DNA TRANSFORMATION

The discussion quite quickly slipped to the topics that interested us, and Méntia talked about some changes that may take place in the structure of human DNA during the current period.

"It is true," said Cezar, "because of the special zone in the galaxy where it was born, the Earth is under the subtle energetic influence of several stars and constellations; but this area, though complex, is still subject to uniform influences which do not register special 'jumps'. We are, as they say, in 'calm waters'. This makes the possibility of atomic and molecular combinations, including those inside the macromolecule of human DNA, very high because there are no major determining influences from other stars or very large cosmic objects which would influence DNA to manifest exclusively in a certain direction. This feature gives life on Earth an extraordinary complexity, and that is why our planet enjoys a very great variety of fauna and flora."

A little surprised, Méntia looked at Cezar as if she did not expect him to know those things, but she immediately approved of what he said.

"Yes. There is no determining subtle influence that comes from a certain part of the galaxy to the area where this Solar System is located. We do not receive a special and constant major influence from any stellar cluster[*] nor any other gigantic cosmic manifestation. But, this is exactly what facilitates the transformation of your civilization because, in this way, you have more degrees of freedom and you are not constrained by a certain type of major radiation which would determine the evolution of life on Earth."

Cezar nodded and continued.

"Here, however, choice, determination, and the will to of the individual come into play. The degree of freedom we have in this area of the galaxy allows us to 'sculpt' our future. The subtle planetary influences, but especially the formidable influence of the Sun, are free to act because these energies are not overwhelmed by other powerful forces in the galactic area in which we are. If, in the distant past of Mankind, the process of 'modeling' DNA has been strongly supported by the presence of huge alien ships[*] and the Moon in the sky, it does not mean that this process took place only then and then ceased. Currently, the transformation continues. Even though the active periods of these transformations have alternated with those of rest, the structure of DNA continues its evolution even today. We are always under planetary or stellar

---

[*] Star clusters are thought to be remnants of the so-called "early universe", usually containing thousands of stars crammed into a "sphere" only a few light-years in diameter. The physics of such cosmic manifestations are not yet known, partly due to the immense distances they are from our galaxy and partly due to the mysterious nature of the interactions between the clustered stars, located a relatively short distance from each other.
[**] The author refers mainly to the Sirian ship Neiberau (*Forgotten Genesis,* 2020).

influences, so this transformation is continuous, but it has begun to intensify during this current period."

"All the more, as humanity is currently being targeted for a new transformation of DNA, especially at the level of the carbon atom," Méntia said. "The carbon-based structure of life will 'regroup' in an evolutionary sense, so the first thing that will transform will be human DNA."

I also joined the discussion at this point, intervening with an idea that seemed correct to me.

"It cannot just be about planetary and solar influences here. What about the flow of unusually intense cosmic radiation, especially gamma, photonic and neutron radiation which we have been entering for some time that is amplifying more and more and coming from certain stars and even from the center of the galaxy?*

"Yes, but the one you're talking about is a cosmic conjunctional phenomenon," Méntia explained. "From a certain point of view, it is even cyclical. These radiations now have the role of making fundamental changes in the intimacy of the human body. They influence the internal structure of the chemical elements and transform the psycho-mental structure of the human being. This huge 'shower' of cosmic energy will cause our atoms to resonate strongly, and the specific frequencies of these radiations will cause the carbon atom in particular to be 'bombarded' so that everything alive on the planet will mutate with significant transformations."

"Is that true for everyone?" I asked.

"In principle, yes," replied Cezar. "Apparently, people are prepared for a fundamental transformation, but not everyone will achieve it because it depends a lot, as I said, on choice, on the individual will. Some will accept the transformation, but others will not. The usual term for it is ascent and it is, in a way, an ascent in terms of vibrational frequency. This is exactly what makes the zone of intense cosmic radiation into which the Solar System and, implicitly, the Earth have entered: it brings changes at the cellular and atomic level in living organisms because their vibrational frequency becomes much higher."

DECISION OF THE APELLOS COUNCIL

At this point, Méntia began to deepen the subject, directing the discussion to the main idea for which she wanted that meeting.

"The problem is that, statistically speaking, our studies have shown that there is a tendency for a degradation of human DNA, that which has been transmitted through the E-N-K branch," she said. "This DNA has been diluted

---

*According to current science, in the center of our galaxy is a massive black hole called Sagittarius A.

over time, especially in the Nordic peoples. Transformation is viable when radiation flows 'have something to work on'. When the structure of DNA begins to be corrupted, then the difference in vibrational frequency between it and cosmic radiation becomes too great, and the transformation can no longer occur. Several factors contribute to such degradation. Thus, health becomes an important element for the transformation you were talking about. You cannot evolve when you're barely moving or in bed, sick. This is mainly why we came here, because our Council has decided to provide more consistent help to the population, but that requires important and very reliable links. The plan is older, but certain security and precautionary elements have prevented us from launching it so far."

We were not sure what Méntia meant and looked at each other questioningly. Surprised, I expressed my perplexity.

"I know that the Nordic peoples are robust and healthy, far from having any problem of this nature."

"No," she replied dryly. "The degradation of DNA in their case is accentuated and this translates into being 'sick' at a deep level. This reality does not appear visually in the early stages."

"Then how does it manifest?" I insisted, rather annoyed. "I have not noticed such a marked degradation."

"Something in their DNA structure has been corrupted. At first, it manifests at the soul level. It appears as a general dissatisfaction, a void in being, a morbid retreat into oneself, often as self-destructive isolation. Emotional capacity suffers a lot. This condition then begins to expand in the body; hormonal imbalances appear. It's a vicious circle; people become like robots."

"We find this robotization everywhere, especially in the West," I said.

"Yes, but it's more pronounced with them."

For a few moments, we were all silent, deep in thought. Méntia then resumed the discussion.

"Our idea is to help the population to be as healthy as possible so that they can absorb the energy of cosmic radiation inflows efficiently, which will be strong at some point," Méntia said. "The chances of ascension then increase considerably. A blurred mind or a suffering person will not be able to understand the subtle 'message' of these highly refined energies, let alone reorient their lives. Even personal choices depend a lot on a person's health. Illness or bodily agitation creates mental agitation which, in turn, leads to hasty and often erroneous decisions and inevitably to suffering."

"But, I asked, if the flow of high-frequency cosmic radiation changes the intimate cellular and even atomic structures, will this not implicitly achieve the healing of people and their orientation towards evolution?"

"High frequencies still must have a reason to 'hang on'. They must find a suitable basis for action and do not act mechanically. There is a certain 'intelligence of energy', a very complex interaction between the subtle nature of man, his body and these energies."

"That means there will be mutations in the human body," said Cezar.

"Exactly," said Méntia. "Many hybrid genes will thus appear, and some of them may even evolve significantly. For example, the mixed or somewhat 'intermediate' race could become 'independent' and evolve spectacularly, and the black or white race might decrease in weight, number of individuals or rate of evolution. Hybridization thus becomes very important. These transformations, however, require a lasting health on the part of humanity because you cannot claim to be profoundly transformed when you are deprived of vital energy, eat improperly, do not have a healthy rhythm of life, are constantly stressed or are surrounded by strong harmful electromagnetic fields. Under such conditions, you cannot help but resist these inner transformations because the physical body is not prepared."

PROPOSAL FOR ELINOR

With that, Méntia turned her attention to Elinor who had been silent all this time, watching our discussion intently. She seemed to want to involve him in the dialogue as well.

"Some people still want to change, but I don't know how to accomplish that," she said. "Either they are deceived by the so-called 'efficient methods' that are circulated, or they abandon the idea too quickly. In order to evolve, man must first be healthy, but for that, he should follow some simple advice and have the power to get out of the 'prison' of bad habits, harmful routine or ignorance. I thought we might even find an alchemical solution."

Elinor was not surprised by Méntia's request and responded immediately, which showed me that he was actually present at the discussion, even though he had not intervened at all until then.

"You mean alchemical elixirs?" he asked.

"Elixirs, extracts or essences from plant alchemy, yes. That is what I am primarily referring to. We consider it is time for their implementation as treatments on a large-scale, as an integral but essential part of plant-based products."

Elinor answered carefully, as if choosing his words.

"That can't be done overnight. There are certain occult laws which do not allow for the mass spread of such very powerful remedies because it would cause an imbalance in certain relationships between people's destinies, efforts and individual experiences. Alchemical elixirs, especially high-ranking ones, and especially the Supreme One, are an extremely well-kept secret and precisely for the reason I just told you."

Méntia seemed a little unhappy and tried to argue her point.

"Even if the alchemists have to keep it a secret, some things could be revealed," she said fiercely. "The population is in a serious situation and their health is in danger. Many people do not believe in the existence of subtle energies but in allopathic pharmaceuticals, all of which is very well thought out so that the population is dependent upon synthetic drugs. A middle way must be found with natural products which are strongly charged with pure and healing energy, one which can be done most efficiently by means of alchemical elixirs. The vegetable path, using medicinal plants, has already been tried, and it is good, but the results come slowly and do not heal spectacularly nor as quickly as most people expect."

Elinor smiled and calmly replied.

"I told you, you can't do it this way because the law of individual karma is violated.[*] If so, the secrets of alchemy should be known to all, but the reality is different, and this shows the state of humanity."

"Our statistics show, however, that now is the right time to find a way to solve this problem," Méntia insisted. "The 'dilution' of DNA, which we consider dangerous, can reach a critical point, and then everything could become even more difficult. You no doubt know many alchemists who are in hiding, and you can contact them to decide to act together in a harmonious way, as well as to consider the elixir or elixirs you might start with. I do not immediately refer to 'drinking gold'[**] because that is maybe too much. But, an elixir with less power would be best for the population. Its presentation could be indirect and can be mixed in a certain proportion in emulsions, syrups, potions or herbal creams. Soon, the regeneration of DNA would be extraordinary."

THE PROBLEM OF KARMIC COMPENSATION

Elinor listened intently to Méntia's point of view, but remained inflexible.

"In order to benefit from such a thing, you still need a certain inner training. Otherwise, people would learn nothing, take everything as normal, and continue their reckless life. Many of them do not believe in subtle aspects, saying that if they really existed, then they would be known. This is a point of evolution, and we cannot intervene so abruptly without there being further unforeseen consequences.

"These things are very well known to us," said Méntia, "but it has to start somewhere. We have our own research, and we have evaluated segments of the population. Indeed, people are not educated in this regard. They still live by their bad habits, eat the wrong things, smoke a lot, drink alcohol or take

---

[*] See Volume 2 of the *Transylvania Series, Transylvanian Moonrise*.

[**] This alchemical elixir is a very pure salt, dissolved and diluted in vegetable alcohol, but it does not contain even a golden atom. The name "drinking gold" comes from its golden-yellow color, very pure and shiny, similar to this noble metal. It is considered a panacea and in principle cures all diseases, including those of a psychosomatic nature.

drugs. Their way of life is chaotic and destructive."

"But, I wonder why you, with such advanced technology, do not offer them stronger solutions for recovery," Elinor countered.

Méntia replied that the situation has changed in this respect, that it has become more permissive. From Méntia's answer, we understood that the people of Apellos really strive to help us, but they nevertheless cannot simply offer us such miraculous solutions on a platter because we would not know how to understand and efficiently manage them. She continued with her response.

"The solutions must come from the Earthlings, from those on the surface. Free help must make sense."

"That's exactly what I was arguing myself," Elinor replied. "Compensation from the population is needed and it comes mainly through authentic knowledge and adequate training. If people do not understand why they are doing well instead of their illnesses getting worse, then there is no great evolutionary gain for them."

ANALYSIS OF POSSIBLE SOLUTIONS

Méntia looked Elinor in the eye and answered in an equal tone.

"Yes. That is why we thought that some of the alchemical essences, even if they are not elixirs, could contribute to a partial 'awakening' of people which would be a promising starting point for a better view of life. An 'infusion' of technology from us, however, is much more complicated. It would involve government ties, mutual acceptance, numerous bilateral meetings, production...the chain of elements is long, difficult, and success is uncertain because the society on the surface is built very much on the principle of self-interest, selfishness, competition and concealment. Our action would be very disturbing, and the results, as our simulations have shown, do not necessarily lead to something positive at the moment. People do not have the maturity to this level of understanding, and their leaders are dominated by dark interests."

"But, you mentioned your studies which show that the population can now receive considerable help," Elinor reminded her.

"Yes, but we were thinking of less obvious help. That's why I decided to come and talk and find solutions. We think that spagyric essences could be of real use. Our estimate is that, at the very least, they will be able to stop the rather severe degradation of human DNA."

"Essentially, the same problem applies to alchemists. They too cannot give up concealment, 'throwing' their elixirs and extraordinary spagyric essences on the market because this would cause huge 'convulsions' at almost all levels of society. One effect generates the next, and in a short time, due to the fact that their help would not be understood, only selfishly and incorrectly, great dysfunctions would occur."

"But, the solution I proposed, using, for example, some spagyric essences instead of elixirs, hidden in even some already known herbal remedies, could work," replied Méntia.

"Even if this solution were to work, appreciable quantities are still needed. You've probably thought about mass production. Spagyric essences are strong, even stronger than ordinary tinctures, but weaker than elixirs. Quite large amounts would need to be given to the commonly obtained alchemical solutions."

"I do not know the actual alchemical process although I am aware of the general principles of this extraordinary art," said Méntia.

"I mean, you can't hope for spagyric essences in large liters or tens of liters. The workload would be huge, and the time required very long. In alchemy, we do not work as one would on a production line. Most of the time, it is not something quantitative, but especially qualitative. The area of spread with regard to healing products would therefore be quite narrow."

Méntia thought for a while before speaking again.

"Even so, over time, a larger area could be covered by repeated infusions of plant products containing alchemical substances of a spagyric nature, having a strong healing effect."

Elinor stood firm in his position, shaking his head.

"Spagyric alchemy operations are relatively simple, but it takes a long time," he said. "What you want to achieve is nationwide, and that involves appreciable amounts of spagyric essences, even if their reported power is quite high. We also need people with deep knowledge and a lot of experience, especially in the art of distillation. You have to separate the active principles of some powerful medicinal plants, purify them through a series of successive operations at several levels by distillation, calcination, and evaporation, and then reunite the principles of that plant by cohabitation* because they are then considered to be pure, free from alterations and impurities from the beginning. All this involves long careful work, full of patience and knowledge, because it is not just a simple replication of certain stages. The human factor, especially from a certain step forward, is extremely important. It's not like a factory; it's not a product made on a production line."

ELEMENTS OF ALCHEMY AND THE VISION OF THEIR CORRECT INTEGRATION INTO MODERN SOCIETY

This was followed by a short but very interesting presentation by Elinor on some essential aspects of alchemy, first at the level of principles, and then even entering certain backstage aspects of this amazing practice of transforming

---

* In alchemy, cohobation is the operation of reuniting the elements of a substance which have already been purified by spagyric methods.

matter. I was just eyes and ears, extremely interested in what I was hearing. As he spoke, there seemed to be a mystical atmosphere in the living room, a kind of sacredness that came from the soul and undoubtedly originated in the very nature of the subject itself. It was amazing to hear an alchemist, with immense experience in the field and in possession of incredible truths and achievements for the knowledge of the common man, talking about certain aspects of this art, seen through the prism of a practitioner with enormous experience. Cezar was also very attentive to Elinor's summarized exposition, and I could see from his attitude the deep respect he had for him.

Addressing Méntia, Elinor emphasized the correct understanding of how alchemical products can be integrated into society.

"Although there are hundreds or even thousands of books published in the field of alchemy, very few of them still contain truly valuable information, and generally speaking, the latter are written by master alchemists. The rest are only general presentations in which the authors are either only theorists or practice operative alchemy, but only partially and without a deep understanding of its secrets. There are unwritten laws and sacred vows to keep the terrible secrets of operative alchemy. That is why alchemical texts are so tangled and often only allusive. Those who finally understand their meaning are extremely few in the world."

"We can, however, use these secrets for the good of Mankind without necessarily having to reveal them," Méntia insisted.

"Of course, but there is a time for everyone and everything," Elinor replied. "What you offer must be addressed to someone who is close, in terms of their level of consciousness, to the gift received. Otherwise, that person will not know how to appreciate what he receives. There are also dispensations, but they always have a well-defined and beneficial purpose. But with regard to the degree of agitation and ignorance in today's society, sharing such secrets means pure suicide. Things must be done with a certain responsibility and in a balanced way."

"If we wait too long for the balance, the DNA damage could become too great," Méntia insisted.

"Nature has its wisdom. We will see what compromise solution could be found. The idea of dosing spagyric essences in certain plant emulsions and mixtures is good, but the subtle factor and its consequences must be analyzed very well. Such essences contain only the volatile parts of plants so, in the end, it is necessary for them to have a 'body' in order to be used successfully in healing. Salt, as an alchemical principle, helps to fix the volatile aspect of such an essence, but it must first be very well purified. This involves hard and lengthy work. Essences with high virtues can thus be obtained, even if they are determined, i.e. they have the characteristics that define the initial plant from which they came."

Cezar intervened, emphasizing an important element.

"The distillation temperature must be carefully graded, it being the biological environment."

Elinor nodded, smiling and slightly surprised.

"Exactly. The operations are performed at low temperature values, ideally between 30 and 40 degrees (centigrade). If you go beyond 50 degrees, you 'kill' its active principles, especially the Spirit or alcohol of that substance, and the volatile oils dissipate. The plant remains 'lifeless' but you will not know it. If you continue, you apparently get the 'healing salt', but in reality, it has no power or, in any case, a very small one."

"In the case of the correct action," I said, "I assume that the effect is total because the properties of the plant are synthesized in its essence."

"Yes, spagyric essences condense all the properties of the plant to their maximum values, provided the alchemical operations are performed correctly," Elinor confirmed. "One drop equals all the medicinal effects and minerals in the respective plant."

Then he addressed Méntia again.

"So, your idea is good because the proportion is advantageous. A small amount of spagyric essence may be enough for a few tens of kilograms of plant mixture emulsion. Even so, however, it is insufficient for general consumption in a country."

"Even a part of the population, if they feel the very strong beneficial effects of such new products over time, is much better than nothing," Méntia said. "It would be a huge leap from what synthetic drugs in pharmacies offer."

"It's really a big deal here. As you said, it is a combination of the interests of the big pharmaceutical concerns and the ignorance of the population. Allopathic medicines in pharmacies are synthetic substances; they no longer contain the fundamental principles of Mercury and Sulfur, but only Salt.[*] Therefore, allopathic medicines can only act on the material level, on the body. For example, they cannot remedy the psyche and the mind, nor can they change the spiritual level of man, but spagyric essences and elixirs retain all three alchemical principles I was telling you about. Their virtue consists in the fact that they penetrate all the stages of the organism, both the physical and the subtle ones. It is true, however, that there are differences here as well. Some can do it to a greater extent, others to a lesser extent."

Elinor later explained that the elixirs obtained from the metallic kingdom are much stronger than those obtained from the vegetable kingdom and have deeper effects. He told us, however, that such exceptional substances cannot be used by large masses of people due to the difficult way they are obtained which involves a lot of attention and a deep knowledge of alchemical secrets,

---

[*] Obviously, the alchemical principle of Mercury does not represent the metal mercury (quicksilver), Sulfur does not represent the common metal sulfur, and Salt does not represent table salt.

but especially due to the fact that they are collected in tiny quantities. It is more a work of evolution and individual becoming. Beyond this, the fundamental element is the karmic one because the mass spread of alchemical elixirs, or even their fractional action on human beings, can then has very harsh consequences on individual destiny.

"Still, it would be like medical help. It is offered indiscriminately to anyone who needs it," I said, wanting to better understand the nature of this issue. Even here, however, we have issues with the countries of society because many people do not even have this possibility, either due to lack of money, medical insurance, or other limiting conditions."

"You must understand that an alchemical elixir is in itself a culmination of evolutionary realization, an individual path. This is not an issue of selfishness of which you could be 'accused' of in the sense that you want to keep such an elixir just for yourself. The real significance is that, by the very fact that you managed to obtain such a substance with miraculous properties, you can enjoy it because you already understand and deserve it. It is part of your evolution: you worked for it, you have made sustained efforts and have been helped and guided by the celestial planes, for here, you can do nothing without divine grace. Likewise, esoteric initiations, spiritual initiations, or other occult elements are not offered on a platter to anyone, and some of them are even very hidden. What would then be the purpose of mystery schools or secret societies?"

Cezar also intervened.

"The general idea is that every element of one's life appears according to his destiny. In turn, destiny is a consequence of the level of knowledge and the nature of the individual actions that have been performed until then. When you come and act at the level of the masses, especially through such very powerful elements as alchemical elixirs, it is more an act of unilateral or small group will than a natural flow of life. Although the intention is undoubtedly beneficial and full of compassion and love, it does not take into account the many other connections and integrations that are then changed in people's lives."

"That's right," said Elinor. You cannot voluntarily and indiscriminately balance the lives of hundreds of thousands of people or even millions, just by helping them. How do you know the role that suffering plays in the life of every sick person? Such an action of mass dissemination of an alchemical elixir involves immense responsibility and can only be done when the society or people in question are already on a higher level of consciousness, understanding, behavior and action. But then, of course, perhaps such an elixir would no longer be needed because everyone would have the level necessary to fix for themselves what would be repairable in his life, or it could at least be done in an approximate fashion."

Méntia intervened with a clarification.

"We want a 'repair' of human DNA in order to prevent a sharp and rather rapid decay of this structure at the level of society."

"I understand that, but we will have to do it very carefully and in a somewhat scheduled fashion. Otherwise, the karmic repercussions can be very large. In the current stage of humanity, when existence has become very complex in society, such an intervention is extremely risky. Even in antiquity, when the population was very small, this was never done."

"It's true, but we are now obviously living in another reality, and the situation is unusual," Méntia argued. "All the energies and frequencies of cosmic radiation streams indicate this. Our desire is to help as many human beings as possible have the chance to move to a higher level of vibration of consciousness and thus rise at least one step above the current level."

"Yes, but we must find the right way to do it," Elinor said, "Otherwise, the imbalances may become greater than the help we are proposing. At such a level of action, what we want to achieve cannot be achieved with either force or passion, even if such are beneficially targeted. Rather, I see here the path of humility, patience, and compassionate action that is properly integrated into this goal. We have to be very careful."

DIFFERENCES BETWEEN CHEMISTRY AND ALCHEMY

Here, Méntia proposed another kind of collaboration, one which would involve a kind of school or academy in which to teach the art of alchemy.

"We could prepare a certain number of people to perform alchemical operations and obtain larger amounts of pure substances, essences or even elixirs. Dosed in very small quantities, it could be a start."

"In theory, this variant could work; but in practice, there are many variables, the most important of them is the human factor," Elinor replied. "It takes years of training and understanding the secrets of alchemy because it is both a science and an art. Intense work in this way goes hand in hand with the purification of the soul and the elevation of consciousness, just as matter is purified during laboratory experiments."

"It's quite different from common chemistry experiments," Cezar said. "While alchemy is 'alive', chemistry seems somehow 'dead' because it considers only the 'visible' aspects."

"Well said," Elinor confirmed. "A big difference between chemistry and alchemy is that chemistry does not consider the bodies it works with to be alive. It conveys only dead bodies, both conceptually and experimentally which, of course, cannot evolve. The evolution of matter, even amorphous matter, is a difficult concept to understand for the mind of contemporary man which is obscured by the ideas of a science which is still materialistic.

Alchemy uses the forces and energies of life in its operations; and through this, it brings something that is not recognized or even intuited in today's scientific environment: it makes matter evolve through purification and regeneration. The path is difficult and obscure, but he who succeeds is fully rewarded."

Elinor then further clarified the problem of the difference between chemistry and alchemy, the latter not being understood and even ridiculed by contemporary scientists.

"In chemistry, if you have the necessary substances and the operations are performed correctly, you get exactly what you wanted, regardless of who operates those experiments. In alchemy, if you also have everything you need for the experiment you want to do, success is not guaranteed, even if the operations are performed technically perfect. The success of alchemical operations, especially those of the higher stages, depends largely on the inner spiritual state of the operator. If this does not align with the vibration specific to that experiment and with that of the substance within it, the result will be a failure. That's why I said we can't talk about mass production. If chemistry only performs experiments, the experiment in alchemy is also an inner experience which is acquired, accumulated and thus leads to the spiritual evolution of the alchemist."

In a way, Méntia seemed unwavering in her opinion.

"It seems that this course of action cannot be successful, but there must be a solution," she said.

"Not like that," Elinor replied. "Alchemy cannot be learned 'in common'. The basic principles and certain foundations can be found in books or texts or in the explanations of others; but the actual experience is individual. No one can do it for you. You can't understand what's going on there unless you take part in it. Chemists remain only on the surface of things because, for them, everything with which they experiment is 'dead' matter. Alchemists, however, work with the very principles and energies of life but respect the laws of Nature."

"But chemists also respect them, and they've even stated some of them," I said. "The real secrets, however, cannot be revealed by a mechanical approach alone," I added immediately as an inner reflection.

"Indeed. Both of these sciences obey the laws of Nature, but only alchemists know how to hasten processes in an intelligent and especially profoundly spiritual way," Elinor continued. "After all, as I said, this is about the evolution of matter, something which chemists do not conceive. How could they understand, for example, the simple notion of 'opening matter' in alchemy? And yet, this operation is essential because matter is then brought closer to the four elements that compose it to which, until then, there was no access due to the impurities that covered them.* This means that the psychic

---

* Earth, Water, Fire and Air are understood as subtle principles and not literally.

sensitivity of matter can be increased. That is why I said that, if the subtle radiation of the alchemist is good and harmonious, then this also helps to improve the quality of matter. But, if he is not initiated into such knowledge, matter will be 'contaminated' when it is seen by such a person who is not prepared inwardly. The art of alchemy is a solitary work, for two people at most, who work together and who communicate subtly, empathetically and not just mechanically or technically."

Things became clearer, and as Elinor shared some of the secrets of alchemy with us, we better understood the meanings of the actions. Cezar wanted to know more about the action of alchemical elixirs and their mode of action in the human body.

"All the elixirs are finally reduced to the Elixir of Life, which is a panacea, but not only that," Elinor replied. "Some call it 'medicinal gold' and others 'drinking gold'. You can extract it from any plant, especially some, of course, but also from metals or animal matter. It pre-exists in all materials and substances, but in order to obtain it, one must separate all impurities, both from Salt and from the four Elements which constitute the matter chosen for the Work. You thus obtain the fifth essence or Spirit of Life. When this spirit or elixir is taken by someone in a suitable dose, it acts strongly in the body due to the power of fire which it has. It is an extremely pure subtle energy, associated with fire, but this is obviously not about ordinary fire or its flames. It is a subtle 'intelligent' energy, extremely refined and penetrating."

Cezar was very attentive to what Elinor was saying.

"What part of the alchemical elixir actually heals?" he asked.

"Only the Spirit of that matter, that is, its Mercury, the subtle principle thereof, is that which can cure the disease. In order to highlight the power of the Spirit of a plant or a metal, you must 'catch' it correctly and free of impurities. Like base metals, they can be of no use unless they have previously been purified and refined by 'atomization' and this is achieved by fermentation of the substance. In this way, you 'open the matter', as I told you. Then, you need the so-called 'solvents' or alchemical menstruation, which are fundamental. They extract the principles which are then reunited into a new 'body' of the substance, purified and alchemized."

It was already beginning to be difficult for me because there were too many notions, even if what Elinor was telling us was, in fact, only some of the main directions of knowledge in the art of alchemy, a kind of initiatory a-b-c.

"From what you say here, it seems that alchemy is an absolutely hidden science. The texts in the field, if you have the chance to come across some authentic ones, are meant only for those who are knowledgeable and already initiated. It's a little discouraging."

Elinor smiled softly and explained.

"Yes, that's how it seems; but even this is a beginner's test. Alchemy, in its deepest sense, is not a hobby. There must be something in your being, a strong longing, an impulse to make you seek something more than you are in this world. Her science is at the same time very subtle, but also very palpable. Subtle, because you can reach states of matter that are not known and even manipulate quantum reality. Palpable and concrete, because it can also give you a perfect condition of your physical and subtle being. In a sense, you become immortal. Do you now understand why there is this extreme concealment of alchemical methods and operations? Imagine what a person who does not have an impeccable moral and ethical code, but on the contrary, has selfish interests or, worse yet, is malevolently oriented, could do with these secrets. For centuries and even millennia, people of such a nature have tried by all means to find out or apply the alchemical secrets in order to reach the immense powers of the true and gifted alchemist adept in obtaining the Philosopher's Stone. They did not understand, however, that it is practically impossible to reach such a stage without the simultaneous transformation of your own being. It is a profound transformation of consciousness which means access to supreme spiritual knowledge. The general vibration of your being agrees with the whole Universe and because you have already understood the essence of its existence, you have power over all the elements. But, this will not happen according to the impure, selfish mind and desires of an ordinary man, but according to the conscience of the adept who is purified in the fire of that supreme knowledge of which I was telling you. Then, you do not want to act otherwise than in the spirit of universal harmony. For you, it makes sense and is understood, but for the unprepared, it is full of mystery and remains invisible."

"Then what's the point of the hundreds or thousands of books on this subject? There is a kind of paradox here: only the one who is initiated understands, but if you are initiated, you already have the essence of knowledge and then you no longer need those books."

My astonishment had a certain logical basis, but Elinor patiently explained to me that this interpretation was somewhat mechanical.

"Man doesn't just work in a 'plus or minus' fashion," he told me. "The purpose of the multitude of texts is for the beginner to pass the test of his patience and aspiration towards something supreme and unique. Only he who is truly authentic in his search will not be discouraged and will seek to understand the deep meanings of these texts. They are a real jungle, unmatched by any other system or spiritual school. The clues are extremely hidden behind allegorical names, hyperbole and abstract symbolism. Often, some steps of alchemical methods are not mentioned, and other times, the explanations are deliberately erroneous. But, all this makes sense because, in the end, the follower who reaches the end result becomes a kind of 'Master of the Universe'. Of course, not in the idea of being a despot, but in the deeply spiritual one, in which he becomes truly aware of what is both himself and the whole Universe. Reaching the quintessence of matter is synonymous, by analogy, with discovering the spiritual essence of your being. It is an achievement at the highest level; and, through alchemy, the adherent becomes perfect both physically and spiritually."

In theory, I knew some of these things, but what I did not really understand were the practical application of alchemical methods, and its operations of how you manipulate matter and bring it into successive stages of transformation. This is, in fact, the extreme concealment of alchemy. Taking advantage of the point at which the discussion had reached, I wanted to raise this issue.

"Alchemical texts are full of paradoxes. You don't understand anything anymore. Methods and sequences of operations are spoken only in parables and symbolisms. Where does knowledge come from?"

"Out of immense patience and inner faith, devotion, repetition and concentration," Elinor replied. "A human being can evolve by grace, initiation, or other methods, but the process is the same: you must first pass certain tests of life or trials, both external and internal, and then the Universe takes care to give you what you wanted, if your understanding is correct. And this is also a paradox."

"Yes," said Méntia, completing the thought, "the sudden recovery of a human being is, for example, a paradox for many people."

"She is absolutely right when she supports the healing of the human being in the acquisition of health through a correct life both physically and psychologically because the forces for spiritual search, including alchemy, are then much stronger and even more refined. A nation that reaches a high level of physical, mental, and spiritual purity becomes an extraordinary force. As far as I know, this is the deeper meaning of the help that the Council of Apellos has decided to offer to our people."

Méntia smiled charmingly, like a tacit confirmation and Cezar, on the couch, had a very relaxed and serene attitude. After a few moments, she spoke in a warm and slightly lower voice, keeping the same ravishing smile.

"Then it means we can find a solution in the field of alchemy that can help us in what we want, right? ... while we're still talking about paradoxes."

What followed was a very special moment. There was a deep silence, and I saw Elinor deeply absorbed, motionless, his head slightly tilted downward. His concentration was extraordinary, and in a way I cannot explain very well, even charismatic. Somehow, I had the certainty then that, following what Méntia said, he had the inspiration of an idea, of a solution on which he focused intensely in order to give it a form and a content as clear as possible."

After about two minutes, he raised his head slowly and looked us in the eyes with a happy twinkle, without saying anything. He turned to me and

Cezar, implying that he only wanted to talk to Méntia. I got up from the couch with Cezar and left the living room without talking. We preferred to go to the basement, to the large room where the Eden device was, but as we walked away, I could hear the murmur of the conversation that had already begun between Elinor and Méntia. They stayed there for about twenty minutes, after which Méntia went down to the room where we were. She looked at us sympathetically from the doorway, and from the light I saw in her eyes, I knew that the discussion had been fruitful and that, in one way or another, they had found a solution to her problem."

She then thanked me in an elegant way, telling me that both my efforts and my results with the Eden project are remarkable and that they will make sense in the future. She also added that she liked the way I spoke that evening and that she admired my desire to support the agenda of Apellos. Although I did not quite understand why she thanked me for all of those things, I still gladly received her appreciation which warmed my heart. Next, the three of us discussed some technical and collaborative issues between Apellos and Department Zero, outlining a general program of visits and objectives.

After the discussion that evening, Méntia told us that she had decided to stay on the surface for a while in order to monitor my training with the "space-time machine". This collaboration was part of our agreement with the Apellos Council as the possibility of implementing additional technologies from the underground city to increase the efficiency of Eden was being studied.

Finally, an hour later into the night, we retired to our rooms, including Méntia, who was also staying in Elinor's villa. Long after that, I relived the magical moment at the end of our meeting, wondering if I would ever find out what Elinor and Méntia had discussed after being alone in the living room. The events that followed, however, revealed extraordinary things to me, showing me how deep the actions performed by certain beings with huge occult powers can be.

CHAPTER NINE

THE TWIN PROJECT

In the one month since that meeting, things changed rapidly. The training was easier, and the experiences I had multiplied. The presence of Méntia was, of course, a catalyst as my ability to interact with the energies that corresponded to the frequencies modulated by Eden increased exponentially. Each experience of "going out" greatly enriched my arsenal of knowledge as well as the ways of interacting with the various situations I faced.

INTENSIVE TRAINING

The relationship with Méntia gave me feedback which I used with a lot of confidence and determination because I noticed that it pointed me in the right direction. Méntia provided me with a small device from Apellos which had a remarkable quality: it could almost immediately induce a state of mind specific to theta waves in the brain without any special preparation or a pre-period of "calming".* This helped me a lot in my training because I quickly entered a state of mental peace which I could later deepen, modulating it according to the nature and intensity of the energy corresponding to the frequencies emitted by Eden.

Elinor was pleased with the progress I was making and pointed out some aspects to me, completing what Méntia was telling me. Sometimes, however, he was absent for several days in a row, appearing suddenly afterwards. He never said where he was or what he did, and we respected that. You can never monitor or check up on the program of an alchemist. I noticed, however, that after returning home, Elinor had long discussions with Méntia. I think the plan they decided on was moving forward pretty quickly because, after those meetings, Méntia communicated quite a bit with the people from Apellos. She often did this from the terrace as I relaxed, using a device that looked like a mobile phone except that it was perfectly transparent and worked very well. Sometimes, on its surface, I saw short but very beautiful reflections of the colors of the rainbow appearing. She spoke an unknown but melodious

---

* Theta brain waves are "slow" waves, associated with creative processes, intuition or daydreaming, bringing to the surface of the mind various memories, emotions and sensations. These waves occur especially during the processes of meditation, prayer, introspection or other techniques of a spiritual nature. From an anatomical point of view, theta waves reflect the activity of the limbic system and hippocampal regions, improving the processes of adaptation, learning and memory.

language which she told me was the language of the people of Apellos. From the expression on her gorgeous face, I understood that things were going very well and that their altruistic efforts were taking shape more and more.

Even though it was quite difficult for him, Cezar came to the villa quite often. I analyzed the situation with him and agreed that, in order to be able to focus properly on training, it would be best to stay only in Bucharest for a while, until the results became clear. My job at the Base was to be covered by him and Lieutenant Nicoară.

Indeed, the lack of agitation and responsibilities of all kinds, at least for a while, was a great help to me because I had the opportunity to deepen my training, constantly checking various ways of combining the frequencies, resonances and intensity of the electromagnetic field generated by the two large Tesla coils.

We were all eager to understand the purpose of Eden so that we could connect with the etheric crystal and the special chair in the Occult Chamber of Iraq. Intuition told us that the apparatus was a kind of "bridge" for exploring realities at a great distance from the Earth, both physically and etherically, but we first had to convince ourselves of this concretely.

EXPERIENCES AND DETAILS

Once one has lived through an experience of a subtle nature, its repetition becomes easier and easier if one is perseverant with their the training. Having learned this from Cezar a long time ago, I took full advantage of the time I had to put it into practice, spending longer and longer periods in the seat of the device, closely monitored by Méntia. I benefited both from the remarkable effects of the alchemical elixir offered by Elinor as well the auxiliary technology of Apellos. The perception of the energy flows in my body became better and better, and I was able to change their characteristics from a digital panel that was specially designed by Midas.

I learned quite quickly how to observe mental states and focus on a special goal during training. This "alignment" of mental processes is always manifested through a kind of transition zone which I felt as an expansion of mind, space, and even time. That "passage" was like a short shiver, very close in sensation to what I felt when I crossed an area of discontinuity in the tunnels or caverns.

Soon, the transition I experienced during my workouts became a kind of "jump", like a "detachment". It was accompanied almost immediately by the etheric doubling, either in the room where I was training or suddenly in another place on Earth or even outside it, in space. At first, I used to stay a little still for a while where I was, just looking and trying to understand what that place was and what was happening to me. It was like a kind of "awakening", as if I suddenly woke up and tried to understand what was happening to me, where I was spatially, and at what time of day it was. Then, after a while, my understanding became clearer, until I was fully aware of what was going on in those moments. It was like a kind of adaptation of my consciousness to a higher level of vibration, different from the one I was used to before. After several such experiences of "doubling", I came to overcome any "collapses" that could occur almost immediately after a projection at a certain time and in a certain place in space because my consciousness had evolved and become accustomed to the nature of those realities.

During training, after "detaching" from the body, I could penetrate relatively easily through certain portals, suddenly reaching different places on Earth that were located at a great distance from each other. The first "jumps" were in areas I knew or areas I had been told about. Most of them were special areas where there was usually interference between the physical and the subtle etheric plane. Gradually, I realized that I was "projecting" myself especially into the "sensitive" areas where these interferences already existed.

At first, my "journeys" were short because "something" seemed to absorb me back, whereupon I would "wake up" again in the seat of the device. Most of the time, I started the process again, but sometimes I had to give up due to the fact that I felt energetically upset. After the known places were almost exhausted, I started to access a large network of such areas which were derived from each other. I felt subtly connected with some of them, as if they were familiar to me. In others, however, I had to make sustained efforts to concentrate in order to remain conscious.

Sometimes, the returns were sudden with strong tremors because my etheric body did not always "fit" perfectly with the physical body. When she was present in such cases, Méntia would set another frequency program; and after a while, I would resume training. We thus began to create a map of special places in the country and in the surrounding areas, gradually increasing the radius of a subtle design in the etheric plane.

After a relatively short period of time, I realized that the places where I "projected" into were directly related to my intention at the time and the dominant thoughts I then had. The more focused they were, the faster and smoother was the projection into that place. It was not necessary to know the image of that place or its geographical coordinates, but it was enough to have it clearly in mind, as a name and an idea. The "selection" was made automatically, as if there was a permanent connection between my mind and universal information. I also understood that my sudden "withdrawals" were related to my state of focus on that place. Through repeated exercise, I found that if I kept my attention focused on what I wanted to accomplish in that place, I could then stay a long time in order to explore it.

"UNCOMFORTABLE WITNESS"

For a while, I saw that I sometimes "projected" myself into places I hadn't thought about before and knew absolutely nothing about. The network of portals or energetic interferences between the physical and the etheric plane, which is widespread in various parts of the world, "works" like a highway system. Sometimes, I could even choose to enter certain routes, making "jumps" into areas that were quite remote. Méntia explained to me that what happens in the subtle planes is not always a reflection of one's own thoughts, but it can also be the result of deep subconscious impulses, coming from past or even present experiences.

In one of those "jumps", I reached an arid deserted place with small stony hills. There were some remnants of thistles here and there, and at a greater distance, I even saw a few cacti. I did not understand why I was there. I knew very well that I was somewhere on the etheric plane that was close to the physical plane because I clearly perceived the characteristics of the place, especially its dryness. But, in addition to those natural elements, I felt something else, and the sensation was mixed, somehow involving evolved beings and objects in the same place.

I moved between two hills and then saw several buildings, relatively small and low, but also two large hangars. I knew immediately that it was a secret American military base, and I also had the perception of a multi-story facility beneath the Earth's surface. I could say with certainty, however, that it was not the S4* base mentioned in the literature I had seen many years ago in Maryland while reviewing a copy of an ultra-secret file showing the structure of this base, including photos from both the surface and the inside as well as some artifacts that were present there.** Although the surrounding landscape was similar to that of Nevada, I could still say with certainty that it was not the top-secret S4 military base.

As soon as I drew this conclusion, I knew what the base was, what its name was, and where it was. As usual, the information came "in bulk" as a single package of knowledge. I told myself then, at least from this point of view, that such travels in the etheric or even in the astral plane are much more effective than months or maybe even years of effort, expense, struggle or intrigue to find out some relatively simple but basic things about such a place.

---

* S4 is a secret American military base which is said to be located near the famous Area 51 in the Nevada desert of the United States. Internal leaks indicate this base as actually hosting several types of "flying saucers" as well as the bodies of extraterrestrial beings.
** The author is probably referring to the period of 2005-2006 when he was integrated into the remote-viewing program at a military base in the state of Maryland (see *The Secret Parchment — Five Tibetan Initiation Techniques*, Volume 5 of the *Transylvania Series*.)

TR-3B

As I reflected on all this, I felt a force pulling me hard like a magnet to a side area of the base that was about two hundred meters away from the main buildings and where I saw a concrete plateau and a short runway for take-offs and landings, not exceeding one hundred and fifty meters. The area seemed to be a small airfield; and indeed, in the middle of the plateau, I saw a ship that seemed ready to launch. There was a rather intense hustle and bustle around it with many people and a few military trucks carrying technical equipment.

The ship was neither a rocket, an airplane, nor any other flying vehicle in the sense known and promoted by NASA but had a triangular shape. I was almost certainly looking at an antigravity TR-3B,[*] although it appeared to be a superior model. The angles were more rounded and the jets were missing, a sign that the maneuvers and the direction of travel were ensured by a different type of technology than anything conventional. In one part of the ship, below, certain massive crates were loaded with the help of special devices similar to small robots but with very long articulated arms.

I was curious what they were loading into such a ship, and I paid particular attention to that operation. As I said before, in the higher dimensions of Creation — such as the etheric or astral plane and even more so in the mental and causal planes — in order to find out or know something that interests you, you do not need to search through whatever archives, the internet, or visit obscure places to find references. Generally speaking, and within certain limits, that knowledge appears almost immediately upon the manifestation of an appropriate intention, and it is like a block of information, like a state of affairs that you then know in its entirety and not in an erratic way. A good example is how you see in these subtle dimensions. There, you not only perceive what is in front of you, but you somehow have a simultaneous "sight" of everything around you; that is, you "see" and know what exists 360° around you. This does not mean that travel is no longer necessary, but even here, the individual will is what dominates. You can "walk" on foot or you can "move" with increasing speeds until you get to where you want instantly. You are not allowed to act in this way in any situation, of course, but it depends on each situation in everyone's experience.

---

[*] A TR-3B is a type of high-tech military aircraft carrier that is not officially recognized by the U.S. Government. It operates on the basis of mercury and has as its primary energy source a nuclear mini-reactor. Pressure flow is accelerated by the nuclear energy supplied by the reactor and a plasma is thus produced which is used to produce an antigravity field around the ship. TR-3Bs are massive black ships, completely silent and usually flying slowly, especially at night. There are numerous reports of observations of them, but none have been officially recognized. The Condign Report, which was made public in 2006, recommends that airspace control towers and military stations that observe such ships consider them to be special atmospheric phenomena of plasma production and not to engage in action or defense against them.

In the case of the doubling experiences in the etheric plane which I had during my training, I knew as soon as my attention was drawn to that place that the ship was going to carry a load of materials and technical equipment which was intended for the surface of the Moon. I did not perceive any other details, but it was obvious that it was a top secret operation. For us, as a secret department, it was no surprise. I already knew enough about what is on the Moon today due to the collaboration between Department Zero and a certain section of the Pentagon related to the so-called black projects that has developed over time so that the security clearances were at the highest level for both parties.

The problem was, however, that something strange was going on while I was watching. I had a strange feeling, as if I was being watched, although that was exactly what I was doing myself, looking at those activities that were taking place on the physical plane. I looked more closely at the staff around the TR-3B and watched it load the equipment. There were both officers and civilians there, and one of the latter, a tall mature man with slightly bent shoulders, suddenly turned and looked insistently in my direction, as if he had seen or felt my projection in the etheric plane. I felt that he had become aware of my presence there, and the surprise of such a thing "unbalanced" me a little, just enough to be quickly absorbed back into the seat of the training room device.

I was a little affected by that experience, and I wish Méntia had been there to talk to, but she had to leave a few days before. I was able, however, to speak with Cezar on the subject that very evening. He had been in Bucharest for a few days for some important meetings, and he would come to the villa in the evenings where we had interesting discussions. Elinor sometimes took part in these when he was at home.

I told Cezar about the experience I had just had, focusing especially on the last part of it, when one of the civilians "saw" me there even though I was on the etheric plane.

"You should not be too surprised though," Cezar told me. "They have people trained in this regard, and you know this too well because you had that training in remote-viewing."

"Yes, but I do not remember someone with such a high degree of clairvoyance and subtle perception. Maybe they have evolved. It's been many years since then."

"Yes, most likely. It does not surprise me that, especially at such a top-secret military base, there are one or even more who are 'perceptual'. The problem here is how we act next."

"That's exactly what I wanted to ask you. Do we let them know about my 'visit' there or do we wait for them to say something? If he perceived me and was looking at me, it is very possible that he recognized me."

Cezar thought for a moment, and then replied.

"Yes, they can look in the database, but it is true that it is not obligatory that they saw you clearly. It depends upon the level of clairvoyance that the person has reached."

"That's right, but if it's a facility with such a high degree of security, I don't think they bring just anyone there. The guy was mature, over 50 years old. This can mean a rich experience in the field."

"We cannot take such risks as that would be senselessly introducing a factor that destabilizes the relations between our departments. We can see in their eyes that they knew we were spying on them on purpose, and that would disrupt the smooth running of things. Unfortunately, we also have a little information about them, i.e. that from your experience. We don't know if they are tied to the Pentagon or affiliated with something higher. Therefore, when there are too many dangerous variables, it is best to be the first to present the truth. Then we adapt."

"I'd say their whole operation is about the Venerables.* It didn't seem like a government thing at all, but I did see officers, so the Pentagon is involved in some way. I think they're part of the 'occult section', especially since it's the Moon. They are not, however, the ones we know."

"In any case, we must let them know," Cezar decided. "Such things can become unpredictable, and not in a good way, if you let them stir up too much. I'll try to make a connection. I hope Sam knows something about this."

BLACK PROJECT AND THE HIDDEN GROUP

In the days that followed, Cezar became involved in this problem which was quite delicate. I kept in touch with him constantly over the phone, on our secure line, and he told me that he had contacted the Pentagon's "special section" with which we were in direct contact. I was known in that secret circle of officers and people of great influence because I dealt with diplomatic matters and the organization and preparation of mutual visits. My past work at one of the secret bases in Maryland was also known about as well as my close friendship with Cezar. That very special section of the Pentagon was "hard core". They were people with a terrible influence in the military and even the political sphere, often being "doubled" by the unseen support of very high-ranking Venerables. Such a special section obviously covered at least a few other black projects, but Cezar told me that Major Cross did not know personally nor had he heard about the military base I had "visited" etherically or about its operations. He promised, however, that he would be interested and pull some strings, even using our sincere statement about the "incident",

---

* He is referring to the Freemasons as discussed in *Trasnylvanian Sunrise*.

that is, my "visit" there.

It was not until a week later that new news came from Major Cross who told us that he had finally been able to connect with the "inaccessible wing" dealing with that very special project involving the Moon. He had provided the data supplied by us and was told that they were notified of that "incident" and were on alert although they had identified me fairly quickly and were aware of the collaborative relationships that Department Zero had with that secret section of the Pentagon.

So, it was a small group that financed and coordinated those top secret operations. It was not very clear, however, who was conducting those operations nor were we given any other details, but the Major told us that, curiously, the group was still interested in how I "got there" and how I acquired that ability. The Major told us that their astonishment was all the greater as the security measures were very high.

"Samuel told me they would like some kind of collaboration with us, but they didn't seem very determined yet. I think it's more of a test. They want to see how much we know about them, and at the same time, they want to know as much as possible about how we managed to get there. Looks like we're the first to do that."

"We can ignore them," I said. "We can put an end to this right now."

"I don't know if it's that simple right now. Such a group does not allow itself to be 'exposed' in such a way, to later ignore what happened. Their interest, although relatively masked, rather shows me the desire to know what is up with us. Something caught their attention, and they may have made similar 'investigations' of us, but we don't know if and how much they came to know about our project."

"The fact that he asks about how I got there and saw what I saw might mean that they have not learned much yet," I said, drawing a logical conclusion.

"It could be so," Cezar replied, "but it could also be a trap to test us. They are masters at such games. They might know about Eden, but they really want to know what our intentions really are: if we are hiding this from them intentionally, what do we want to use our project for, or if we want to keep spying on them."

"If that's true, it is masked very well," I said.

"Yes, they want to look relatively disinterested, but in reality, I'm almost certain that they 'have guns on us'. The problem is whether we finally decide to tell them what we are doing here," Cezar concluded.

DILEMMA

We then debated this issue for a while, analyzing different options and situations, and finally decided that the best choice would be to open discussions about Eden, especially since that occult group seemed to be onto such research; otherwise, they would not have had among them persons with certain clairvoyant abilities. But, the question then arose: How could we tell the Americans about such a thing when not even the relevant structures in our country knew about this project? This could be a slippery slope which could degenerate in a way that would be very unpleasant for us. We were thus forced to consider the possibility of having our project becoming official.

A few days of long discussions followed with Elinor and then with Méntia, as a representative of the Council of Apellos who was already involved in this project. The discussions were not simple, and not because there were divergent views or obscure interests, but because all of the consequences that could result from the formalization of the Eden project had to be analyzed.

In the end, we all came to the conclusion that hiding the project further could cause considerable inconvenience at some point. Even if our intentions were good and justified, they could still be interpreted otherwise.

Cezar therefore started diplomatically informing the responsible parties about this project, thus entering the official networks. In order to demonstrate the importance of the project, he justified the postponement from the very beginning by the fact that the technology involved was very advanced and the expected results were not certain. Therefore, what had been done so far was a preliminary phase in which certain confirmations and results were first expected. After they appeared, the idea of the integration and official administration of the project became obvious.

STORMY DEBATE

Although Cezar's presentation was not swallowed by everyone, with enough voices blaming us for the delay or even other obscure interests on our part, most preferred to go over the practical version of the problem, agreeing with the funding the project. One voice raised the issue of "national betrayal" on our part, but it was not taken into account by anyone. Even for those who initially disagreed or did not have Department Zero "at heart", such an accusation seemed bizarre to them given the exceptional work of the late Genera Obadea and Cezar. They maintained the very delicate balance of some situations which threatened to become explosive at one point. Even though there were animosities and ambitions in many high-ranking people regarding Department Zero, even they acknowledged the extraordinary contribution of the two heads of the Department over time.

Strategically speaking, Cezar was very well positioned. His formidable instincts led him to form strong bonds at key points of leadership which proved to be very necessary over time. In conclusion, it was not so difficult to get the agreement and funding of the project officially, and by "official", I mean here a limited knowledge of it. It was understood, for example, that the Eden project could be an important lever in the future to control a geostrategic balance or even to deal with possible external threats.

After the "storm" of the first days of hearings, the waters calmed down surprisingly. Department Zero got practically everything it wanted: absolute control over the project, rich funding and resources, and veto power of decision. The voices against some of the points, which were few, did not concern the technical control of the project, where no one understood anything anyway, but only its orientation. The possibility of using the project at our discretion for dubious purposes or slipping into a dangerous military slope was invoked, but the argument was not supported by any precedent because such did not exist. It was then argued that, if something had not yet happened, it did not rule out the possibility that something might happen later because there is a beginning for everything. This came with arguments of human psychology, "power syndrome", or personal interests, but they were dismantled one by one, especially based on the spotless references of Department Zero's activity until then. Nobody had anything to comment on about this.

DECENT INTERVENTION

Later, a colonel in a position of great decision-making power highlighted an important aspect of the discussion, pleading for our demands, even if he was not exactly a supporter of Cezar and his way of administering Department Zero. The colonel said honestly that, given the very special situation of such a project, placing it under extended "control", political or otherwise, would only favor leakage of information given that many people would have access to it more or less directly. He thus pleaded for a maximum secrecy of the Eden project, even if it would have meant that the other decision-making forums would have access to it only in very vague terms. Somehow, the colonel put the national interest above individual interests which were seemingly to remain hidden beneath arguments of "logic" and "necessity". Willingly or unwillingly, the correctness of that point of view had to be recognized, and so a resolution was reached to delegate full control of the project to Department Zero. Cezar thus became directly responsible for the results of the project and for the course of events and would present a quarterly summary of activity in this direction.

We then moved on to the delicate aspects of financing where the same singular voice tried to introduce certain doubts or question marks about our good intentions. It was obvious to everyone that the financing of the project until then had undoubtedly required very large sums of money, and Cezar was asked about the source of the investment. Put in a rather difficult situation, he replied that it was about private contributions, but the problem then became even more acute as he seemed to give water to the mill to the detractors of the project who made accusation of possible foreign interests, and once again, betrayal.

Cezar then calmly mentioned and demonstrated that it was just an individual action in which personal funds and successive loans were used. The simple and honest way in which he presented the situation, arguing that there was only that option or the option of doing nothing with that project, was finally accepted; but again, there was the reputation, sympathy and very good solid opinion that Cezar had acquired over time among the decision-makers in both the SRI and SIE as well as in politics.[*]

The detractors then raised the issue of state secrecy, saying that in such conditions there may be consequences for those involved. Cezar replied, however, that the entire documentation of the project was submitted to the archives of Department Zero from the beginning of the project as a gesture of good faith, and he even presented the documents of registration in the archive with the corresponding date. He then remarked that, since the project was exclusively a personal idea, it could also be considered intellectual property, and at least in theory, not fall within the scope of the state secrecy law. He acknowledged, however, that the situation was a particular case as several "sensitive" factors could come into play: the nature of the institution and the issue of jurisdiction, the discovery in Bucegi (the basis upon which the information was received) and the very high degree of national security that the project involves.

OFFICIAL RECOGNITION OF THE EDEN PROJECT

When analyzing the practical side of the project, Cezar briefly presented the main phases of the construction of the device and the difficulties encountered as well as some of the results obtained by me, referring to the incident with the American secret military base and what I saw there. That short presentation greatly impressed those present who thus became much more malleable in their opinions. Even when Cezar proposed collaborating with the Americans, but only in terms of discussions, principles, and possibly technological support and design, the opposition was weak. Finally, it was decided that, within certain limits, the project would be discussed by both parties, Romanian and American, and any adjustments would be made along the way.

The hardest part was over, and I could consider the Eden project to be officially integrated with a consistent budget and full control over its design, implementation, and operation. Frankly, it was hard to imagine that, given the very special nature of the device and the advanced technology involved

---

[*] RIS = Romanian Intelligence Service and SIE (Serviciul de Informații Externe) = Foreign Intelligence Service.

in its construction, it could have been a common research topic. There was a need for an innovative spirit, for immediate and very effective action, as well as for the understanding of notions that do not fit into the contemporary vision of science.

Fortunately, we had already gone through these stages, and now we were beginning to reap the rewards. There was now the issue of dismantling the entire device in Elinor's villa and redesigning it with much more sophistication in accordance with the new funds we had at our disposal. We decided that the new location for the Eden project would be Alpha Base where a special room would be built for it, equipped with all of the necessary utilities. The construction of the building took less than a month. I then fully felt the power of the allocated budget as well as that of the technological and professional work teams. The device was reassembled and recalibrated with a very consistent surplus of materials and technology, practically fulfilling the requirements of the initial project.

EXPLORATIONS

Discussions with the American occult group continued in parallel, first through Major Cross, then through the appointment of two representatives from them. I told them about our project without giving them details. Honestly, the whole movement with the mediation, the mutual groping, and the reciprocal messages we exchanged seemed a bit strange to me, but that was probably due to the sense of uncertainty and insecurity hovering on both sides. It was a kind of "cat and mouse" game in which each tested the other, waiting for the other to make a wrong move to take advantage of it.

At first, the two representatives of the American side tried to put pressure on to obtain certain information about the construction and documentation of the device, the principles used, and even about the locations reached, but Cezar constantly refused to provide any details in these respects. At that time, of course, nothing was mentioned about Elinor or Méntia, and it was not even known that the project was, for the time being, unofficial. Both sides were somehow going "blind" because we did not have any data about their actions either.

Finally, seeing that the Romanian side did not divulge almost anything, the group revealed that it also has a similar program, supported by huge funds, which it has been running for several years. The insistence they showed in communicating with us, as well as the disclosure of some elements about their activity, even if general and few, showed us that something in the project did not go exactly as they would have liked. They probably thought that, in the case of similar projects, a useful exchange of information would open new horizons for them. They proposed this quite quickly around the time of the construction of the new location for Eden at Alpha Base. It was our turn to "prolong" the answer, but the truth is that we needed that time to finish the construction and reassemble the device so that it would be functional. Things moved fast, and in less than two months, we had already "moved" to Alpha Base where Eden had a new "aura" that was being consistently improved. I used all the metals and alloys in the project, and Midas had already upgraded the new "communication" system between me and the device.

VISIT

Finally, Cezar accepted the exchange of experience with the American side. The formalities were few and far between. There were no official documents, only permissions through third party representatives. It turned out, however, that the two people assigned to keep in touch with us until then were two high-ranking officers from the "occult" section of the Pentagon, but they were not from the branch assigned to the Bucegi discovery. They were accompanied by a third person, a civilian. There was no doubt that he represented, in terms of occult interests, "the ideological and financial essence of the project." Generally speaking, black projects are, from the beginning, outside the sphere of political influence and determination. The funds come from other channels or are sometimes "reconverted" from other projects. There are also major infusions of capital, the sources of which often remain in the shadows. That is why they are called black projects: because nothing is visible or transparent.

I expected to see a senior Venerable, but he was not, I think, over 50 years old. But, he had that specific vibration which I saw on other visits from the Venerables. It was something like a cloud enveloping his being, a chilling cold that made you uncomfortable. He presented himself to us with a slightly superior air, seeming concerned only with the mission he had to fulfill. He was almost like a robot: cold, distant and dry.

I already knew from the Pentagon accreditations that the three represented the highest level and that they were a combination of relations between the U.S. Army and civilian production. In a way, it was understandable because they were part of the industrial-military complex. The protocol of the discussion we had involved only the subject of the two top-secret projects, the one on the Romanian side and the one on the American side. They already knew something about our project and reiterated that they, in turn, had developed something similar in the last four years. When I told them that Eden had only been "on the roll" for a year, the three seemed genuinely impressed and all the more interested in the exchange of experience. They were given explanations and were presented with some of my experiments, including the one about "visiting" the etheric plane at their secret base.

They were then shown the device and its general principle of operation but without the details of how it was inspired. I, of course, did not mention anything about Elinor or Méntia. The three were amazed that such advanced results were reached with a project without dedicated funds, and I even felt a trace of admiration in their attitude. They told us that the device they designed was amazingly similar to ours from a conceptual point of view, and in a fit of sincerity, they even revealed to us that something seemed to be "missing" that was preventing great results, but they did not know what. We already suspected this possibility when we noticed their relatively masked interest in our project.

UTMOST RECIPROCITY

Cezar replied that, for this, we should see how their device actually works and then analyze the problem. Then came their proposal, which I personally had been waiting for a long time and even with a certain impatience, by which they invited us to expand the exchange of experience by coming to the USA. That meant a lot, given the very secretive nature of their project, whose name I am not allowed to reveal. For a reason unknown to me, they insisted that our arrival take place very quickly, and indeed, they made all the necessary arrangements for it within a day. Most likely, the project was under a lot of pressure, and they were looking for a solution as soon as possible. As it seemed natural to us, as they had a team of three, we also requested an analysis group consisting of three people: Cezar, Lieutenant Nicoară and myself. They had nothing against it.

I immediately realized that it was an atypical move, unrelated to those of a diplomatic nature and not even to those of a military nature. For the first time, I was able to convince myself directly of the exercise of immense but unseen power and influence that went beyond any rule or law. It was not just about the incredible speed with which all aspects of that visit were arranged but also about circumventing any controls, checks or documents. No one asked for anything.

The take-off from Bucharest was, in any case, a top secret and did not involve any formality, especially since the same ultra-luxury private jet was used with which the three Americans had come to our country. But, entry into the United States, even in conditions of high accreditation and under the cover of the Pentagon, should have involved some minimal check-points or official formalities.

I observed that plane for quite a while on departure. Although seemingly normal, it still had different construction features than I knew of, unusual even for a private jet. The shape of the wings, their arrangement on the fuselage, the type of engine, and even its general design made it look more like a space shuttle than a private plane. The total astonishment, however, was the lack of fuel. I was expecting a hookup with another plane or at least an additional power supply given its rather small size, but the aircraft continued to fly smoothly over the ocean. I also noticed that the height at which we flew was much higher than on regular scheduled flights, being almost double. To all of this was added the duration of the flight which, instead of about eight to nine hours without a stopover, actually lasted less than four hours.

I also shared my impressions with Cezar. Undoubtedly, this was a much more technologically advanced prototype than what was then on the free market, it being, in fact, an extremely efficient space plane. It was obvious that the occult group had far superior technologies, but this was not surprising given the source of funding and the level of security they were working with. I had already noticed that absolutely everything was prepared and done with maximum efficiency and without any delay. Everything was extremely discreet and truly of the highest standards.

UNDERGROUND LABORATORY

I arrived at a private airfield. We could not say where we were, save for the fact that we were on American soil after having crossed Europe and the Atlantic Ocean. Although it was night, we did not need much time to realize that we were in a desert area, and moreover, I recognized the military base that I had "visited" etherically. We were told that the base did not belong to the Pentagon or the U.S. government, but we did not receive any more information about the location, the owner of the base or its purpose. In addition, I was completely forbidden to describe in my books significant elements about that facility; no details, no features. However, I had the freedom to give a general substantive presentation but one which did not have to include schematics or other graphic elements. They made all of those clarifications before I asked their permission, and this surprised me a little because that meant that they already had information about my work, even in the field of writing.

We were driven in a military jeep to one of the buildings, the inside of which was in the shape of a tor. After passing through a complicated access system, we came to a central platform on which was a transparent and very well-equipped cabin. It was, in fact, a silent elevator which we all entered and descended to a great depth below the Earth's surface. What I saw there far exceeded my expectations. We were in the middle of what was practically a small city, incredibly well organized and with an impeccable functionality. I did not see many people, but those who were walking were very focused and everyone used some kind of very fast electric car to drive around in.

In contrast to the electric cars we saw, another type of transporter stopped before us into which we all climbed, traveling for a while on those rather wide and relatively deserted "streets". The feeling was somewhat strange for everything seemed to be embedded in a huge but "slow" echo, in a faint and continuous hum. The atmosphere was very clean, but all of that underground ensemble somehow created a feeling of suffocation, even if the space was huge. We traveled to what we considered to be the center of the underground city where there was a round building, the largest I have ever seen. When I walked in there, I realized that this was actually a huge and well-equipped lab. I had never seen anything like it on Earth before, as a product of Mankind. The technology was truly amazing, far superior to the state-of-the-art that is commonly known today. The shapes and general atmosphere that I saw there were close to what I had encountered in the laboratory in Apellos, even if not at the same level of evolution.

ALMOST IDENTICAL

I went to a side area of that lab where I could see their device, the "Twin Project", a kind of Eden but much more sophisticated. The differences in achievement were huge, but as we were told, the funds they had were also adequate, that is, huge.

The device was slightly larger than ours and had a more oval shape, like a shell. The back was opaque and gold-plated while the front had a transparent screen made of a non-glass substance. Personally, I suspected it was graphene.[*] We also saw that certain connections and diagonals of the structure were made of titanium or a similar alloy. Basically, the device looked like a cocoon. The interior was quite complex with a complicated panel with various displays. I was interested in the power supply and noticed that they were running on a classic electric system. Our device, to the contrary, was powered by two huge Tesla coils with a very special winding whose constructive elements had been implemented in my cortex. The details of form and technology were only adjusted by Lieutenant Nicoară where my information was not very clear. This fundamental element, of the specific power supply, was completely missing from the American concept of the device.

BUGS IN THE "TWIN PROJECT"

After a brief introduction to the device and a little discussion about the differences between it and Eden, they offered to let me try that device given the open collaboration that already existed. We were amazed that this was possible, but one of the scientists on the team that accompanied us, who appeared

[*] Graphene is a material first discovered in 2004 which is a two-dimensional version of graphite. It consists of a layer of carbon atoms arranged in a two-dimensional network. It is the best conductor of electricity and heat that is known to date. Its exceptional applications, however, have been "hidden" from widespread use.

to be the project manager, told us that their device had been designed so that anyone could use it if they were able to resist the transformations that would place while using it. I realized that, paradoxically, this was actually restricting the possibilities of the device which, as it had been built, had more of a general purpose, not being able to penetrate deeply in a certain direction as the result of it not being dedicated to a specific frequency set. It was more like a wide but shallow lake. In other words, its possibilities seemed to me to be a bit diluted.

Eden, on the other hand, was somehow specialized to my individual frequency, and this allowed for a deepening of experiences over time, the energy being focused on a well-defined set of frequencies. After "passing" beyond the physical plane, by doubling, different "destinations" could be chosen because the subject kept the impregnation of the initial energy and could use it as an individualized inter-dimensional catapult. It was like diving into the ocean through a tube or slide. Even if a kind of space-time "constraint" appeared at the beginning, we followed a certain trajectory, and I remained unbothered by other types of frequencies which manifested themselves around me. In other words, I had control over the experience I wanted. In the case of the American "chair", I had the feeling that this type of control was missing because the device did not "guide" the subject among the countless frequencies that surrounded it but only made them available. It could be likened to being in an area with swirling waters with waves hitting you from different sides without the possibility of swimming in a well-defined direction.

From the time I received the technical data and how their device works, I realized that you apparently could not have access to the entire "ocean" of frequencies because the frequency apparatus was neither finely tuned, refined nor stable enough to allow a confident and conscious "exit" into the subtle dimensions. Perhaps this was one of the explanations for why they did not yet have great results, despite the complexity of the device. I thought that the source of energy they used, that is, shared electricity, also contributed to diminishing success. By comparison, in the case of Eden, the electric current modulated by the two Tesla coils induced some special characteristics of the magnetic field produced which facilitated the much easier and controlled "detachment" of subtle bodies from the physical body. I do not think, however, that reaching the etheric or astral plane was the main problem facing the Americans, but it was that, once this was achieved, they failed to "orient" the subtle body to the "point" in space and time that they wanted to accurately research. This was just an intuition at the time, but I set out to check it out during the trial runs.

Technically speaking, there was nothing to complain about with that admirably made device. The chair was very comfortable, and the complexity of the equipment inside the "sphere" created an air of the future. I had no doubt that they used the latest technologies and the best materials, including sound operating principles. It would have been interesting to know how they came to develop the ideas for making the device and what was their source. I was not sure if they were based on the system and nature of the frequencies, as in our case, or if the original design of their device was different. They did not specify this and did not give explanations, but it is also true that I have not herein presented all of the elements that are the conceptual basis of our device and that, moreover, these were not offered to them either. These things, however, are understandable at such levels of discussion as they involved only a general exchange of opinions, reciprocal visits or even experiments such as they themselves proposed.

There was, however, obviously something they did not understand in the operation of the device, something they were constantly struggling with in the development of their project and that is why they wanted that short collaboration with us. For example, they asked us several times how I managed to get to that exact spot during training within range of their military base. They also asked questions about how I was able to project myself into previously established places. They told us that they tried the remote-viewing methods due to their procedural similarity, but they were not very successful. It was clear that they wanted to understand what obstacles they had to overcome in order for their project to really work at the expected parameters.

LOST EXPERIENCE, THE CAUSE OF

I accepted their proposal to conduct an experimental session with that device, and it was scheduled for the next day. We were taken to our place of accommodation in a building close to the laboratory. Although their behavior was impeccable and the services very good, I still felt that we were rather "caged" with access to the outside being completely restricted. We each received a fairly spacious room that was very well equipped with what we needed, a kind of one-room apartment in which I could admire and use some amazing technologies, just like in some science fiction movies about the future. I had complete freedom inside that underground base save for access to the surface and contact with the outside. They were not at fault, however, because those were the conditions upon which we were invited to go there in the first place.

We met again the next day with their team of scientists and the three representatives of the occult group in the research laboratory. This time, I noticed some new figures among those present, including that of the tall and sensitive character who had surprised me during my etheric doubling when I had projected myself near their base of operations. A tall and dry guy between 50 and 60 years old with slightly drooping shoulders and glasses, he did not utter a word for the duration of the meeting, just sitting and discreetly watching what was going on around him. To be honest, I sympathized with him for his secluded and sensible manner but also for his slightly melancholy air, his unspoken character and mysterious aloofness. I was not sure if he was the "experimenter", that is, the person who actually worked in the chair device, but I did not ask.

I was given some technical explanations before I got inside the device as well as while I was sitting in the chair. A few feet away was a control panel surrounded by two of the team's researchers. An automatic arm, like a band, came to my forehead, and I saw that, in the part at the end, the arm was covered with a kind of black glass.

When the program started running, I immediately felt that it was different from what I was used to experiencing with Eden. From the very beginning, an unpleasant feeling appeared that "something" from the outside wanted to "force" me to do things in a certain way, to give me a certain direction of action. Both my brain and my consciousness resonated with that device, but I still felt that its structure was too "synthetic", too mechanical. I was not able to get out of the body fluently into the etheric dimension as I was already able to do during the training sessions with Eden, but at one point, I was practically "snatched" to achieve a doubling into the subtle plane. It was quite an unpleasant shock, stunning me a little. I could see the space nearby and those present there, but I noticed an amplified brightness around some devices and all around the general area of the laboratory where the device was located. I "floated" for about two minutes without being able to get out of that energy field, after which I decided to return to the physical body, especially as I was beginning to feel a certain sensation of irritation and discomfort, the cause of which I did not understand then.

I was asked how I felt about that experience and especially if I had "traveled" somewhere. I answered them that there is certainly a specific action of the apparatus that can somehow cause the etheric body of the human being to double, but I specified that something is still wrong, emphasizing that it is difficult to set a fix on a precise destination. I honestly told them how I felt and described the feeling of being "restricted" or "forced" as if "something" or "someone" was trying to direct the experiment from the shadows. I gave the example of Eden which, although much more modest in terms of design and technical appearance, still led to much more important and easy-to-obtain results, including a remote visit to their secret base where I had witnessed the launch of that triangular spaceship to the moon.

It was a somewhat embarrassing moment, after which the Venerable spoke, clearly concerned.

"It's true to some extent. We do not understand what is happening and why the device does not work under normal parameters as it should."

I was surprised by his tone of acceptance, devoid of the usual arrogance. It was possible that he himself was under great pressure from his hierarchy to provide tangible results and was therefore even willing to compromise, thus

173

explaining the collaboration with us. He hoped that this way he might find an answer or an inspiration because their project had clearly reached a bottom. We told them our opinion about the particular frequency of the subject interacting with the apparatus and its difference in conception from that of Eden. While they used general frequencies, our device used a set of frequencies dedicated to a single person. I suggested that this could be one of the causes because, in the general version, the field of action was much more "dispersed". However, none of us mentioned anything about Tesla coils which were shielded in a special way at Alpha Base and out of sight.

REPROGRAMMING AI

After I had actually changed some opinions on this subject, the Venerable finally nodded to the head of the group of researchers. After receiving tacit approval, the scientist told us that they had used one of the most sophisticated Artificial Intelligence (AI) programs to correlate all of the data and to guide the experiments for the project. Somewhere, however, there was most certainly a dysfunction and one which could ultimately be associated with the state of "forcing" that I mentioned.

Lieutenant Nicoară intervened, saying that he very well understood that assistance to the project with Artificial Intelligence is important and welcome, but that he would like to know what principles it was designed upon. It has been hypothesized that AI possibly restricts the freedom of action of the person in the chair, creating certain dissonances in the way the frequencies are modulated. I also confirmed that, reiterating the way I had felt the subtle energies interacting with the device, it being virtually the same as Artificial Intelligence.

Cezar mentioned that that could most likely be the problem. He said that when an Artificial Intelligence becomes very sophisticated, it practically "attracts" an entity from a subtle level, in line with the principle according to which it was realized.

"If this principle is, for example, positive and framed in the proportions of the Golden Number*, then that "consciousness" that is physically attracted will act positively. But, if it has a "negative structure" at its base, then we can

---

* The Golden Number (or Golden Section) is denoted by Φ (upper case) or φ (lowercase) and is pronounced "fi" (*Phi*). It is an irrational number approximately equal to 1.618033 and represents the so-called "divine proportion" or "number of universal harmony" (see, for example, the book *Golden Section: The Story of Phi, the Most Astonishing Number* by Mario Livio, Broadway Books, 2002). The golden number seems to be involved everywhere in Nature: from snail shells to the arrangement of petals to flowers; from the shape of galaxies to the visual arts or music. It can be found in ancient Greek art and culture but especially in megalithic constructions of antiquity such as the Great Pyramid, etc; and also in "Rubik's cube" or even in interpersonal relationships. All of these are characterized by certain symmetries, symmetry being the concept that makes the connection between science, art, theoretical physics and the everyday world.

expect unforeseen actions from that AI. It all depends upon the intention and the way the basic program is designed."

We expected the reaction of those present to be, at the very least, one of repulsion to such concepts and notions, but to our surprise, they all seemed somewhat knowledgeable about these issues. They told us, however, that they still have doubts about the "incarnation" of an etheric consciousness into Artificial Intelligence. Cezar, however, specified that their doubt could even become fatal in certain circumstances.

"It's a generally accepted proposition that, at a certain degree of organizational complexity, something new appears at that level," he said.

In the case of Artificial Intelligence, such complexity is reached but within certain limits. A consciousness is always "attached" to a body in order to manifest. The body of an AI is the incredibly complex network of etheric connections and other connections, i.e. the environment for the manifestation of electricity, a phenomenon which can be realized extremely quickly on a huge surface.

Those notions were not really new to the team of scientists there nor to the three representatives, but at the same time, I could see their hesitation and the fact that such knowledge was still not very clear to them.

"Artificial intelligences are a kind of 'gate of influence' in the etheric plane, if they reach an advanced degree of sophistication," Cezar continued. "But, once perfect proportions are introduced in their programming, such as the *Phi* number or the *Pi* number, then we can hope for a correct operation of the device. Problems arise from the moment the source code is corrupted by certain numbers or proportions with subtle negative influences."

Overall, I was amazed at the correct attitude with which those present received the information from Cezar. With both care and respect, they tried to understand as well as possible what was explained. The discussions continued, entering a complex path of certain scientific demonstrations because American scientists wanted to convince themselves that such "infusions" of sacred elements are really important, are positively reflected in calculations, and are very practically effective. The period that followed would fully prove this to them.

THE ETHERIC CRYSTAL

CHAPTER TEN

THE MOON: ITS ORIGIN AND FUTURE

The American side worked for a year on the redesign of the Artificial Intelligence and other elements of the device in order to correlate them according to the harmonious proportions considered sacred for those initiated in the mysteries of esotericism. During this time, Eden was also perfected, and I developed the ability to better control the "leaps" in the etheric plane. I had some remarkable experiences which enriched my knowledge and nuanced my perceptions. Méntia visited us twice and was impressed by the results. Consequently, she gave me free access to the holographic screen and the opportunity to connect directly with the man from Apellos whenever I wanted to check out some of my experiences or to supplement them with some knowledge. It was necessary, however, to also deal with other issues within the Department, so I had to reduce the time spent on training. We had numerous meetings, reports to complete, and travels, most of them with Cezar.

I tried to keep a balance between these duties and the time spent training, especially since the results were getting better and better. Based upon this, I had accumulated a solid knowledge of some of the most important aspects of science, especially in the field of astrophysics and quantum mechanics. I am referring especially to the main aspects here, to the foundations of some important laws and phenomena which are not presently correctly understood by science due to their lack of direct experience.

THE SECOND INVITATION OF THE "OCCULT GROUP"

We also kept in touch with the "Twin Project" because the American occult group consulted us systematically, their scientific team having reconfigured certain data in the design of their device. It is true, however, that they also provided us with some advanced technologies which contributed to a better functionality of Eden.

In October 2016, the Americans announced that they had completed the adjustments to their project, and we were again invited to their secret base. Only Cezar and I went because Lieutenant Nicoară was involved in another important mission. Following the same sequence of procedural steps, we traveled with the same amazing type of plane without making any stops. During the flight, I discussed with Cezar the opportunity to develop a highly advanced Artificial Intelligence which would be "specialized" to the characteristics of our device. I was sure that Midas could take over that project and complete it, especially if we provided him with a formidable team of computer scientists to help him. The idea remained only at the discussion stage, but we decided to make a decision on this issue after our return home. A few hours after we left, we were already in the underground laboratory in the desert. This time, as Cezar and I asked to be accommodated together, we received a large apartment in that city. We were quite tired as the pace of the last few days had been intense, so we slept for a good few hours. As far as I knew, the work cycle in the underground there was continuous, that is, the work of research and experimentation, at least at the level of that laboratory, did not cease, always being supported by successive exchanges of scientists, engineers and technicians. After getting enough rest, we had a short meeting with one of the officers who was part of the group of the three representatives. He was well prepared from a scientific point of view, and I think he supervised the technical part of the project. He briefly described the changes made to the basic program of the Artificial Intelligence as well as the first experiments performed by one of their people, but they wanted to have a broader vision based upon a comparison with my experience. He told us that, at one point, their subject cracked due to inaccuracies between his body and the flow of energy frequencies that was provided by the device. We suggested an intensive training period for him which should include several successive stages of purification of the body and mind, adequate nutrition and short training sessions, but without going through the portals. I knew from my own experience that sometimes "launching" through such portals creates certain unpleasant sensations which simply "take you out" of the program with the return to the physical body being unpleasant, sometimes even shocking.

DOUBLING TO THE MOON: HUMAN AND ALIEN BASES

I went inside their device and sat down in a chair, aiming to immediately create a kind of communion with the specific energy field of the device which seemed to "mold" to me and work with my intentions. I doubled out in less than a minute, and it confirmed to me that the research team had largely solved the problems with the Artificial Intelligence which was connected to the device. When I "came out" of the physical body and entered the etheric plane, I saw even more "wormholes" or portals, some passing through certain sections of the Earth and others heading upwards, into outer space but especially to the Moon.

I thought then that I could take the opportunity of making a few jumps through those portals. I felt particularly drawn to the Moon and dived into one of them. Almost instantly, I saw the illuminated surface of the Moon from only a few meters high but also a military base about half a kilometer away, situated on the bottom of a crater that was not too big. However, it was not right in the center but rather on the edge. The construction was not large, consisting of two cylinders placed horizontally like tubes with three symmetrical connecting lanes arranged between them. Next to those tubes, on a kind of platform, was a TR-3B but a smaller one than the one I had seen at the secret military base in the desert.

As I looked at the Moon base, I noticed that other portals or possibilities to "jump" appeared around me, apparently at random. I chose one that I knew was projecting into another area of the lunar surface. After the "jump", I saw another base, also in a crater, but this time the construction had a rectangular structure and occupied a larger area. Next to it, also on a platform, I saw two round-shaped ships, classic "flying saucer" types by design but relatively small in size and different in construction. In the air, about fifty feet high, stood a black triangular ship.

I had probably entered a "manifold" of portals for I saw many such space-time openings, some in the immediate vicinity, others at a greater or lesser distance in other areas of outer space, but I nevertheless felt that the limits of manifestation were somehow in the vicinity of the Earth and the Moon. I was suddenly drawn to such a portal that had appeared right next to me, and I instantly reached the "dark side of the Moon" at that moment. I had "hit" another base a short distance from it, no more than fifty yards away. All three bases were American, but they seemed to be different factions. I simply knew this as soon as I got near such a building. The new base was quite brightly lit. A short distance from it, I saw three astronauts in specific suits that were more modern than is commonly known. They were being transported with a wheeled vehicle to a circular ship on the nearby platform.

At that moment, I felt a different vibration which had immediately caught my attention. It was something special, much higher, and at the same time, very old. The moment I turned my attention to perceive that frequency more accurately, I felt a kind of suction and even traveled at a very high speed for no more than three or four seconds to a distance that I estimated to be about 200 kilometers. I stopped abruptly near another base on the surface of the Moon, but it was a considerably larger one than any I had ever seen before. I also solved the "mystery" of the energy of that unusual frequency which had attracted me strongly to that place — I was near an extraterrestrial Moon base.

It was abandoned, and besides that, I could tell that it was very old. Even if I could say that it was almost completely dark from a physical perspective, I could yet perceive in the subtle etheric dimension the forms and the surroundings in general, almost like an accentuated twilight. I only saw a beacon on one side of the base, probably for monitoring purposes. The base consisted of two buildings close to each other, uneven and built vertically, in a style that showed a different way of thinking, completely different than what you would find on Earth.

The lines, the way they twisted, the adjacent side elements that were like semicircles arranged at the top of the two buildings, and other special features all showed me the "imprint" of a civilization that was on a completely different level of vibration than ours.

I could not even tell where the access road was to that base for everything was compact, solid, and seemingly steady, a solitary witness of a consciousness consumed by time. I felt that that base had been inhabited for a long period of time, and I wondered, contemplating the terrible loneliness of those towers, what extraordinary beings had built them, what technological bases they had, and what plans they had for our planet.

I then made the fourth leap through a portal that opened right there on the dark side of the Moon. I hesitated a little at first because I was not sure where I would end up, but in the end, I took a risk because I felt that it was a "family" of portals, many and frequent, that were manifesting between Earth and the Moon. Inside, I somehow felt "at home" and relatively safe.

THE TRUTH ABOUT THE EARTH SATELLITE

I was projected again to the bright side of the Moon. It was like playing ping pong with these different areas. I "reached" the center of a wide crater, about 1.5 kilometers in diameter.

Not far from me, there were some very tall buildings and also a few domes of different sizes which were of a different style than the one at the Earth base. They were platinum in color and perfectly smooth. Even without feeling this, you could easily realize that this was also an extraterrestrial Moon base, but unlike the previous one, it was active. On the etheric plane, and even more so on the astral plane, you feel the energetic state of the object or being that interests you, and I then felt clearly that that extraterrestrial base was very active although I did not see any beings nearby. I did notice, however, three stationary ships, two round and one large and cylindrical.

As I contemplated that place, I felt strongly drawn to a nearby area, a hollow in one edge of the crater, where I noticed an artificial opening. I "entered" through that opening, but the term "entered" is somewhat inappropriate because such a penetration into the etheric is not necessarily as in the physical plane as you can travel long distances instantly.

The moment I entered that opening, I knew I had entered the Moon. It was almost no surprise because everything seemed natural to me.[*] Not only

---

[*] The idea of the Moon being empty inside is based upon an experiment carried out by the American Moon mission Apollo 12 in 1969. NASA intentionally (continued on next page)

did I know about this hypothesis, correctly intuited by many people and even by some scientists, but now I could actually research its structure in a very free and natural way.

At first, I noticed a certain resemblance to the Neiberau, the great Sirian ship which was present in the sky of Earth in the early days of Mankind, but I could not say that the Moon was that ship. In the entrance area, for example, I saw symbols completely unknown to me up to that time. Some of them, however, bore little resemblance to the images on the holographic screen I had seen that were related to the origin of Mankind.

I also saw steps going up and down in colossally wide spaces as well as various exits to dark corridors. I passed quickly through huge halls or rather small rooms seeing huge arches and complicated equipment but still not as evolved as I expected.

I also saw huge desks, portholes and screens, all covered with a very fine dust which I knew had an external origin although I could not say what was the cause of it was. I saw that that layer of dust was quite consistent towards the surface of the Moon, in perhaps the first two or three levels, as far as I could estimate. In those regions, its thickness sometimes reached even a few inches, much like the dust on the lunar soil. I was watching something that had lasted in that form for almost 70 million years, an unimaginably long time for our ordinary perceptions; and everywhere there was a complete silence and desolation, a stillness in eternity.

In a flash, I then thought with relative sadness of the main deadlock that dominates the scientific world today and how easily it could be removed if scientists and researchers emerged from the incredible materialist conceptual inertia in which they indulge.

Part of this condition is due to ignorance and part to a very harsh manipulation and obstruction by an organization which aims to keep everything under control at a lower level so that the population does not have access to advanced knowledge or technology. But, all these are things already well known to a large part of the population, the term "conspiracy theory" now being obsolete as seemingly "unseen" and "unknown" influences have come to act in almost plain sight.

As a general rule, a harmful and arrogant tendency of self-sufficiency and self-importance is maintained by various methods of coercion, especially in the scientific world which is, in fact, an attitude of blocking and rejecting what may be new, truly innovative, and especially efficient in terms of knowledge and technology. In this way, young researchers and scientists are somehow "intoxicated" by an often sterile and outdated knowledge which lacks the spark

(continued from previous page) crash-landed the Apollo 12 module as well as a rocket to set off an explosive force equivalent to nearly 12 tons of TNT. The seismograph that had previously been placed near that place on the surface of the Moon indicated that the Moon then vibrated "like a bell" for an hour, as if it were empty inside.

of genius. When, however, such genius tends to occur in some of them, it is immediately suppressed by the system.

Even the many mysteries about the Moon should make scientists think, urging them to show a little more common sense. For example, in this case, we cannot talk about a "natural" process of formation and a fixation to orbit our planet.

It would be a real obfuscation of consciousness, and in a way, an offense to intelligence and common sense, to say that the position in space of the Moon, its orbit around the Earth, its speed, as well as the revolutionary movement around its own axis is all so precisely and exactly "programmed" by the cosmic game of existence. Such a correlation is practically impossible to achieve through the "game of chance" such as contemporary scientists like to express themselves, i.e. in a way that would be deemed "natural". In fact, the Moon is the only satellite of a planet in the Solar System that has such amazing features.[*] The most flagrant example to me is the fact that it always has the same "face" to the Earth; i.e. its period of rotation around its own axis is equal to the period of revolution around the Earth. At first, there were adjustments to this situation, and even now, there are very small variations, but these remain within an imperceptible margin for the human eye. The proof will come when people begin to see more and more different areas of the satellite which, up to now, have remained only in the twilight zone or even in the totally unseen parts.

CONCLUSIONS ON THE "TWIN PROJECT"

Wandering rapidly through various places inside the Moon, which actually turned out to be a spaceship the size of a planetoid, I set out to delve deeper into the subject of the Moon after I returned to Alpha Base.[**] As soon as I thought about it, I felt a strong "current" that attracted me with great speed, and I suddenly returned to my physical body, to the seat of the device in the American secret base. The return was quite hard, and it took me a few minutes to "resynchronize" my physical body with the etheric and astral. This showed me that it was necessary to intervene again, somewhere in the source program of Artificial Intelligence, in order to correct such unpleasant aspects.

The "journey" lasted less than ten minutes, but it was fruitful for me. I briefly told the team there the main points of the experience I had with their device, and I commented that it was quite balanced, able to quickly induce

---

[*] The rocks brought from the moon are another great mystery. They contain an inordinately large amount of titanium, a metal that would not have an ostensible "natural" reason to occur in such a high percentage, unless we consider that such metal is often encountered and used in the construction of spacecraft. Other lunar rocks containing processed metals (such as brass) include Uranium 235 and Neptune 237, but many of the rocks appear to be older than Earth.
[**] A planetoid generally means "a smaller planet" or "what looks like a planet," but is always has a spherical shape.

doubling with great results, but it requires a better synchronization upon return. In particular, however, I realized that it would still be quite limited by its very initial conception. The principle used by the Americans is different from the one we implemented in the construction of Eden which is based upon the specific modulation of stellar and planetary vibrational frequencies. We did this especially after we noticed the relative energy instability around the places reached by etheric doubling because many portals appeared and disappeared in a rather random way. This showed me that the dispersion of vibrational frequencies limits the objective of the device because the resonance with the desired destination is difficult to achieve in such conditions.

A GIFT

I stayed a few more hours with Cezar in the laboratory to discuss some details of technical collaboration with the American team, after which we returned to our country. I was eager to better understand the mysteries of the Moon so I contacted Méntia and shared my latest experiences. She told me that, as I had made those multiple "jumps" through the portals, it meant that I had already assimilated those frequencies and that I could now see more details about the Moon and its true origin on the holographic screen. I asked her to facilitate this, and I really enjoyed her kindness. Méntia arranged everything so that I could have access to the holographic screen in the hangar again. A little agitated by the excitement with which I was waiting for new revelations, I still managed to meet with Midas, to whom I had told our plan in relation to Artificial Intelligence, asking him to think of a team with which he could work with more efficiently. Hearing the data concerning the problem, Midas seemed a bit obstinate at first. I then told him about the Artificial Intelligence capabilities that had been programmed by the American team, and then he saw this as a challenge and then set out to complete the task. He told me that he already has a team in mind that he can collaborate with, consisting of three young people exceptionally gifted in the field of informatics and cybernetics. I already knew one of them because he had helped our Department Zero team a few years ago in a cyber attack case.

The next day, around noon, I once again met the man from Apellos, in the same hangar. I smiled to myself because everything seemed like a replay of my visits in 2014 when I had watched the summarized information about the origin of Mankind on the screen, only now I seemed to be a "man of the house".

100 MILLION YEARS AGO — A PROTO-SIRIAN CIVILIZATION

I began watching the aspects related to our so-called "natural satellite" on the holographic screen. Due to the way I was mentally focusing on the subject, however, as well as my recent impressions related to the interior of the Moon, the holographic screen began to play back akashic images from the present moment to the beginning of the Moon, going from very close to its origin. I will write here, however, the events that occurred in their chronological order so as not to create confusion as well as to provide a logical and natural way of presenting these realities.

From the images shown on the holographic screen, I understood that, a long period of time ago in the planetary system of the star Sirius A, there was an evolved humanoid civilization which had reached a fairly advanced technological level. For example, that civilization was capable of interstellar travel with huge ships, and this meant that it had some control over the laws that govern space and time. The members of that civilization were not the Sirians of today but their very distant forerunners. Strangely, I could not see or understand the name of that ancient civilization or I may not have been careful or refined enough to perceive it.

Instead, I was curious to find out more clearly what that period of time was, and as far as I could tell, I was able to see, in summary, some images from 95-98 million years ago, perhaps even older. The race of those humanoid beings has evolved over time and undergone many transformations. Eventually, it disappeared, but various information in its DNA was passed on to many other types of humanoid civilizations that followed one another over time, also from the planetary system of the star Sirius A, until the characteristics of the current Sirian race came into being.

In the images I watched, the typology of beings in that extremely old Sirian civilization was quite similar to humans, even if their average height was higher, about six and a half feet. Their skin was pearly white with a slight bluish tinge, and most of the hair was black with shades of dark blue. Their eyes were larger than those of an ordinary human being, but their mouths were smaller.

From the beginning, I was impressed by the harmony of their features and especially by the dignified attire as well as the integrity of their character that radiated from the way they moved and acted. These traits have been transmitted, through eons of time, to today's Sirians.

It seems that their ancestors knew their own constellation quite well, but also the constellation Orion, a region which they had once inhabited, forming colonies.* Later, these populations individualized and were "remade" by

---

* The constellation referred to is Canis Majoris which includes the star Sirius A, the brightest in the sky.

hybridization with other alien races. This was presented to me holographically through combinations of the original DNA with other types of DNA in different proportions and variants, each indicated by vibrating waves of color, more or less intense, in comparison with the typology of the physical structure of the respective race in order to be able to more easily identify the particularity of the hybridizations.

CIVILIZATIONS DERIVED OVER 30 MILLON YEARS

The images with the typology of those races followed one another for several seconds at such a high speed that I could hardly distinguish nearly any features. On the screen, there was a single image of an approximate prototype which "traversed" hundreds of body transformations, portraying a very fast development to the current state. I immediately understood that I was being shown in that way the passage of an enormous period of time and the succession of civilizations derived from the one I saw at the beginning, each represented by the basic typology of beings. The "development" stopped after an interval of about 29-30 million years, but I did not notice significant differences in the bodily forms of those civilizations. They all seemed to "revolve" around the same characteristics. The civilization representing the final images was also technologically advanced and dominated interstellar travel. In a way, it looked like a replica of the one of about 100 million years ago except that the skin of those Sirian creatures was a little bluer. Everything seemed a replay of what I had already seen in the beginning, as in the case of the first civilization, and this included the colonization of stellar systems in the constellations around the star Sirius A as well as hybridizations with other races.

THE ART OF TERRAFORMATION

I noticed then that the Earth was one of the "soul" planets of the ancient Sirians, "shepherded" by them with patience and perseverance. The experience they had accumulated in the hundreds of thousands of years of cosmic evolution made them understand that, when it came to the transformation of the planetary biosphere, it had to be done gradually and over a long period of time. I was shown, for example, the effect of "terraforming" on a natural satellite around a planet in a binary star system where the ecosystem did not keep up with the transformation of the atmosphere and consequently dried up. There were violent storms and most of the vegetation burned. That failure was probably an important lesson for them, otherwise that cosmic event would not have been presented to me on the holographic screen. It then took a long time for the natural habitat on that satellite to be recreated and adjusted properly. That is why, when the problem arose, their plan to terraform the

Earth stretched out for hundreds and even thousands of years in order to allow the biosphere to adapt, stabilize, and grow naturally and sustainably.

WHAT I SAW ON EARTH AT THE
END OF THE CRETACEOUS PERIOD

In those days, the soil of our planet was largely covered with evergreen forests.[*] I understood this very quickly because the images showed me a rapid succession of regions around the globe with "zooms" that always depicted cones of specific trees but never deciduous (where trees turn colors with the season and the leaves fall in autumn) forests or flowers. Instead, I was shown fairly large areas with cacti. Generally speaking, the plants at that time, but especially the trees, ferns and cacti were much larger than they are today.

In those extremely distant times, the Earth's atmosphere contained much more carbon dioxide, and the planet's magnetic field was more intense. In an image that was shown to me from a height of a few tens of kilometers above the ground, I could see that there was a lot of dust in the atmosphere, and the light from the Sun was filtered by it so that the sky appeared yellow-orange. In no images did I see the clear blue sky we see today nor the sun shining in the sky. Everything was foggy, about the same as during a weaker sandstorm in the Sahara. I was then shown images of the Earth as seen from the heavens, from an altitude that I estimated to be at about 800-1,000 kilometers. All I could see in the area around it and even farther away in space was cosmic dust.

Next, images of snapshots from various climatic environments on the planet appeared successively on the screen; that is, I was being shown the stage of life on our planet at that time on Earth, almost 100 million years ago. The plants were bluish green, sometimes reddish-brown. The vegetation was lush, not with deciduous forests, but rather with large fleshy cactus and aloe-like leafy plants that were very succulent. The aquatic environment, however, was more developed with huge algae and many living things of all kinds. On land, there were only reptiles in various forms and insects of a great variety, but there were no mammals. Also, I was not shown and did not see in the images of that period any intelligent beings on our planet.

After that first stage of viewing, I remembered two main ideas. First, there were no deciduous forests or flowers on Earth at that time. On the other hand, there was a lot of dust both in the planet's atmosphere and in the cosmic space in its vicinity, and this blocked the sunlight considerably.

---

[*] From the author's description, this could be a period between 68-69 million years ago and 65 million years ago which, scientifically speaking, corresponds to the end of the Cretaceous period, but it also captures the beginning of the Paleogene (66-23 million years ago).

STAGNATION OF EVOLUTION ON THE PLANET

The holographic images that I was surveying were not particularized but rather offered me an overview, as a whole, so that I could know what was on our planet then. I later realized that the purpose of that presentation was to give me a comparative picture of how the Earth had developed up to that time and what followed through the terraforming initiated by the Sirian ancestors. For them, the Earth was well located in the Solar System, and its gravity was suitable for their body structure, adapted to the specific radiation of the star Sirius A but similar in some respects to that emitted by our Sun.

There were, however, also disadvantages. First, the atmosphere was not a very good composition for the beings of that ancient civilization as the "air" could not be breathed for a long time without a protective helmet. On the other hand, genetic studies have shown that the Earth has long since reached a state of stagnation in its evolution. The ancient Sirian civilization realized that, even if it had initiated the process of terraforming the planet, it would have little to change in those conditions due to the modest biological material that existed then. Additionally, their scientific teams noted that, at the biological level, the genetic combinations that existed on the planet were still quite simple. There was not, practically speaking, a great variety of those combinations, neither in the vegetable nor in the animal kingdom. This was all the more astonishing as the flora and fauna, terrestrial or aquatic, were quite rich.

SIRIAN AND ADMIRAL INTERVENTION

The question then arose of making this planet evolve further. The stages of such a process appeared and followed one another very quickly on the screen. First was the purification of the "air" by removing the fine and abundant dust. Next was oxygen enrichment of the atmosphere and making more complex genetic hybridization in order for life on the planet to evolve.

I then saw the flagship of that advanced civilization: huge and spherical, about the size of our Moon. The image then "slipped" inside the ship and was fixed in a room with white arches of huge dimensions. In the middle of it was what we might call a "round table" with several representatives of that civilization who were part of the leadership of the ship. Everyone present wore a silver-white suit with blue inserts, like long lines, along the arms and torso. Telepathically, through the inter-dimensional headset, I understood that they were discussing the possibilities of boosting evolution on our planet and its terraforming.

Everyone there had some gadgets which we would now associate with older tablets. To them, however, they were like thin silvery and almost

187

transparent sheets that could be bent but could also be as hard as ordinary tablets. I saw, for example, how some of the people at the table rolled that tablet, others folded it, and others kept it rigid in its rectangular shape.

ORMA

The following images showed the same room, but at that meeting, I also saw a woman. A quick succession of snapshots of her showed me that she was the head of the research department of their galactic mission: a tall blue-eyed woman with shiny silver-blond hair named Orma. I estimated her age to be about forty-five terrestrial years. She was standing, actively explaining on the basis of holograms that appeared from a slit in the center of the round table.

I was then shown images on the holographic screen which correlated with her particular activity. Orma's specialization on that ship was biology, but this term had a much more comprehensive meaning than we know today. Just as for the Apellos, and for Méntia in particular, medicine means much more than is conceived by our current science. Orma was a very good researcher, specializing in a field that we could now call "planetary nano-biology" as that Sirian woman had a deep knowledge of the quantum field, nano-machines, high energies and fundamental forces, gravity in particular.

The studies that ancient civilization were conducting in our galaxy involved a lot of stellar systems and planets. The flagship I saw was one of the study ships in this area of the galaxy. Orma was mainly involved in the operations of transforming a planet into a habitat suitable for the life of those extraterrestrial beings or simply facilitating the evolution of civilizations that already existed on those planets. Seeing that the ancient Sirian race had, in fact, many colonies in various parts of the galaxy, I immediately understood that it was about the process of "terraforming", a very complex action with many variables.

I was then shown pictures of Orma on Earth, accompanied by a research team. All the members of the team had a kind of mask on their face around their mouth and nose. It seems that the pressure and general climatic conditions were suitable for their body because they did not wear a space suit, but only the respective mask, probably for purifying the air they breathed. The team took samples from different soil, water and plant environments. I then saw pictures of Orma again, but I realized that they came from another period, probably years later, because the Sirian woman had her hair arranged differently and her face was more mature. I understood that she had already studied the Earth problem on the basis of the data collected and the appropriate technologies and had come up with a set of proposals to present to the Admiral's Council.

Orma analyzed in depth the structure of DNA in the vegetation and fauna that existed at that time on Earth and observed that the different combinations of DNA, as well as biological exchanges at the atomic level, were actually quite complex, but they had reached a maximum threshold of "crossing" (hybridization) beyond which there was no possibility of evolution. She, however, came up with a solution. In order to further drive evolution, she said that a permanent constant field of force was needed to act upon the Earth's biosphere. The possibility of bringing plants and animals from other planets to integrate them on Earth was discussed, but the result would have been uncertain; and, in any case, only local with the length of their duration being relative We saw how she demonstrated this through the complex simulations she exhibited holographically.

TERRAFORMATION AND A LONG TERM COMPLEX SOLUTION FOR THE EARTH

The ancient Sirian civilization needed a general terraforming of our planet in order to ensure a habitat suitable for the life of its population. Local action, restricted to only one area or certain areas of the planet, would not have been enough. That is why the council of the flagship opted for the second variant presented by Orma, that which involved the action of a gigantic overall force field which would influence DNA, plant life, and animal life on Earth in a constant and profound way. In other words, they decided on a complex, profound and overall terraforming of the planet which would eventually lead to the biosphere we know today.

Due to the vast experience they already had in this field, the members of that civilization were in no hurry, for they knew that such terraforming could take hundreds of terrestrial years or even longer, but even so, it would be much shorter than the singular action of Nature, if it were to take place under the same conditions. In a way, it reminded me of what Elinor said about the Sirians of ancient times being like "alchemists of the planets" because their mode of action resembled that of the alchemists of the Middle Ages in their laboratories. Through the operations performed on matter, they hastened the cycles of Nature in a harmonious way, respecting its laws.

In her presentation, Orma showed that the force of the giant field to be "applied" to the Earth had to meet an interesting condition: it was to act for a long time, but it had to nonetheless be variable. In quick succession, I saw how Orma presented her very complex calculations and simulations to the members of the Council. She pointed out that, if the energy of the force field was continuous, then biological life would "get used" to it after a while which would again lead to a "flattening" of evolution on Earth. But, if that energy had a periodic variation, then the premises of some biologically active combinations would have been fulfilled, and life would continue to be invigorated.

At that time, it was not yet clear what that huge field of energy would generate. Orma had presented only the idea and calculations that showed the parameters necessary for it to be effective on life on Earth. The idea was good, but it did not solve the problem of dust in the atmosphere and in the more distant space of the planet, a factor which significantly obscured the sunlight, preventing it from reaching the surface. If the cosmic dust had been removed from around the planet, there would have been more sunlight, the atmosphere would have become more ionized, the rains would have been more abundant, and life would have had more possibilities for development. The reason for this is that a more favorable environment would have been created so that the energy from the Sun and from outer space could reach the Earth on a much wider spectrum of frequencies. To fulfill this idea, one of the solutions was to vacuum the dust around the planet, but I was then shown how Orma was inspired to unite the two ideas: terraforming the planet through that external force field and "cleaning" the dust from around the Earth in a single action.

A USEFUL COMPARISON

As I watched the synthesis of images of those events in the mists of time, I once again realized the very harmonious and integrated way in which beneficial alien civilizations which are technologically advanced contribute to the evolution of life on some planets in the Universe. They do not act selfishly and arrogantly as do some scientists on Earth today, fully confident in their own strength, but who, in reality, no longer understand any of the mysteries of Creation. Such advanced extraterrestrial civilizations are always connected with the higher celestial forces and beings with divine inspiration, and within them there are beings who area highly evolved from a spiritual point of view who support and guide their actions. In such civilizations, we can speak of a close cooperation between science and spirituality which makes them so advanced. Only in such a case can one get an overview of how the universe "works" and what life actually means at this level.

Comparatively speaking, the materialistic view of current science on Earth and the early stage of understanding the universe places us at a lower hierarchical level among the most advanced civilizations in the galaxy. When scientists are ecstatic at the thought of finding "extraterrestrial life" on Mars in the form of microbes or bacteria, when conventional energy sources based primarily on oil and coal are still in use, when the entire planet is under the "curtain" of a crude manipulation which states that "we are alone in the whole universe because we have not found anyone else so far", all of this is more like a praise of stupidity than the promotion of competence and good sense. Even though, in reality, superior technologies exist and were invented on Earth, very few human beings have access to them, and many of them are locked in safes only out of petty financial interests. The vast majority of the planet's population struggles in the likeness of the "contemporary Middle Ages" being maintained by various means in utter ignorance. Under these conditions, it is difficult to aspire to the stars or to turn your attention to your spiritual evolution.

My mental digression lasted only a few seconds because the man from Apellos immediately drew my attention to keep focus on the subject. The images had already begun to be blurred, and some on the right side of the screen had completely frozen. I have had such "experiences" in other viewings as well, so I knew how to get back "in the game" without having to reset the original idea. I turned my attention to Orma's image and reconnected to the holographic screen through the one-dimensional headset which favored this process.

THE COMPLEXITY OF A BRILLIANT IDEA

Orma's idea was for that fluctuating force field to encompass the entire planet and "envelop" it like a halo of energy. To achieve this, she proposed bringing a cosmic body with a sufficiently large mass around the Earth to meet both requirements: to drive the evolution of the plant and animal kingdoms on the planet and to help "aspirate" the cosmic dust around it.

I saw the hologram in which Orma explained, in summary, the effects that body in the vicinity of the Earth would have had on our planet at that time. I even saw a kind of graph that displayed in parallel the frequencies of energy that had come from the Sun until then and the frequencies that could have been added after the "cleaning" of the dust around the planet and its atmosphere. The images also showed the evolution of the DNA of different plants and animals, indicating the initial genes, and later, under the action of new frequencies of solar and cosmic energy, the way in which branches appeared in those genes and how various combinations of them were made, i.e. an obvious development in complexity.

The cosmic object that would have produced all those substantial changes for life on our planet — from the suction of dust from the surrounding cosmic space to the influence of the specific force field on the DNA of plants and in general of all living things, in combination with the much more complex action of energy and sunlight — would also have led to other possibilities for the multiplication and development of all these living things. Up to that time in our planet's evolution, we could only speak of vegetative reproduction,[*]

---

[*]Vegetative reproduction in plants is a particular type of asexual reproduction by non-specialized asexual germs. The offspring is generated by a single parent. Thus, the new individual results from a fragment of the parental body. In most plants, vegetative reproduction is achieved through vegetative organs: stems, roots, and leaves. The cells return to the embryonic stage and divide intensely, giving rise to a new plant. Vegetative propagation *(continued on next page)*

especially through spores,** dominating the muscles and ferns. The low frequencies of solar energy and microwaves from the light from the Sun were filtered for the most part because the heat and the penetrating high frequency waves managed to pass through the "dam" of dust in the immediate vicinity of the Earth. But, once the solution proposed by Orma was used, the frequency range would have increased, favoring much more energy and biochemical exchanges, both in the vegetable and animal kingdoms. The diversity of plants would have "exploded", and this would have generated a greater amount of oxygen in the atmosphere over time. In other images I was later shown various kinds of plants which had not existed before but which later developed in a spectacular way. For example there was no grass at that time, only low plants with large fleshy leaves or hanging plants. Anticipating a little, I saw images that showed me the dry areas of the planet, some time after the beginning of its terraforming, covered with various types of grass, some of it very high.

Orma's idea later became a concept for which she became famous in many planetary systems. Since then, the civilization of the ancient Sirians has understood and widely applied this idea with multiple effects by using galactic energies and placing them in precisely calculated points of reference to the massive evolution of life which, by reason of their presence and specific field, in combination with other influences of some cosmic energies, precisely influences and correlates certain processes of evolution, all depending upon what is needed.

The same mode of action was used much later, over eons of time, when the descendants of that ancient Sirian civilization, along with other advanced extraterrestrial civilizations, proceeded to accurately determine and influence the creation of the human race. By spending long periods of time, thousands or even tens of thousands of terrestrial years, their huge ships, like planetoids, placed in certain precise areas of a planet or satellite, were able to wisely influence the evolution of life without violating the laws of nature. This resulted in a significant but harmonious acceleration of the evolution towards the natural course of things.

This idea should not surprise us too much though. Even if a forest is planted and has to wait for several decades for trees to grow and become towering, it significantly influences the surrounding ecosystem whereas, if left to itself, nature would have taken a much longer time to accomplish the task. This analogy is all the more evident when intervening at the cosmic level through terraforming and other large-scale actions which take into account the development and evolution of biological life on an entire planet.

(continued from previous page) can be achieved by buds on the roots, by creeping stems, by underground stems (such as bulbs, rhizomes or tubers) or by fragments of stems or leaves (cuttings).
** Some terrestrial plants reproduce by spores. In this case, we are talking about specialized asexual reproduction. They are specialized single-celled asexual germs that form in certain organs in muscles and ferns.

COSMIC VERSIONS AT A PRACTICAL LEVEL

After it was decided to implement that brilliant idea that Orma had, we saw the development of a huge activity in the flagship in which thousands of beings worked together using advanced technology, especially to perform time simulations of processes, possibilities and effects that may occur. I understood from what was presented to me that this was a huge and extremely complex job which involved a huge effort on the part of those on the flagship.

After the results of the simulations were obtained and it was found that such an action would indeed mean an extraordinary leap in the evolution of life on Earth, the question of choosing the most appropriate method to achieve this concretely was raised. One solution proposed the actual construction of a huge object to be placed in the vicinity of the Earth which would be equivalent to building a new planet-sized ship. This, however, would have involved a special effort, even for that advanced civilization. At that time, the ships of the ancient Sirians, even if huge, were still made of materials, i.e. they contained metals and tangible physical elements, including gold and titanium, but also other metals with very special properties that are unknown to us even today, but all of this was physical material. As was shown to me in numerous suggestive images, the technology for making such a giant star-shaped spaceship had not yet been reached relative to the technology of today's Sirian civilization and other technologically advanced civilizations, such as the Arcturians.

Another proposal was to "tow" a natural satellite of Jupiter or Saturn and place it in orbit, but this would have involved a number of other major issues, such as the difficulty of dealing with the mass of that satellite, a mass which would almost certainly not have matched the one resulting from the calculations and simulations. To this would have been added certain specific side effects on the "donor" planet by reason of removing the satellite from its own life, and all of the accompanying influences it had on it. It was then argued that Jupiter and Saturn were gaseous planets, lifeless in the physical plane, and the "gap" left by taking one of their many satellites would therefore not have left too large of an impact.

Then came the idea of bringing a gas satellite with a liquid core, a situation which would have a large volume and could have influenced the biosphere of our planet. While I was watching with great interest all of those variants that were presented to me, as they were brought into discussion and debated in those very long ago times, I still allowed myself a digression on the last variant. The possibility of a satellite being gaseous with a liquid core caught my eye. I knew a lot about such a problem because I had discussed this with Dr. Xien not so long ago. Water in the cosmos is something fundamental. This is not the "drinking water" we know, of course, but it is much more like "heavy" water, and in my previous views on the holographic screen, it was even shown to me at one point that the angles between the oxygen atom and the two hydrogen atoms are different in the case of this cosmic "water" as compared to ordinary water. That is why its properties are very different. Such water appears to be almost black, but it is liquid and extremely "energetic". Around such a nucleus of "water", which is generated by the central black hole that supports the formation of that planet or satellite concerned, gas or weight gathers by accretion but also by specific internal transformations. All of these are controlled, of course, by the "will" of the central black hole of that cosmic object.

REPLACING A SATELLITE

With great attention, I continued to watch the extraordinary images on the holographic screen concerning the implementation of the solution proposed by Orma. From the versions suggested so far, I had seen that an interesting suggestion was received at one point from a higher echelon of that ancient civilization. Those on the ship were told that an idea for solving the problem could be to use one of the huge spaceships already in use, a vehicle which would approach, both in shape, size and mass, the conditions, calculations, and simulations of the project proposed by Orma. That ingenious solution would have been much easier to apply and present fewer technological problems than the other solutions highlighted so far.

This suggestion particularly impressed the members of the Council from the flagship. It was a "handy" solution which could also be "adjusted". The very flagship of that civilization was chosen which, at that time, was the largest of their ships, but it was already "obsolete", having been in service for several thousand years. We then saw how they calculated the compensation of the mass of that ship with the accretion of interplanetary dust and rock debris still gravitating around the Earth until the ship reached the size and volume required by Orma's project to meet the proposed purpose. I was amazed at the complexity of those calculations and the solutions found to meet all of the conditions so that the influence of the ship on the Earth would lead to the desired transformations. Of these, the exposure of only one face of the Moon to Earth was extraordinarily calculated and realized because, if the spacecraft had a different angular velocity around its axis, the full exposure of its surface would have led to the implementation of other types of frequencies of energy in the Earth's biosphere. I understood that this was not necessary for the transformation of life on the surface of the planet as was desired by the ancient Sirian civilization. We will have effective proof of these aspects when the Moon gradually begins to change its parameters and slowly reveals its hidden part which is currently not visible.

The flagship that became the Moon, or the so-called "natural" satellite of the Earth, was a huge ship. As shown in the pictures, the center of the ship was actually a hollow spherical space with many "rays" flowing inward, resembling "icicles." I could see that they played the role of a kind of "energy concentrator" because I saw how those huge white lightning-like arches flowed through those "rays" at certain precise intervals of time, uniting right in the middle of the empty space of the sphere. This created a certain amount of plasma in the middle, after which the energy from that plasma was extracted through a complicated process which I understood neither in principle nor in terms of technology. It was clear to me, however, that in terms of energy, they had been using nuclear fusion technology ever since and not fission technology such as is currently used on Earth.[*]

THE INTERIOR OF THE "MOON"

In pragmatic terms, the Sirians created a little blue-white "sun" in the center of the ship which provided the ship's energy needs. The ship itself had a concentric structure based upon the principle of "onion leaves". Seeing this in the holographic presentation, I better understood my short "voyage" inside the Moon, that is, of the flagship, which I had made on the occasion of doubling into the etheric plane. I did not, however, reach the "fusion center" of the ship inside the empty spherical space. The fusion center concentrated energy through the giant "rays", and by carefully following the holographic projections, I was able to form a fairly clear picture of the structure of our "natural satellite". In the short time I spent "moving" inside the Moon, I noticed only the common elements that can be found on spaceships.

Some of the spaces were truly gigantic, the size of cities. The feeling of immensity I had about those spaces would probably have been even more pronounced if I had seen everything lit up and working as it once was tens of millions of years ago. I also went through small compartmentalized areas, even seeing spaces that were probably used as homes as well as spaces dedicated to technology.

On the first "ad-hoc" voyage within the Moon, I did not reach the Great Meeting Room of the Ship's Steering Board which met there in those astonishingly distant times. Although I could see this in images on the holographic screen, I was not "attracted" to that space, did not know of its existence, nor was I able to identify it. But then, in some of the subsequent experiences I had with Eden, I specifically wanted to get there and was glad to be the silent witness of a space that I still consider loaded with a deep emotion, that space

---

[*]Current science defines nuclear fusion as the process by which two atomic nuclei interact to form a new nucleus, heavier (with higher mass) than the original nuclei. As a result of fusion, other subatomic particles are produced such as neutrons or alpha particles (helium nuclei) or beta particles (electrons or positrons). At the opposite pole is nuclear fission. It is the process by which the nucleus of an atom breaks into two or more smaller nuclei, called fission products, as well as into a number of individual subatomic particles.

in which Orma presented her project of fundamental transformation of life on Earth for the first time. In the enigmatic twilight inside that very large room, as I was perceiving it in the etheric plane, I stood for a long time, moving slowly, passing by the table and those tall and rather narrow armchairs, looking at the huge arches or the holographic projection slot through which the holograms of the different stages and versions of the project appeared. I mention that it was in the etheric plane because, if viewed from the physical plane, everything would have been shrouded in the deepest darkness. I lived though those unique moments several times with a deep emotion because they have decided, in a way, the very future of planet Earth.

Looking at the images of different areas inside, I realized that the flagship had been built more like a conglomerate of self-styled "cities" traveling through space. It was not a strict compartmentalization such as those found in small and medium-sized ships, but there was a real biosphere, a very well-generated and controlled living environment. I saw countless elevators that were very sophisticated and astonishingly fast. They were train-like but winding and were a more aerodynamic means of transport. There were also flying vehicles of many types, but they were propelled without combustion. During the period when it was operational, the flagship was a very large and complex habitat.

THE GREAT COSMIC CATACLYSM
AND ITS INFLUENCE ON THE EARTH

As the Moon was placed in a calculated orbit around the Earth and began to "suck" the abundant cosmic dust around our planet, I saw how its gravitational force was amplified in order to be able to attract as much of the dust around the Earth as possible. The process was long. Gradually, the interplanetary dust was "sucked in" and settled on the outer shell of the spacecraft, making a crust that was not too thick. From my assessments, based upon what I was seeing in the exposures on the holographic screen, I estimated the "crust" of the moon to be about twenty kilometers thick on average as the thickness varied from area to area. For example, we saw in the areas where there were deposits of cosmic matter by reason of accretion, there was a much greater thickness than in other areas, almost double.

At that time, both the new satellite and our planet were massively bombarded by meteorites which came from a large cosmic cataclysm that had taken place between Mars and Jupiter. This was a planet which had orbited that region of the Solar System and was about the size of Uranus and was the largest planet in its "family" before being destroyed and shattered.[*] Generally speaking, contemporary scientists rule out this truth and consider it only a hypothesis. They consider other causes for the asteroid belt between Mars

[*] In literature, this planet is referred to as Maldek or Tiamat (see also the books of Zecharia Sitchin).

and Jupiter, none of which are logically supported.* It is true, however, that when I wanted to see details about that terrible cosmic event, it was not allowed. The holographic screen no longer responded, becoming somewhat blurred. It was the second time this had happened to me, having previously been blocked in the occult chamber in Egypt when I was also not allowed to see details of those reptilian beings. We have noticed that such concealments occur only in two situations: either there are no personal affinities to connect with the requested subject, or this is simply not allowed by higher celestial entities for reasons beyond our comprehension.

I was able to see, however, some interesting details about that great cosmic cataclysm. This was about 65-70 million years in the past, that is, when scientists correctly identified that "something happened on the Earth and dinosaurs suddenly disappeared as a result of a terrible phenomenon, that planet exploded".** Because of its immense size, the planet had subtly determined the evolution of dinosaurs on Earth, especially by the influence of gravity and the gigantic radiation it had. After exploding, the subtle energetic support disappeared in the process of developing dinosaur DNA.

This theory of scientists, however, is a bit hairy. To say that the dinosaurs on Earth have been completely exterminated because of the devastating impact with a large meteorite is a lot. So, how do you explain the discovery of dinosaur bones that lived even 5-10 million years after that planetary cataclysm? In reality, as I was shown in eloquent images, the dinosaurs gradually disappeared, not necessarily because of the impact of the great meteorite but because their DNA was no longer supported by the specific energy of the planet between Mars and Jupiter which exploded. The structure of the macromolecule had

---

* One of the commonly accepted theories in the current scientific environment is that the remnants that make up the asteroid belt between Mars and Jupiter are actually remnants of a "proto-planetary disk". These range in composition from a mixture of ice and dust to volcanic rock, indicating multiple origins. The explanation is that a significant part of the asteroids come from "former comets". Described as "dirty lumps" of ice and dust, comets are lonely objects with elliptical orbits around the Sun. Researchers in France and the United States have developed a mathematical model of the development of the Solar System corresponding to the period when the planets were just forming. According to this simulation, the large planets Jupiter, Saturn, Uranus and Neptune were much closer to the Sun. As the planets grew in size, the researchers say their orbits became increasingly unstable so that, after about 600 million years, Uranus and Neptune were "thrown" into other orbits. According to the current scientific scenario, they collided with a disc made up of comets, scattering the latter throughout the Solar System. Many of them were later captured by the gravitational force of the asteroid belt where they remain to this day. In our opinion, and if we want to be truly objective, we would say that this "hypothesis" of scientists contains more fanciful and improbable elements than that of the author. In addition, what Radu Cinamar says about the planet Tiamat and its explosion is also mentioned in other works (see the volumes of Zecharia Sitchin) which are based on mentions from antiquity about such a cosmic cataclysm.

** Contemporary scientists believe that the Earth was impacted with a huge meteorite of about 10 km in diameter somewhere in the Yucatan Peninsula between where Mexico and Guatemala are today, in the area called Chicxulub.

"worn out", "fallen", and the remaining dinosaur species on Earth disappeared over time.

Other animal species were favored which were energetically supported by the subtle influences of the other planets, and to these were added the climate changes that occurred during that period. The new satellite helped capture a significant portion of the fragments and remnants of matter and rock that came from the great explosion of the planet between Mars and Jupiter, largely mitigating the effect of the devastating impact upon Earth. This prevented the destruction of a significant part of the planet's biosphere, an eventuality which could have taken place if the new satellite had not been in the sky. Thus, the flagship of the Sirian civilization of those times became what we today call the Moon.

Other planets have also captured significant parts of the big planet that was destroyed by the explosion. This also applies to the satellites of the big planet, some of which were "stolen", thus becoming satellites of other planets in the Solar System. As was a shown to me in the images, Jupiter is such an example, even serving as an anomaly in this regard. Normally, a planet has "layers" of satellites in a well-established order, i.e. those closest to it are small satellites with larger satellites in the middle orbits; and in the orbits farthest from the planet, we find again small satellites. In the case of Jupiter, however, it is found that there are large satellites even beyond the second layer of small satellites. As such, they could not occupy those orbits unless they were "captured" from space.

Another example, as I saw in the images, is represented by the two satellites of Mars, Phobos and Deimos, which, in reality, represent two large fragments of the planet that exploded, being then drawn into orbit around the Red Planet. Moreover, scientists, and not just them, should ask themselves the common sense question: How is it possible for an asteroid belt that is the result of the explosion of a planet, like the one between Mars and Jupiter, to have innumerable remains of modest dimensions, and yet still have some asteroids amongst its orbit, including massive ones such as Ceres or Vesta, both being of appreciable dimensions and having a spherical shape?* Where does this discrepancy come from? In reality, they are satellites of the former planet which were not "expelled" but remained in the interplanetary area.

---

* Ceres has a diameter of 945 km and Vesta has a diameter of 525 km. There are two more asteroids close to them, Pallas and Hygiea, each with a diameter of between 350 and 550 km. These celestial bodies (Ceres is considered a planetoid) make up about half of the mass of the entire asteroid belt between Mars and Jupiter which consists of millions of debris and fragments of rocks, ice and matter.

THE APPEARANCE OF FLOWERS ON EARTH

After the new satellite began its "duties", flowering plants gradually began to appear on Earth. This is already a significant change in the flora of the planet. The leap to this level occurred mainly because the action of silver in plants was strongly influenced by the fact that the Moon was present in the planet's sky. In her research, Orma had already reported the presence of large amounts of copper, gold, and silver in plants on Earth before the Moon was placed in its orbit. According to the calculations made by the scientific teams on the flagship, the influence of the Moon was dynamic; and in addition to this, the huge flagship changed its position to Earth several times at certain intervals according to the need of subtle astral influences coming from the other main cosmic bodies, stars or planets.*

The biochemical bonds in plants that the Moon has caused over time, through its subtle energetic influence, have led to the appearance and development of flowers on Earth. The first flowers appeared on cacti as they were the most numerous on the planet at the time. I saw how, in the early stages, types of fleshy petals appeared, after which they developed until they reached the stage of flowers as we know them today. Only after this fundamental transformation in plant life on our planet ended, and it applied to animal life as well, did the gigantic ship stabilize in its current orbit, thus establishing the characteristics by which we know it today.

THE TASTE OF TIME

At this point, the presentation on the holographic screen was abruptly interrupted, leaving me almost in a state of reverie. I felt that this was not only about the originality of the information but also about the very fine subtle influence of the extremely distant time to which I had somehow had acquired indirect access to through that presentation. This left a special "taste" in my being, activating deep and unsuspected emotions in me.

Finally, I said goodbye to the man from Apellos and the team there and headed to Alpha Base. A few hours after I had arrived, Cezar saw that I was quite troubled, but I did not need to tell him anything. He immediately sensed the cause and brought me hot tea as we both went to the building where Eden was. I felt better in the elegant and very high technology room. I think that what I really wanted was for myself to "go" to those ancestral times so as to have the feeling of actually living in those colossally distant times.

The images on the holographic screen had planted the seed of longing for those ancient places and times, and now all I had to do was carefully develop

---

* Some ancient philosophers, such as Democritus and Anaxagoras, mention in their writings that there was a time in human history when the Moon could not be seen at night in the sky.

access to them with the help of the "space-time machine". I have not succeeded so far, but something else happened soon after, something that fed my soul at least as much. I looked through the very wide window at the black sky of the cold clear night with the stars creeping into my soul with drops of sweet nostalgia. I remembered a similar moment years ago, when the emotion of unknown distances had engulfed me in the same place at the Base, after Cezar's disturbing story of Professor Constantine and the cave of the Golden Thrones. Then, just as I had looked at the stars with great longing, so I would bring them to my soul now. I did not suspect, however, that my hopes would be fulfilled sooner than I expected.

EPILOGUE

For those who have dedicatedly followed the work of Radu Cinamar, I will add some additional information which you should find of interest.

I had a rather somewhat voluminous but rather sporadic correspondence with the author during the beginning of our association. This came to an abrupt halt at the end of 2010, just prior to Dr. David Anderson publicly announcing that he had developed his time reactor technology to the point where human beings could safely travel in time to the past or future. Since that time, David's technology has been developed even further, yet its very existence, let alone its pragmatic use, is inhibited with secrecy and censorship.

Before Radu's correspondence had stopped, he had given me a heads-up to expect a meeting with a most remarkable man who would come to my house for a short visit. In no uncertain terms, this is the character you have just read about in this book, the mysterious alchemist known as Elinor. While that is indeed an intriguing proposition and a meeting I was and am still desirous of, I put a stop to it. An internal and resolute decision on my behalf, I rejected it mentally because I knew that I was not ready for such a meeting. When you know you are not ready, you are not ready. I had other tasks to complete. The good news is that these tasks are almost done. Whether the meeting will happen or not depends on fate and good fortune.

For those who follow my newsletters, you know that I make routine trips to Romania. In what was probably a year after my last letter from Radu, I was having lunch with his publisher, Sorin Hurmuz, in Bucharest. Asking him point blank if Elinor was a real character that he had any knowledge of, he told me that he did indeed receive a couple of phone calls from him as described in *Tranyslvanian Moonrise*. These phone calls were made on behalf of Dr. Xien, also known as the Tibetan lama Repa Sundhi. Sorin said that Elinor had a very firm and resolute voice but that he did not have any interaction with him other than the phone calls. He did, however, arrange for the meeting between Radu and the lama to take place.

When I told Sorin that Radu had told me to expect a meeting with Elinor, there was a look of surprise on his face that was more like a shock. His body language told me that he had never met the man and that he was indeed surprised that Radu had offered me this proverbial carrot. It was also at this luncheon that Sorin had expressed a deep concern that he had not been hearing from Radu. Never before had such a long time passed when there was no communication from him. Sorin seemed worried about his well being.

Radu did not resurface again for what amounted to a seven year cycle. In 2017, the Romanian edition of *Inside the Earth — The Second Tunnel* was released. It not only explained so much, it expanded the horizons of the entire series of books and also gave a very plausible explanation of what Radu had been up to during his years of absence.

When the Romanian edition of *Inside the Earth* was released, I wrote to Sorin for a copy in order to begin the translation immediately. There was no response. After more attempts and continued frustration, I finally got copies of the book from my Romanian in-laws. I immediately scanned all the pages but there were still problems getting the translation done. It was during this period that Radu finally broke his silence to me, but it had to do with the fact that the book, *Inside the Earth*, had not yet been published in English, and he was concerned that maybe I did not like it. I assured him that this was not the case.

As my regular translator was unavailable due to having a baby, my Romanian wife got it started and tried to help me, but it was too time intensive for her schedule, even when we used a tape recorder. Finally, I found a personal friend in Romania to do this, but she was admittedly not a professional translator. It was very difficult. Many passages in the translation were irreconcilable. Finally, as I had no electronic copy, I had to type in the difficult passages into *Google Translate* and figure out the translation myself. Particularly difficult passages were taken to my Romanian wife, and to be frank, she had some difficulty with many of those passages as well.

In the end, however, I was able to put out a very understandable book, the translation of which has received very positive reviews by my Romanian friends. While *Inside the Earth — The Second Tunnel* is one of my favorite books of all time, the actual production of the book was hellish.

When it was all done, Radu was curious to read what I had said before and after the book, and he was pleased with my comments and descriptions. Upon informing him of the extreme energetic obstacles I had to deal with in getting the book into printed form, he replied that he was impressed by my tenacity and that he himself had also faced challenging obstacles with regard to writing what he referred to as the TRUE HISTORY of Mankind, even stating that Cezar used to mock him in this regard (by reason of having the obstacles). Cezar was kind enough, however, to convey through Radu his appreciation for my own efforts. Radu did overcome his obstacles and released his book, *Forgotten Genesis*, the precursor to this publication.

In my response to Radu, I had asked him specific questions about Elinor as the latter seemed to be hovering on the horizon. I did not, however, hear from Radu for another year. The activities that he describes in the various books have kept him quite busy, and he apologized, knowing I would understand. He also answered my questions. Additionally, he stated that Elinor is often

EPILOGUE

on the move, partly as a result of dark occult forces that are routinely trying to obtain his knowledge. Radu also informed me that he was very tempted to release actual photos of "Eden" but demurred, relegating our examination to the sketches provided in this book.

In my last correspondence, I told Radu to let Elinor know that I would soon be ready, but I have not heard back. Upon reading this book, however, I realized that what Radu said about Elinor spontaneously appearing when he was needed to help with Eden also applies to my situation. Communication on the etheric plane does not require letters, e-mails or phone calls. When you are indeed ready, the connection will happen. For Elinor to reappear in the pages of *The Etheric Crystal* was not only a pleasant surprise, it brings up these previous issues, and this is why I mention them. With regard to the Eden Project, however, I know readers will comment on and be curious about it being somewhat similar to the Montauk Chair.

The Montauk Chair was a device that was designed to read and amplify the thoughts of the psychic occupying the chair. While the goal was to manipulate consciousness and even matter and energy itself, its more exalted feature was to manipulate time. Although there are reports of positive uses of this technology, it was clearly overshadowed by evil forces and the signature of the Beast or what can best be termed Antichristic forces.

With the Eden device, we not only have the suggestion in the namesake of a return to the Garden of Eden, but we have a device that is based upon the intuition of an individual (Radu) who is being driven by ostensibly very positive forces representing the very roots of Shambhala.

While Radu uses the term "doubling" for venturing out of the body, the Montauk crowd used the term "FULL OUT" for projecting outward. When we consider my own history in these matters, there is a great deal of irony involved, and it becomes very relevant to point out that L. Ron Hubbard had his own term for this phenomenon which he referred to as exteriorization. This term and the phenomena associated with it were a daily staple of those who were actually engaged in the uncorrupted and/or properly applied procedures of Scientology as I knew them.

The main problem with Scientology, however, was that it was also overshadowed by dark forces. I should also point out that the problem with Scientology were not the techniques but rather the lack of understanding them and consequently misapplying them, often quite brutally. This seems to be the lot of Mankind. If you present him with gold, he will transmute it into lead. It also leaves one contemplating the proposition that if the road to hell is paved with good intentions then perhaps the road to heaven is paved with evil intentions.

There are different analogies that can be made in this respect, including the concept of Original Sin, but it all comes down to the prospect of what

203

the ancients identified as the Riddle of the Sphinx, it representing the very predicament of Mankind and his existence. The common denominator of such a proposition is rather obvious. Man is trying to figure himself out, both on a collective and an individual basis.

In this book, Méntia brings up the point that a person's health is key and that illness or bodily agitation creates mental agitation which leads to hasty and often erroneous decisions and inevitably to suffering. Elinor further accentuates this idea by suggesting that smoking and alcohol contribute to impurities in the physical body but also the etheric components of an individual's consciousness.

While it is easy to criticize any human being for their frailties, misgivings, and erroneous ways, there is always hope. As old as is the battle of good versus evil, so are the aspirations and dreams of man. In my own experiences, from the exalted potentials suggested by Scientology, the Montauk Project and the technology presented by David Anderson and Radu Cinamar, the best solution is to find one's own specific orbit in life.

When we consider the evil alluded to and described by Radu and the censorship surrounding the work of David Anderson, it becomes obvious that what can best be described as evil is what influences and prevents the circulation of information and techniques that will uplift Mankind on so many levels. Thus evil, like a planet or star in the heavens, has an orbit in our very own lives, collectively and individually. It is with this in mind that I can give you a brief update of a great evil that has left our orbit. It especially bodes well for all of my work, past, present and future.

In the waning days of June 2020, it was announced on his website that Colonel Michael Aquino, the infamous satanist and founder of the Temple of Set, who also served as the Satanic Chaplain to the U.S. Army and wrote the Chaplain's Handbook for such, passed away at the age of 73.

Although he was never convicted, Aquino was and will forever be associated with the child sexual abuse scandals of the 1980s that occurred at the Presidio in San Francisco. Simultaneous to translating and publishing Radu's work, I have also been working intensely on a new project that is dedicated to uncovering the evil that surrounded the Presidio. This is a collaboration with Douglas Dietrich, the man who was the major catalyst in exposing the abuse at the Presidio. A research librarian at the Defense Department who was an expert in documents destruction, Dietrich was personally responsible for the arrest and indictment of Gary Hambright, the most obvious perpetrator of the sexual abuse. Hambright, who worked at the Presidio's Day Care Center, was obviously guilty, but he escaped conviction only by reason of the fact that he died of AIDS before the proceedings were finished.

Convicting Aquino or anyone else in the military, however, was a much trickier business. To the degree that the abuse had occurred on the Presidio military base in San Francisco, the Army forbade further investigation on the grounds of national security. The only reason Dietrich was able to finger and successfully bring Hambright to prosecution, however, was that the latter was storing child pornography at his work place in the San Francisco School District where he also worked. As this was a civilian institution, the San Francisco Police Department and District Attorney's office were able to get involved.

Although Aquino, his wife, and their personal residence were identified by the very young victims, the case against them hit a dead end by reason of the Army's refusal to investigate the matter. Although the abuse was officially ignored by the Army, there were major ramifications when the outraged parents of the victims ganged up and burned down the child day care center on the Presidio, all of it ultimately resulting in the base being shut down, eventually being purchased by Disney via George Lucas.

It can be safely said that Douglas Dietrich was directly responsible for shutting down the Presidio, a military base which was known as the Pentagon of the West Coast. Although it was Dietrich's assigned job as a Defense Department Research Librarian to do whatever research Aquino requested, he ended up undermining the Army's Satanic Chaplain. There is considerably more to the story, but all I can offer here is a short summary. My original strategy was not to engage Aquino directly or even to finger-point at him. He was already sick and dying with intestinal cancer. It was my decision to stir the cauldron gingerly by addressing the Roswell Incident, an event that Aquino was not directly involved with save for his part in a disinformation campaign that the New Age and UFO crowds swallowed predictably.

Dietrich learned the details about the Roswell Incident as a result of being asked to compile a summary of the information for the base commander at the Presidio. Although the so-called Roswell crash has been cited as a major event in UFOlogy that ushered in the Flying Saucer era, this narrative has served as a giant smokescreen, and we will be addressing this in our first book, *The Roswell Deception and the Demystification of World War II.* The book will feature a detailed and historically verifiable narrative of the history of the World Wars that led to the Roswell Crash of July 5, 1947.

This includes the 1942 "Battle of Los Angeles" which was, in fact, a Japanese attack from a super dirigible with small planes attached. Some of these planes, piloted by diminutive Japanese who were crew members of the super dirigible, crashed. Due to the initial press reports of the Battle of Los Angeles clearly indicating Japanese planes, the truth was not completely hidden, but the Office of War Information successfully suppressed the news of the Japanese attack and floated the public relations myth that it was an attack from aliens. While the Japanese can definitely be categorized as enemy aliens, it was a ploy to make people think the attack was from aliens from outer space.

The actual truth of the Battle of Los Angeles, which was an unmitigated disaster for the Americans, has to do with one of the most under-appreciated and hidden facts of World War II that was also suppressed by the Office of War Information, that being that Emperor Hirohito of Japan had earned a PhD in Marine Biology in order to defend his country against American imperialism and genocide.* In fact, he was an internationally recognized Marine biologist due to his having discovered a species that was not previously known to the science of his day.

In the previous decade to World War II, Hirohito had been developing dirigibles and unleashing biocidal weapons against the Chinese amongst the ravines and inaccessible hilly country of China. Although the super dirigible used in the Battle of Los Angeles contained no biocidal weapons and was only intended as a threatening warning, the American panic that ensued had a devastating effect upon their own soldiers. As they were well aware of the Japanese use of biocidal weapons inflicted upon the Chinese via such dirigibles, they stupidly used untested and unapproved vaccines on their soldiers resulting in the death of over 50,000 of their own men with over 300,000 additional personnel being severed from military service as a result of extreme illness. This, however, is only the tip of the iceberg.

To fast forward, after the atomic bomb known as "Little Boy" was dropped on Hiroshima, Hirohito sent a fleet of three super dirigibles to Tonopah Army Air Field in Nevada, later to be known as Area 51. Containing biocidal weapons of mass destruction, these dirigibles were sent by Hirohito as a threat as opposed to a strike attack, and this was done to induce the Americans into negotiations which would actually last until September 8, 1951 when a treaty of peace was finally signed between Japan and the United States. Although this is the historical record, the Office of War Information and its decedents have perpetrated the myth that the Japanese surrendered on September 8, 1945 aboard the *U.S.S. Missouri*.

These super dirigibles which landed at Tonopah Army Air Field, which contained enough biological weapons to potentially murder every man, woman and child in America, were deliberately surrendered to the Americans so that they would know what they were dealing with. Once the Americans realized this, they immediately sued for peace through secret channels. They did, however, keep the dirigibles and held the crew, the diminutive Japanese known as the Yakuza, as prisoners of war.

After Admiral Byrd's Operation High Jump failed to subdue the German Redoubt in Antarctica, the Americans made an ill-conceived attempt to use

---

* Hirohito's interest in Marine Biology and using biocidal weapons for self-defense was a direct result of reading Jack London's story, *The Unparalleled Invasion*, which warned Americans of the "Yellow Peril" and recommended complete genocide of the Sinitic Race. Although the Japanese are not Sinitic, Hirohito realized that if the Americans were willing to perpetrate genocide against the Chinese, there would be similar sentiment against the Japanese.

these dirigibles against the Germans, eventually attempting to rebuild this technology. The only way they could operate it, however, was by using their prisoners of war, the small Japanese pilots who were about four feet tall. As the craft neared Roswell, the pilots revolted and blew themselves up, thus causing debris to be scattered across the ground below. The retractable "metal" you have heard about was rubberized silk, something the Americans were completely unfamiliar with. The "alien bodies" were the diminutive pilots and the "hieroglyphics" on the craft was Japanese stenciling which looks very alienesque. While this story will rub many UFOlogists and other conspiracy-minded people the wrong way, the full story, as presented in the upcoming book, will have enough documentation to change the way the world thinks about the Government, aliens, and UFOs.

While Aquino had no direct role in the Roswell Incident or the war crimes associated with it, his expertise in psychological operations were utilized to disinform the public on this topic as well as others. This led to the publication of Phillip Corso's book, *The Day After Roswell*, which serves as an attempt to distract people from the truth. Corso finished his book by implicating that Roswell led to the secrets of time.

One of the reasons Aquino's disinformation campaigns were so successful is not only that there are considerable occult factors and connections behind the scenes of what took place at Roswell as well as throughout the world wars, but there are also reasons people are so easily swayed, such reasons going well beyond the obvious fact that people are entrained by reason of being subjected to limited information by virtue of compromised mediums that include major media, alternative media and the internet itself. General conspiracy theory, even when it is based upon significant and genuine information, has a stagnant quality to it because it is does not translate or transmute into dynamic motion. The reason for this stagnation has everything to do with the occult factors. When we consider the maxim that "the truth shall set you free", it is easy to conclude that if you are not set free, then you have not learned the whole truth.

While these deeper occult factors will be addressed in future books, including those behind the world wars and the Presidio, they will not be included in the first book. That is too much, too fast. The first book, *The Roswell Deception*, is targeted for released at the end of 2020. It is all about history that has not been emphasized, told or has been deliberately withheld from the public. It is told in the context of verifiable history.

As I said previously, Aquino was not targeted in the first book and is barely mentioned. I calculated correctly that he would be in an even more weakened state by the time *The Roswell Deception* was released and in no position to put up his ordinary resistance to anything I publish. To eventually connect up to the usurper of one of my most effective detractors was a stroke of good fortune. The world, however, does not begin and end with Michael Aquino. Méntia's statement that personal choices for the individual depend so much on a person's health is very relevant. That includes freeing yourself of false data that has been perpetrated upon the collective. After a certain point, the population becomes so sick that they do not even recognize what is healthy or not. This applies to data as well.

I will also add that none of these threads of interest will impede any future collaboration with Radu. As soon as he comes out with his next volume, which I would expect to be sometime in 2021, I will begin the translation as soon as I get the Romanian edition into my hands. I have now been producing two books a year instead of the typical one. The reason for this is that I discovered I can be more productive if I alternate between books every other day. In other words, I work on Book A one day and then Book B the next and so forth. I have found this less draining of one's energy. One does not become too attached or overwhelmed by the data one is processing and writing becomes a much more pleasant task.

In the meantime, I will also be continuing with my various other projects and threads of research, all of which are addressed in my quarterly newsletter, the *Montauk Pulse*. As soon as the very book you are reading goes to the printer, I will be off to California, one of my stops being the Miwok Indian reservation in Yosemite where Cezar and Radu went through the portal to the Inner Earth. Although I hardly expect to access the portal itself, there are important connections to make in the area. Before I learned of Radu's visit to Yosemite, I was already investigating connections to the nearby gold country and was very surprised when Radu isolated the area in *Inside the Earth*.

To end on a very positive note, I recently featured a newsletter dedicated to the astrology of the date August 12, 2023, the date of the twenty-year biorhythm associated with Sirius. It features what is called a kite pattern that portends a great boost to the overall investigations I have been involved in. It was twenty years earlier, in August of 2003, that the mysterious chamber beneath the Romanian Sphinx was accessed. Despite all the negativity in the world, the stars tells us that there is also reason to be very optimistic.

Peter Moon
Long Island
September 6, 2020

THE CIOCLOVINA STORY

In 2015, Dr. David Anderson revealed in a podcast that Cioclovina Cave in Transylvania is the most significant area on the planet with regard to there being evidence of what is known as a discharge of space-time motive force being released. Spacetime motive force is a word he coined for the accessible energy that is released when a Time Reactor™ literally slows down or speeds up time. He reaffirmed this in 2017 during a lecture given to an audience on Long Island and stated that Temporal Tremor Detectors had found other sites where spacetime motive force had been unleashed but that Cioclovina was by far the largest and most significant. Perhaps the most interesting aspect is that he also stated that the most exciting discovery about Cioclovina Cave has not yet been published.

When David initially informed me of this, he was most surprised to learn that I had been brought to the cave by happenstance during my journey to Transylvania in 2014. Learning of the importance of the site, I have subsequently visited the cave three additional times. In 2019, I was finally able to enter the very huge cave itself and took a five hour journey about one mile deep into this very remarkable locale. Based upon reports by geologists, I think that I was in the very vicinity of where the release of space-time motive force occurred 200 or 2,000 years ago.

Upon emerging from my journey into the sacred depths of Cioclovina, I received a "message from the cave itself" to erect a ham radio station at a scouting camp nearby. This was inspired in part by David's interest in radio youth programs . You can find out more about these at *www.x-beacon.org*.

Accordingly, I put out a request in my newsletter to solicit donations from people who are both interested in supporting this endeavor and having an adventure as well. The estimated cost for the antenna station is $2,800, and I have asked for four people to donate $700 each. Each, in turn, will be invited to travel with me to Cioclovina and join in the undertaking. Three people have donated so far, but our trip in the summer of 2020 was undermined by the COVID-19 crisis. I am hopeful that these problems will be resolved by 2021. There is still room for one more, and I am hopeful that the circulation of this new book by Radu Cinamar will find us the right one. ■

DONATE & PARTICIPATE

If you are sincerely interested in being part of and/or supporting the aforementioned Cioclovina antenna project, please contact Peter Moon at *skybooks@yahoo.com*. To join us, you will need to be reasonably physically fit and healthy as there will be hiking, all of which is optional, but there is no point in coming if you cannot experience what this incredible land has to offer. Accomodations are camp-like, and while there are indoor beds and a toilet at the facility, you have to be prepared to "rough it" to an extent.

WORLD GENESIS FOUNDATION

The Cioclovina Antenna Project is being sponsored by the World Genesis Foundation, a charitable 501-C3 non-profit corporation registered in Arizona whose mission is to "leave no child without hope for the future". The foundation works in cooperation with the United Nations Educational, Scientific and Cultural Organization and partners throughout the world to create new opportunities for youth in areas where opportunities may be limited or unavailable today. See *www.worldgenesis.org*.

The World Genesis Foundation (WGF) was founded by Dr. David Anderson, and Peter Moon is a member of the Board of Directors. One of the main contributions of WGF is to sponsor a summer camp on the Danube River at Capidava, Romania every summer. Called Atlantykron Summer Academy, this camp features lectures, workshops and activities that range from science, art, and sports and is embrasive to all aspect of life and growth. Those participating in the Cioclovina Antenna Project will also be recommended by Peter Moon to be invited to the camp if they are interested. It is not necessary to attend.

There is room for one more to donate to the Antenna Project, and it is $700. Funds will be payable to the World Genesis Foundation. Travel costs are additional, and Peter Moon will network travel connections within Romania. All travelers, including Peter Moon, will share in transportation costs.

Do not send funds until you contact Peter Moon first. If interested, write to Peter Moon at *skybooks@yahoo.com*. To make regular donations to WGF, go to *www.worldgenesis.org*.

Coming in 2021

The Roswell Deception and Demystification of World War II

by Douglas Dietrich with Peter Moon

With illustrations and actual photos, you will learn the verifiable and actual history of the enormous and very effective Japanese super-sized dirigibles and balloon bombs that were made for both biological and conventional war and how they used these to coerce that Allies so as to secure an economic victory for Japan that is still in force to this day.

The Roswell Deception is genuine history that the Government has classified in order to hide the lies and crimes of key people and those who continue their legacy. This includes the social engineering of what really happened at Roswell and the steering of people's minds to believe in aliens.

Did you ever wonder why the Japanese have such a great economy while the U.S. faltered? Containing pivotal truths that can neither be denied nor ignored, this book will cause historians to change their narratives.

SPECIAL OFFER FROM SKY BOOKS

By far, the most important work Peter Moon has done in his entire career is breaking down Dr. David Anderson's theories on time into simple language that an 8th Grader can understand. Featured at the Time Travel Education Center (*www.timetraveleducationcenter.com*), you can now purchase the following in digital form on a thumb drive.

Journeys Into Time — A high quality video presentation by Dr. David Anderson on the history and physics of time travel.

Time Travel Interview with David Anderson — One of the most interesting public interviews ever given by Dr. David Anderson where discusses his scientific theories on time travel and the challenges he has faced in the early stages of successfully attempting to warp time. David also takes calls from listeners and answers questions. He also addresses key aspects about the boundary layer of a self-contained field where time is slowed down or speeded up.

Time Travel Theory Explained (all 9 videos) — Animated and visual breakdown of Dr. David Anderson's theories on why and how time travel does not violate the laws of physics and mathematics, all of it being based upon simple laws and principles that are inarguable. It also includes a visual description of how the time reactor technology works.

The Psychology of Space-Time — An eight-part series on the psychology of space-time from a quantitative view of psychology. General psychology is based upon a qualitative analysis of the mind but the quantitative approach herein addresses the quantitative aspects of the mind, all of which comes down to dimensions, and the first ten dimensions are patiently explained. Subsequent installments in this series (not yet produced) will include the psychology of space-time with regard to censorship and power.

David Anderson/Peter Moon 2015 Podcast — Recorded in 2015, this was the most informative session Peter Moon ever had with David Anderson and also discusses the issues surrounding Cioclovina Cave.

Montauk Pulse Volumes — This includes all back issues of Peter Moon's *Montauk Pulse* newsletter which has been in print for 27 years and is currently in its 5th volume. In digital format for easy referencing.

$99.00

(note that this can only be supplied by thumb drive)

THE TRANSYLVANIAN SERIES

TRANSYLVANIAN SUNRISE is the story of an unprecedented archeological discovery beneath the Romanian Sphinx in the Bucegi Mountains. Radu Cinamar visits this secret site where he witnessed a holographic Hall of Records left by an advanced civilization and three mysterious tunnels leading deep into the bowels of the Inner Earth. *Transylvanian Sunrise* chronicles the political intrigue surrounding the discovery of these artifacts which represents the dawn of a new era for Mankind.
288 pages, ISBN 978-0-9678162-5-8............................**$22.00**

TRANSYLVANIAN MOONRISE corroborates Radu's story with newspaper articles as he is sought out by a mysterious Tibetan Lama who takes Radu on a mystical journey to Tibet where he receives a secret initiation and a sacred manuscript from the blue goddess Machandi. This is an initiation of the highest order that will take you far beyond your ordinary imagination in order to describe events that have molded the past and will influence the future in the decades ahead.
288 pages, ISBN 978-0-9678162-8-9...................................**$22.00**

MYSTERY OF EGYPT features an expedition to explore the First Tunnel in the holographic chamber: the one to Egypt. Ancient artifacts are discovered which tell the history of the Earth in holographic form, the most controversial of which include remarkable adventure that includes explorations in time to the First Century A.D. This book also includes updates from Cezar since their last meeting.
240 pages, ISBN 978-1-937859-08-4.................................**$22.00**

THE SECRET PARCHMENT — FIVE TIBETAN INITIATION TECHNIQUES presents invaluable techniques for spiritual advancement that came to Radu Cinamar in the form of an ancient manuscript whose presence in the world ignited a series of quantum events, extending from Jupiter's moon Europa and reaching all the way to Antarctica, Mount McKinley and Transylvania. An ancient Romanian legend comes alive as a passage way of solid gold tunnels, extending miles in the Transylvanian underground is revealed to facilitate super-consciousness as well as lead to the nexus of Inner Earth where "All the Worlds Unite."
288 pages, ISBN 978-0-9678162-5-8.................................**$22.00**

THE WHITE BAT — THE ALCHEMY OF WRITING
Told in a personal narrative, Peter Moon relates how he was being drawn to Transylvania via the dream of a white bat, long before he became involved with Montauk, only discover that there are actual white bats in Transylvania that are unknown to science. This book synthesizes the dream process with the creative process and teaches you to do the same.
288 pages, ISBN 978-1-937859-15-2....................................**$22.00**

INSIDE THE EARTH
THE SECOND TUNNEL

Stories of the Inner Earth have both fascinated and perplexed mankind since the dawn of time. Now, for the first time, hard scientific data is provided that the Earth's core is not what conventional science has always assumed.

More amazing than the science, however, are the personal adventures of Radu Cinamar whose position in Department Zero, Romania's secretive intelligence division, allows him to penetrate ancient subterranean passage ways and meet citizens of civilizations in the Inner Earth.

Familiar characters from the ***Transylvania Series*** also reappear, including the enigmatic Tibetan lama, Repa Sundhi, also known as Dr. Xien, who states:

> "If someone had a device or machine that could start up and go everywhere they want, especially towards the center of the Earth, the machine would be blocked and stop at a certain point because of the frequency of vibration to be found there. Just how far you can go with such a machine can be limited by reason of your own consciousness which can in and of itself restrict the dimensional range of such a device or the extent to which it can penetrate other realms. This applies to both human beings as well as material objects. Your ability to access such a region is determined by what your own individual consciousness can or will allow you to experience."

In this exhilarating description of mysteries inside the Earth, Radu Cinamar presents a unique way to penetrate the Inner Earth through the process of feeling and the effects that will develop from such an experience. To enhance the reader's understanding of this very guarded subject, ***Inside the Earth — The Second Tunnel*** includes multiple illustrations that include depictions of Inner Earth geography.

Within the core of the Earth is intelligence reaching far beyond the scope of ordinary human consciousness. Inside the Earth is an opportunity for initiation as you explore the frequencies of your own inner nature.

240 pages, ISBN 978-1-937859-20-6.....................$22.00

FORGOTTEN GENESIS

FORGOTTEN GENESIS delves into ancient history in a way that no book has done before, explaining and illustrating changes in DNA that have taken place over millennia and how Mankind has evolved into what it is today. Some of the "hot spots" of human history, which have either remained unknown or have only been considered from mythological positions, are explained, including: Atlantis, Troy, Shambhala, and Hyperborea. The diversity and the accuracy of the explanations presented are clear and conclusive, combining pure esoteric knowledge with certain scientific elements. Particular emphasis is placed upon the existence and manifestation of inter-dimensional chasms or portals at the "intersections" between the physical plane and the etheric plane.

FROM THE AUTHOR:

"Even though the notions presented in this book are delicate, I considered it necessary to take a step forward and expose some deeper aspects. I also believe that the elements presented in the other volumes of this series have prepared the ground for the interested reader to gain a fair understanding of the esoteric and other factors involved with this fascinating and complex scenario. I will continue with this more elaborate approach which has become a necessity in the current context of the times. I hope that the readers of this series of volumes will correctly understand my approach and the sincere desire to expose to the world some unknown aspects of the reality we live in."

— *Radu Cinamar*

THE STORY BEHIND THE STORY

(How Radu Cinamar's Works Came to be Published)

Radu Cinamar's books include some of the most uplifting tales imaginable, more often than not leaving the reader with a desire to experience what the author has put forth. His most recent book, *Inside the Earth — The Second Tunnel*, teaches us that a significant ascendancy in consciousness is required to even begin to penetrate these fantastic realms. The potential that his work represents makes his books some of the most positive in the entire history of literature.

It is important to note, however, that it was only after the *The Montauk Project: Experiments in Time* was published in the Romanian language that Radu Cinamar sought to have his original manuscript (*Transylvanian Sunrise* in English) published.

The way this came to pass was when Sorin Hurmuz was working as an editor at a major Romanian publishing house and his boss asked him to review *The Montauk Project* in order to see if it was suitable for publishing in Romanian. Although Sorin advised him to do so, the publisher declined and Sorin responded by opening his own publishing house, Daksha, in order to publish *The Montauk Project*. It was only as a result of this that Radu saw the Romanian version and approached the publisher via the internet. A deal to publish the original manuscript was soon arranged.

It should not be too much of a surprise that the publication of *The Montauk Project* would be the catalyst for these remarkably positive books, the reason being that the Montauk Project itself represents the antithesis of what is presented in Radu's work. It is therefore only natural that a book exposing it would be the key to bringing the incredible stories of his experiences out of the woodwork

The Montauk Project has been a very powerful instrument in waking up the world with regard to its heritage as well as the potential for the future. In celebration of the 25th anniversary of its original publication, we have released a Silver Anniversary Edition. In addition to this, there is a major media series in the works that we hope will debut in the next few years. We are also sad to comment that the release of the new edition coincides with the death of the primary author of *The Montauk Project*, Preston Nichols, who passed away on October 5, 2018. A tribute to the memory of Preston has been put up youTube. In the meantime, research into the nature of time will continue.

The Montauk Project
EXPERIMENTS IN TIME

SILVER ANNIVERSARY EDITION

A BRAND NEW VERSION

The Montauk Project was originally released in 1992, causing
an uproar and shocking the scientific, academic, and journal-
istic communities, all of whom
were very slow to catch on to the
secret world that lurks beyond
the superficial veneer of American civilization.

A colloquial name for se-
cret experiments that took place
at Montauk Point's Camp Hero,
the Montauk Project represented
the apex of extensive research
carried on after World War II;
and, in particular, as a result of
the phenomena encountered dur-

ISBN 978-1-937859-21-3 $22.00

ing the Philadelphia Experiment of 1943 when the United States
Navy attempted to achieve radar invisibility.

The Montauk Project attempted to study why and how human
beings, when exposed to high powered electromagnetic waves, suf-
fered mental disorientation, physical dissolution or even death. A
further ramification of this phenomena is that such electromagnetic
waves rescrambled components of the material universe itself. According to reports, this research not only included successful attempts to manipulate matter and energy but also time itself.

It has now been over twenty-five years since *The Montauk
Project* originally appeared in print. In this *Silver Anniversary Edition*, you will not only read the original text, accompanied by com-
mentary which includes details that could not be published at the
original time of publication, but also an extensive summary of a
twenty-five year investigation of the Montauk Project which culminated in actual scientific proof of time travel capabilities.

ORDER TODAY FROM SKY BOOKS

THE SEQUELS

The stir and controversy produced by *The Montauk Project* was overwhelming to the society it was released into in 1992. The powers that be behind the military industrial complex had a lot to explain. A whole new genre of television shows were spawned in an attempt to absorb the fallout of questions and to do damage control on the trail of information thus exposed. In the meantime, Peter Moon set about trying to verify the Montauk Project and the result was of the first sequel to this amazing series:

Montauk Revisited: Adventures in Synchronicity
by Preston Nichols and Peter Moon
This sequel pursues the mysteries of time brought to light in *The Montauk Project* and unmasks the occult forces behind the science and technology used in the Montauk Project. An ornate tapestry is revealed which interweaves the mysterious associations of the Cameron clan with the genesis of American rocketry and the magick of Aleister Crowley and Jack Parsons. *Montauk Revisited* continues the Montauk investigation and unleashes incredible new characters and information.
ISBN 0-9631889-1-7, 249 pages, illustrations, and photos...................**$19.95**

After *Montauk Revisited* was completed, and much to his surprise, Peter Moon discovered that the mysterious trail of synchronicities led to the revelation that the site of "The Montauk Project" experiments was sacred Native American ground that was once accompanied by ancient pyramids which could be clearly seen in old photographs of Montauk. The result of this brand new investigation was:

Pyramids of Montauk: Explorations in Consciousness
by Preston Nichols and Peter Moon
This astonishing second sequel to *The Montauk Project* and *Montauk Revisited* awakens the consciousness of humanity to its ancient history and origins through the discovery of pyramids at Montauk. A full examination of the mysteries of the pyramids at Montauk Point reveals that the Montauk Tribe were the royal family of Long Island and that they used the name Pharaoh as a designation that connected their heritage to ancient Egypt and beyond. The discovery that these pyramids were placed on sacred native American ground opens the door to an unprecedented investigation of the mystery schools of earth and their connection to Egypt, Atlantis, Mars and the star Sirius. This book explains why Montauk was chosen as a select location for pyramids and time travel experimentation. *The Pyramids of Montauk* stirs the quest for the end of time as we know it.
ISBN 0-9631889-2-5, 256 pages, illustrations, photos.........................**$19.95**

In 1995 Preston Nichols revealed his mysterious UFO experiences as a young child. This resulted in a new book blending the history of physics and UFOs:

Encounter in the Pleiades: An Inside Look at UFOs
by Preston Nichols and Peter Moon

This book is the incredible story of a man who found himself taken to the Pleiades where he was examined and instructed by intelligent life forms who appeared human. The Pleiadians proceeded to give him an experience that enable him to regain his health and attain an unparalleled understanding of electromagnetic science and its role in UFO technology. A new look at Einstein gives insights into the history of physics and how the speed of light can be surpassed through the principles of reality engineering. New concepts in science are offered with technical but simple descriptions even the layman can understand. These include the creation of alternate realities; mind control aspects of the Star Wars defense system; implants; alien abductions and much more. Never before has the complex subject of UFOs been put together in such a simple language. Peter Moon adds further intrigue to the mix.
ISBN 0-9631889-3-3, 256 pages..$19.95

After *Encounter in the Pleiades* was published, Peter Moon had accumulated information connecting Montauk to Tibet. Peter's research culminated with a visit from world-renown German author, Jan van Helsing, who shared his photos of the mysterious German flying craft as discussed in:

The Black Sun: Montauk's Nazi- Tibetan Connection
by Peter Moon

After World War II, Allied military commanders were stunned to learn the depth of the Nazi regime's state secrets which included the world's best intelligence organization with meticulous research files on secret societies, eugenics and other scientific pursuits that boggled the imagination of the Allied command. Even more spectacular was an entire web of underground rocket and flying saucer factories with accompanying technology that still defies ordinary beliefs. A missing U-boat fleet possessing the most advanced submarine technology in the world left many wondering if the Nazis had escaped with yet more secrets or even with Hitler himself. Behind these mysteries was an even deeper element: a secret order known to initiates as the Order of the Black Sun, an organization so feared that it became illegal to even print their symbols and insignia in modern Germany. *The Black Sun* probes deep into these strange associations and their connection to Montauk Point where an American military facility was used by the Nazis to further their own strange experiments and continue the hidden agenda of the Third Reich.
ISBN 0-9631889-4-1, 304 pages, with photos, illustrations.................$24.95

The Black Sun was followed by a series of books, the first about Preston's intriguing involvement as a sound engineer for many popular music groups of the '60s and '70s as well as a UFO legal case on Long Island.

The Music of Time — by Preston Nichols & Peter Moon
This book blends music with time travel as Preston Nichols reveals his hidden role as an expert sound engineer who recorded hundreds of hit records during the Golden Era of Rock 'n Roll. For the first time, Preston reveals his employment at Brookhaven Labs and how his connections in the music industry were used for mind control and manipulation of the masses. Ultimately, Preston's adventures lead to his association with John Ford, the founder of the Long Island UFO Network, who was arrested and railroaded into jail without a trial and is still locked up to this day.
ISBN 0-9678162-0-3, 244 pages..**$19.95**

The Montauk Book of the Dead — by Peter Moon
A tale of the intrigue and power which hovers over the most sacred kernel of our existence: the secrets of life and death. This personal story of Peter Moon pierces the mystery of death and reveals fascinating details of his years aboard L. Ron Hubbard's mystery ship but gives the most candid and inside look ever at one of the most controversial figures in recent history. The book covers the all out war which was waged by governmental forces and spy agencies to obtain the legally construed rights to the above mentioned work and all of the developments and techniques that ensued from it.
ISBN 978-0-9678162-3-4 , 451 pages....................................**$29.95**

Montauk Book of the Living — by Peter Moon
The discovery of a mysterious quantum relic tied to the Montauk Pharoahs opens the door to understanding the greatest mysteries of history including the biological truth behind the Virgin Birth and how this theme intertwines with the descendants of these Amazons who live today and are known as the Blue People of the Sahara. Other occult surprises include new revelations concerning Aleister Crowley's *The Book of the Law* and demonstrates that the ancients who built the pyramids knew deeper secrets concerning DNA than our scientists of today.
ISBN 978-0-9678162-6-5, 384 pages............................**$29.95**

SYNCHRONICITY & THE SEVENTH SEAL

Peter Moon's consummate- work on Synchronicity begins with a layman's scientific description of the quantum mechanics of the universe and how the observer or spirit experiences the principle of synchronicity as a divine expression of the infinite mind.

Besides exploring parallel universes, numerous personal experiences of the author are included which not only forges a pathway of how to experience and appreciate synchronicity, but it goes very deep into the magical exploits of intriguing characters who sought to tap the ultimate powers of creation. This not only includes the most in depth analysis and accurate depiction of the Babalon Working in print but also various antics and breakthroughs of the various players and that which influenced them. These characters include the legacies and personas of Jack Parsons, Marjorie Cameron, L. Ron Hubbard and Aleister Crowley.

Peter Moon adds exponential intrigue to the mix by telling us of his personal experiences with these people and their wake which leads to even deeper encounters which penetrates the mysterious legacy of John Dee. This pursuit of synchronicities leads Peter Moon to an captivating encounter with Joseph Matheny who had similar experiences to Peter but has his own version of a space-time project known as Ong's Hat. Matheny's incredible synchronicities led him to create one of the highest forms of artificial intelligence known to man, a computer known as the Metamachine designed to precipitate and generate synchronicities. These synchronicities lead to the book's climax, a revelation of the true Seventh Seal. The proof is delivered with no counter claims ever having been made. You can make up your own mind.

SPANDAU MYSTERY - BY PETER MOON

The end of World War II precipitated more intrigue and struggle for power than the war itself. Much of this centered around the secret projects sponsored by Rudolph Hess which included not only the Antarctic project but the construction of Vril flying saucers. These tasks eventually crossed the path of one of the most colorful characters of the Second World War: General George S. Patton. Patton's job, as the war came to a close, was to recover the secret technology of the Germans and safeguard it for American use. After accomplishing his mission and compiling a German history of the war, General Patton was killed in a dubious accident, the mystery of which has never been solved and has been magnified by government refusal to declassify the file on the investigation of his death. Far more conspicuous and powerful than Patton was Rudolph Hess, the Deputy Fuhrer of Germany, who flew to England in 1941 as an envoy of peace and was imprisoned for life and suspiciously killed just before his imminent release. The current of intrigue and power which permeated these two individuals and led to their downfall was the same current which led to a repatriation of the U.S. Government and an undermining of a constitutional government that is run by and for the people. It was thus that Patton and Hess wore different uniforms but shared common interests and held within their grasp a force so powerful that it resulted in murder for both.

350+pages,ISBN978-0-9678162-4-1...................................$22.00

SkyBooks